WORLD ON FIRE

Also by the author
(with Senator William S. Cohen)

MEN OF ZEAL: A CANDID INSIDE STORY
OF THE IRAN-CONTRA HEARINGS

Shankly's Village

Shankly's Village

The Extraordinary Life and Times of Glenbuck and Its Famous Footballing Sons

Adam Powley & Robert Gillan

First published by Pitch Publishing, 2015

Pitch Publishing
A2 Yeoman Gate
Yeoman Way
Durrington
BN13 3QZ
www.pitchpublishing.co.uk

ISBN 978-1-78531-070-6

Typesetting and origination by Pitch Publishing

Printed by TJ International, Cornwall, UK

Contents

To the people of the forgotten village
For Jo and the girls. Thanks for
putting up with another one.

For Joanne, Danielle, Courtney, Rory,
Lucy and Colby-Patrick.

Acknowledgements

WHEN the authors began research for this book in 2012, we knew the story held considerable promise. What we did not know was how extensive and wide-ranging that story would be. What started as a profile of a little village and a handful of its players mushroomed into a much broader tale taking in a social history of football in Britain. Not only that but it would involve the rise and decline of coal mining, post-industrialisation, politics, professionalism, the nature of mass spectator sport, and even a brutal and cowardly murder.

We have attempted to tell the saga not just of Glenbuck and its players but what their legacy has been – for players, fans and the game in general. Hopefully that story has not ended and Glenbuck will be revived. It's high time it was.

It has been a privilege to research and tell the tale thus far. We hope we have done the village and its footballers justice, but none of it would have been possible without the enormous help, assistance, advice, time, and generosity of a whole host of people – literally, too many to mention. In time-honoured but heartfelt fashion, we really could not have done it without them.

So in no particular order, and with requests for forgiveness if anyone is not included, we would like to thank:

The Glenbuck interviewees and contributors: Ian Bone, Peggy Bain, Elsa Brown, Matt Vallance, Stewart Burns, Bobby Ward, Billy Ward, Bill Hastings, Marion Johnstone and the indestructible Tom Hazle. Extra thanks goes to James Taylor, Barbara Alexander for giving us such an insight into her uncle 'Willie' Shankly and for the photos, tea and laughs. To Sam Purdie – you've been the third author of this book. Many, many thanks.

The other interviewees and expert voices, advisers and facilitators: Martin Cloake (cheers mate), Ian St John, Ian Callaghan, Peter Hooton, Tony Evans, Professor Russell Griggs, Ian Campbell-Whittle, Paul Brown, Andy Boo, Mario Sozzi, Mark Brophy, Matt McDowell, Andy Mitchell, Mat Snow, Julie Welch, Chris Carline, Karen Gill, David Peace, Barry Graham, Ronnie Esplin, Seb White, Bill Donnachie, Kenny Ross, Heidy Verónica Gutiérrez Banegas, Sean Hurl, Jon Emmans, Michael Calvin, Norman Giller, James Morgan, Bob Goodwin, Martyn McLaughlin, Ray Simpson, John Litster, Andy Lyons and all at WSC, Rob Burnett and all at *Mirror Online*, Charlie Lambert (UCA), Carrie Dunn (UEL), and the staff of various archives including Robert Burns Memorial Archive, Mari and all at the Cumnock Library, The Baird Institute, The Mitchell Library, The British Library, Brighton and Hove Libraries. Gratitude is also due to a number of authors and biographers, particularly those of Bill Shankly: John Roberts, Dave Bowler, Stephen F. Kelly, and Oliver Holt.

Big thanks to Alex Jackson, Peter Holme and Gordon Small at the National Football Museum archive at Preston North End, Matt Phillips and David Barber at the FA, and Richard McBrearty at the Scottish National Football Museum.

The media offices of a number of clubs have also been invaluable so thanks to: Colin Farmery at Portsmouth, Jim Brown at Coventry City, Iain Cook at Arsenal, Jon Rayner, John Fennelly and the much-missed Andy Porter (RIP) at Spurs, Alan Futter on Croydon Common, Paul Wharton and Billy Smith at Everton, Duncan Carmichael at Ayr United, Mark Stephenson at Mansfield, Robert Reid at Partick Thistle, and Laura Mansell at Aston Villa.

We are indebted to the many superb fans' websites. Dozens have provided information, confirmation and illumination but it would take up too much space to reference everyone. So, with advance apologies for not citing any that really should be thanked, we would like to highlight Accies Memory Bank, Paul Joannou's Newcastle History, LFChistory.net, kjellhansen.com, Mike Curno and Steve Dean of the wonderful Plymouth Argyle site Greens on Screen, Stewart Franklin and Chic Sharp of 'Gersnet.

Almost finally, Jane and Paul Camillin at Pitch Publishing have been troopers. Thanks also to Paul Moreton, Duncan Olner, Derek Hammond, Paul Dalling and Dean Rockett.

Last but definitely not least the army of sports journalists past and present who tell the great story of football.

Adam Powley and Robert Gillan, August 2015

Chapter 1

Memory

THIS is a kind of ghost story. It begins under an icy-blue winter's sky, in a valley of silence, where there is an eerie, haunting presence.

Visit the place and you never feel quite alone. In the imagination there are ghosts passing by on the cold breeze, others standing stock-still along the sides of the glen and open fields, and some lingering deep underground. These ghosts lurk over your shoulder as you climb the sloping track. They cannot be seen, nor heard, but it feels like they are here all the same. They make you stop and think, "What on earth happened here?"

It is a ghost story of memory and lives retold. It is of people conjured up in fading photographs, the written word, and impassioned conversation. They are still talked about now, decades or more after they were flesh and blood. Walking this same path, treading those fields; working their lives to a stub in the dark holes underground.

They made an impact, these determined men and women, and their families. Their home has gone, erased without care or compassion from the landscape. It is as if a giant hand has simply smothered and smoothed away any remnant of habitation. Virtually nothing is left – just a few stones and the lumps and bumps that give the barest indication where buildings, a school

and dozens of homes once stood. Where people once lived. All that life has gone now. But the memory lives on. Those ghosts have not gone. This village is not quite dead.

This is Glenbuck. It is a name largely forgotten, now. A woeful neglect considering what took place within its unique, isolated world. Narrow your eyes, now, and try to imagine those past people calling and shouting in the middle distance, on a soggy bog of tufted grass flattening out from the road and the sides of the low glen.

It is an unkempt field left to nature's devices. But here, not that long ago – a few generations at most, and still within living memory – men and lads played the game. They ran, chased, tackled, dribbled, and scored. They would battle, fight, strain every muscle and wring out their last grain of energy in the fiercest of contests, cheered on by their family, loved ones, and pals who made up the most partisan of home crowds.

On this now sorry, forlorn field, players were sown, nurtured and grew out of the land, blossoming into champions. Fifty of them, out of a seed bank of talent barely ten times that number. Such a rich concentration of quality has never been equalled. Some among their number would scale the heights of football. One of them even came to almost define it.

They made Glenbuck the most remarkable place in the history of the greatest game. It is the village of football. If a sport is supposed to have a home, it might as well be here. Not the grand arenas of Wembley or Hampden, and definitely not some glass-fronted office in Switzerland, moneymen manoeuvring and manipulating behind its darkened windows and in cavernous underground lairs floored with lapis lazuli. If football does have a heartland and yearns for a true spiritual home, Glenbuck, with its memories and sombre, forgotten pitch, is as good a place as any.

'Hotbed' is a chronically overused term to describe heartlands of sporting prowess and popularity, but Glenbuck unquestionably met the criteria. Football for many in the village was a way of

life: not just a means of leisure and escape from the grim graft of physical labour, but vital for a sense of physical and emotional wellbeing, and identity.

The story of how Glenbuck became so committed to the game and such a vibrant footballing community is as remarkable as the people behind it. Out of the barest of resources they put their own clubs together, seizing upon football's opportunities with a zealous commitment to the sport. Football rescued men from the drudgery and physical hardship of tough manual work in many places across Britain, but few devoured the chance with such alacrity as Glenbuck men. They learned the game, honed their skills, and found a ticket out of the village and away for better prospects.

This is not to say that the village did not imbue pride in its inhabitants. It was their home, and its isolated position and situation generated a strong local loyalty. Tucked off what is now the A70, it was not a place passing travellers would have much reason to detour to. Remote and exposed, it was crushingly cold in the winter; many of those famous footballers would recall with a shiver how dreadful the cold season could be in Glenbuck. But the shared experience of eking out a living made Glenbuck what it was. Thus developed the tightest of close-knit communities.

Collective survival had been stitched into its fabric from the foundation of the village. It was built on coal, literally and metaphorically. The black seams that ran through the surrounding Ayrshire hills were too tempting to leave in peace beneath the shallow soils, and so people endeavoured to quarry the riches by the Stottencleugh Burn. First, sometime in the mid-1600s, by gaining meagre spoils from the deposits close to the surface, supplementing their bare subsistence as they and their families strove to make a scant living off the land. Later, as technology improved and the twin demands of the Industrial Revolution and capitalist profit provided a hunger for coal that never seemed to be sated, mining made its unmistakeable impact.

Pits were opened, shafts were sunk, and the village grew until it was a busy, industrious community of 1,700 people. People no longer sifted the surface for coal but were taken down – way down, into the earth to bodily hew the coal from the rock in deep, cramped passageways and rudimentary openings. It was pitiless work that took men's lives with almost casual indifference. Some of them are still lying there, buried deep underground after roof falls killed and then entombed them.

Those living on the surface resided in an unprepossessing environment. Even Glenbuck's proudest sons and daughters would not claim it was ever anything spectacular or charming to look at. The main street, a couple of terraced rows, low cottages, the church and schoolhouse threaded around its industry, some shops and a pub were all it amounted to.

The Ayrshire hills provided a ruggedly impressive backdrop, looking down on the nearby Glenbuck Loch. 'Loch' is a fanciful descriptive for what was a man-made body of water, formed by a dam to serve the mills at nearby Catrine, but it has become a wooded, sylvan calm that betrays its dangerously ice-cold depths. Yet if the immediate area wasn't pretty, and existence was almost unremittingly hard, it was certainly a living, lively place, full of people making the best of challenging circumstances.

From it sprang that half-century of professional footballers. Not all were great; many were, in the more literal sense, journeymen who ventured far away to maintain their modest careers. But they all made their mark and some carved it deep. There were those who made the relatively short trip to play for the clubs of Glasgow and Scotland's central belt; the players who gave fine service to clubs in England's industrial heartlands; the two Sandys who found glory down south among Londoners and triumphed in the greatest competition of the age.

And, most famously, there was the diminutive right-half who drew on the experiences of his club and international career to forge an even more successful life in management. In the process

Bill Shankly would utterly transform one of England's great clubs, turning it into a globally renowned institution, while providing the broader game with so much of its spirit, purpose and character. He set the highest of standards that few of his successors anywhere have even hoped to equal, but they all work now in the shadow of his deeds and words.

Bill Shankly's famous – almost infamous – misquote has been tiresomely overused and abused, but it is an inescapable facet of the man. He was said to have said, of course, in response to a discussion about the wider significance of the game that, "some people believe football is a matter of life and death, I am very disappointed with that attitude. I can assure you it is much, much more important than that."

It was originally uttered with tongue firmly in cheek. People close to him who heard it first hand knew that for a fact. A man who had seen first hand how hard, brutal and cruel real life could be would not actually have thought a mere game was of greater significance. But there was also in the renditions of the quote an acknowledgement of the all-consuming passions football generated, and the seriousness that could overwhelm its adherents. Fan, player or manager, Shankly recognised and articulated how central football was to working-class people.

That was in turn a reflection of his own political outlook. Shankly, like the village that made him, believed in socialism. Not the esoteric theorising of Marxist philosophy, or grand command of the progress of civilisation, but the practical, ground level application of collective endeavour for collective reward. It was a utilitarianism that governed his outlook on that most team-focused of sports, and a direct product of the environment in which he was raised.

Glenbuck was a place resolutely left of centre. It couldn't be anything much else given the nature of its existence and the economic relations to which its people were bonded. It was not a communist enclave, nor a place of revolutionary ferment, but the people of Glenbuck certainly knew whose side they were on. The mines made this an unsigned but binding contract. People could die from their work and needed to depend on their neighbours and workmates to mitigate the risk of danger, or at least attempt to ensure their loved ones were looked after if they were severely injured or lost their lives. It is no surprise that the village that was nourished on the shared experience and the essential collectivism of mining for coal should provide so many men committed to a sport that depended on those same principles of working and functioning together.

Now those mines have gone. The people who worked them have departed, the surviving relatives and descendants resettled in the nearby towns of Muirkirk, Douglas, Cumnock and beyond. Those local places used to treat Glenbuckians with mutual suspicion and not infrequent enmity, but now they are part of the modern locale of quiet small towns with neat municipal housing and well-kept private homes. Those who were born in Glenbuck, or can remember it from family connections, are inevitably dwindling in number but still speak with a fierce pride for their lost home.

One is Sam Purdie. A barrel-chested, brawny man with a voice to match, he is now 79 but fit, energetic and full of enthusiasm. A former miner and oil man, an activist, campaigner and general go-to man for all manner of things, he writes of and recalls Glenbuck like no one else does. He can talk for Scotland and anywhere else besides. He waxes lyrical and forceful on any number of topics, reflecting his broad interests and areas of knowledge, and holding a listener in a kind of willingly captive grip.

One cold wintry day in the now deserted Glenbuck, Sam Purdie is back. From the car parked just off the modern A70 highway, Sam walks accompanied by two fellow travellers, past the black-stoned memorial close to the trees bordering Glenbuck Loch. The stone is inscribed with gold letters, paying tribute to Bill Shankly. This is the great man's memorial, placed fittingly near the site of his former home village.

People come from all over the world to see it – football pilgrims of many denominations, paying homage to one of the game's legendary figures. A few scarves in Liverpool red are spread around; some flowers hang wearily by the granite sides.

Sam and his companions stop to look and pause before continuing up the sloping track, the sides of the low valley surrounding them, the fresh but faint icy breeze making a barely heard whisper. The footsteps end. There is silence and stillness as the group look up the road to the gently winding lane, the bumps and lumps and that boggy, forlorn field. Sam has stopped talking now.

The moment is broken with the most stupid of stupid questions. "Ask a stupid question, Sam. But how do you feel coming back here now?"

There is a lament of sorts, some hesitant voice-cracking words about the sadness of it all and then silence again. It's no real answer but it speaks volumes. There are ghosts here, listening in. Theirs is a story to be told.

Chapter 2

The Glen of the Buck

BRITAIN is an old country. Many of its villages, towns and boroughs can trace their habited origins back to Anglo-Saxon and ancient tribal times, some still further. Glenbuck is not one of them. It only existed as a recognisable place for barely three centuries, and in terms of population it never amounted to much more than a modest village of around 1,500 people. Yet for such a small place, it made a big impression. Glenbuck's light burned fast but bright.

For all the extent that it shined, casting such a glow over the sport of football, Glenbuck never was particularly striking to look at. Today, there is a fashion to extol a community's virtues with signposts that celebrate its visual charm or grand, centuries-old heritage. Glenbuck has a history alright, but its most loyal sons and daughters would have struggled to champion any gleaming aesthetic qualities. Even during its heyday, there would never have been any 'best kept village' awards, let alone now when there is no real evidence of habitation, to admire or otherwise. Glenbuck always was a tough, rugged, nuggety little backwater that scratched an existence for a good part of its 300-odd years. And yet its people produced their own kind of glittering beauty.

What is left of the village lies in the valley of the River Ayr. This vital waterway gave its name to the county and a town at its mouth, as it flowed from the Southern Uplands into the Firth of Clyde. The region has an extensive and rich history, and the area around Glenbuck shares in that past. Neolithic peoples made their presence felt initially in what would have been an extensively wooded landscape, before successive waves of settlers played their part in turning the area mainly into pasture and moorland.

Archaeological digs and surveys have uncovered the presence of wild ox and wolves preserved in peat. A bronze axe head was found at West Glenbuck dating from around 1500 to 1150 BC. The Romans, Celts, Vikings, and more recent tribes have all vied for Ayrshire's considerable resources. It has been, and remains, productive agriculturally, and was a focus of intensive and often heavy industry from the late 18th century. It also boasts a storied and illustrious past, as the reputed birthplace of Robert the Bruce and, more certainly, the home county of Robert Burns.

Ayrshire's most famous son, Burns was born in Alloway just to the south of Ayr in 1759. His poetry, songs, and brief but vibrant personal life have captivated the imaginations of generations of Scots and many beyond. As a child of tenant farmers, his emergence from an upbringing of rural poverty to fame and renown as an adult enabled him to rub shoulders with the great and the good of 18th-century Scottish society. His aspirational life story, political outlook, and willingness to write in the native dialect resonated with the people of his home county. His determination for self-improvement through learning, art and culture would influence and inspire many, including people in Glenbuck. Bill Shankly was an ardent fan of Burns 'the Bard of Ayrshire'.

John Loudon McAdam, of roads-building fame, was another notable Ayrshire personality, prominent in mining and a tar-making enterprise near Glenbuck. Alexander Fleming, the discoverer of the anti-biotical properties of penicillin that did so much to save so many lives, was born in Lochfield, near Darvel just a few miles from Glenbuck. By complete contrast, Elvis Presley once paid a visit to Ayrshire, flying over the valley and touching down at Prestwick Airport while returning to the USA from army service in 1960. The only time 'The King' set foot on British soil was when he made a very brief regal stopover in a place that was once dubbed the Kingdom of Scotland.

Such world-renowned figures famed in wildly differing eras contrast with the more specifically local story of the Covenanters. The county was a fulcrum for their activities in the 17th century, and with significant relevance for Glenbuck. A mass spiritual and political movement of Presbyterians, the Covenanters rejected the imposition of Anglican religious practice. They were fundamentally opposed to the concept of any mortal man having primacy over religious belief, in this case vested in the power of the monarchy in the shape of England's King Charles I. Opponents signed a 'national covenant' in 1638 to formalise their objections.

Amid the foment of the English (and Scottish) Civil Wars, the tumult of conflict with England and eventual union, colonisation and war in Ireland, and the ongoing broader struggle for religious ascendancy between Catholicism and Protestantism, the Covenanters were central to the biggest political, religious and military events of their age. Loyalties and the issues that gave rise to them switched and evolved, but in essence, the Covenanter period was about power and rule. Subjected to persecution and often brutal repression in what became known as 'The Killing Time', a number of Covenanter martyrs were commemorated in Ayr, including Glenbuck.

Their monuments and memorials dot the countryside, often in the most windswept and evocative places. In the Glenbuck village church there was a stone plaque in memoriam to prominent local activists. Included among them was John Brown. His home lay two miles further up the hills from Glenbuck, an isolated place even by Glenbuck terms. He was executed on the spot by agents sent to stamp out the Covenanters. In florid terms, in 1918 *The Scottish Field* described his demise two centuries before: "The Covenanter, pale but resolute... his wild-eyed wife and her clinging bairns a short way off, the line of red-coat dragoons with their muskets raised, the stern-faced officer's word of command, the flash and the report echoing among the hills, and the tumbled heap left when the smoke blew away. No sound is heard at the spot now but the cry of the lonely peesweep and the bleat of the sheep."

Other locals suffered the ultimate sacrifice for their beliefs. One was Thomas Richard from the parish of Muirkirk that incorporated Glenbuck. By various accounts, and as told in *Jardine's Book of Martyrs,* Richard was subjected to the kind of persecution redolent of witch-finder trials. He was a Covenanter and a likely member of the network of militant religious campaigners, treated as rebels and fugitives by their opponents and remorselessly hunted down. Deceived by undercover agents into confessing his religious ideals and loyalties, Richard was summarily executed.

The inscription on his grave in nearby Cumnock read:

> Here lies the corpse of Thomas Richard, who was shot by Colonel
> James Douglas, for his adherence to the Covenanted Work of
> Reformation, on the 5th day of April, anno 1685.
> Halt passenger! this stone doth show to thee
> For what, by whom, and how I here did die,
> Because I always in my station
> Adhered to Scotland's Reformation
> And to our Sacred Covenants and laws,
> Establishing the same, which was the cause,
> In time of prayer, I was by Douglas shot,
> Ah! cruelty never to be forgot.

The mention of Colonel Douglas (who ordered the execution rather than personally carried it out) illustrates the deep-seated family lineages that persisted in the area since medieval times, and which would last for centuries more. Back in the 17th century, in a world of clandestine meetings, state surveillance, dangerous intrigues and bloody violence, it was a grim period for Glenbuck and the surrounding area.

The episode even has a macabre early link with football. James White was another martyr who met his death in 1685 when he was shot and killed by a troop of dragoons who had discovered White and fellow Covenanters in secret prayer in a farmhouse near Kilmarnock. In a gruesome twist, White's head was hacked off and used as a football by soldiers in one of the most ghastly impromptu kickabouts that can ever be imagined.

Covenanters from the region were also either banished or emigrated to America, where they played a part in founding a number of colonies in the Carolinas.

If such history suggests Glenbuck and its neighbours were places of great tumult, the reality is more prosaic. Glenbuck was a quiet place only occasionally ruffled by the outside world. It was sited right at the source of the Ayr and close to the border with Lanarkshire. Stretching out from the Ayr valley and off the Edinburgh–Ayr road, the village cleaved into a spur of the heather-topped Lowther Hills, part of the Southern Uplands, and nestled below Hareshaw Hill (on some maps labelled as 'Glenbuck Hill').

The land itself was owned by the Douglas family, one of the great clans whose presence punctuates Scottish history, frequently in the arena of battle. Via conflict, marriage and the machinations of the landowning class, the Douglases and their various offshoots and familial alliances came to hold domain over huge swathes of territory.

The Douglases and their relations (the Earl of Mar is traced to one such lineage) have often been associated with the glens and mountain passes of the area romanticised by folklore, and their tales drew the inevitable attentions of writers. In 1913 (as recalled by the former editor of the *Muirkirk Advertiser* James Taylor), *The Scottish Field* colourfully described the exploits of Lord James, springing from the hills above Glenbuck to crush the English Garrison in Castle Douglas, round about the time of the Battle of Loudoun Hill in 1307. It was a period in which the armies of England, Robert the Bruce and William Wallace would have passed through the area as the various conflicts ebbed and flowed. Two centuries later, the Earl of Angus, according to legend, defied King Henry VIII by claiming he could hold his own, "on the skirts of Kirnetable [nearby Cairntable Hill] against the whole English army".

There was similar local excitement caused by the Jacobite Rebellion of 1745–46. On their ill-fated return from Derby, a detachment of Bonnie Prince Charlie's army released at Glenbuck an outspoken prisoner they had taken in Dumfries, one Robert Paterson – the famous 'Old Mortality', who was, ironically, immortalised by Walter Scott. Paterson was a stonemason who devoted his life to carving memorials for Covenanter martyrs.

In more peaceful times, parts of these Douglas lands and estates that encompassed what would become Glenbuck were used for hunting, and indeed gave the future village its name. 'The Glen of the Buck', or 'Buck Glen' betrayed its characteristics as a place where there was substantial game and in particular, deer. David Pettigrew, in his excellent study *Old Muirkirk and Glenbuck* describes how, at the height of Douglas powers in the 14th and 15th centuries, the family and their noble guests were so prolific in their hunting activities that the land became bereft of the animals that gave it its name. Much of the associated woodland was also stripped away, leaving a largely bare and unpopulated landscape.

It left Glenbuck as a remote, isolated and largely inhospitable place. Exposed on the flanks of the valley, it was bleak and viciously cold in winter, making it an environment that was later famously likened by Bill Shankly to 'Outer Mongolia'. Quite why, 300 years before Shankly's time, people would have wanted to settle in such an unwelcoming place is unclear. Pettigrew suggests the then belief that its land was more fertile than already cultivated areas close by, prompting a handful of families to try and farm it. There is also the possibility that readily available coal that could be picked from the surface drew in settlers who were likely poor and very desperate. Perhaps it was simply the inevitable consequence of a human instinct for migration or more specific, localised economic circumstances.

Whatever the real reason, by the middle of the 17th century, Glenbuck began to make its mark. There is recorded evidence of a settlement in 1650, home to 40 hardy souls who eked out a bare subsistence, combining small-scale surface mining with a basic level of agriculture.

Their homes were made of wood, and they relied in part on the barter system. The Military Survey of Scotland of 1747–55, undertaken after the Jacobite rising of 1745, was the first proper survey of mainland Scotland. It noted in rather cursory terms of Glenbuck that there were 'Cole pits, in the east'. The land around it was unpromising and often waterlogged.

Water was in fact a distinct feature of the little glen, bubbling up from springs and running off the catchments on the hillsides, forming into streams and burns and heading into the nascent River Ayr. It was this plentiful supply of a natural resource that provoked Glenbuck's next phase of development, with the establishment in 1760 of a textile works by the New Mills Weaving Company of Lanark. Weaving needed water, and Glenbuck had plenty of it.

The advent of textiles manufacture here even led to Glenbuck being described as a 'weaving village' by *The Scottish Field* in 1918. Its correspondent was dismissive of the attempts by villagers to build an industry similar to Robert Owen's model factory at New Lanark: 'The weavers of Glenbuck made an ambitious start upon the same lines. The social experiment, however, by reason of the common frailties of human nature, which Socialist Utopians are so apt to overlook, proved no less disastrous here than elsewhere, and the building set up by the weavers remains, with fallen roof and empty windows, a monument to their enthusiasm and disappointment.'

Textiles production was a major industry in Scotland at the time, but subject to fluctuations in growth and decline, resulting in a volatile relationship between the authorities, mill owners, and their workforces. In one brutal dispute sparked by a cut in wages in 1819–20, dubbed the Radical War, the leader of one weaver group, James 'Purlie' Wilson, came to prominence in gruesome circumstances. A resident of Strathaven, 13 miles from Muirkirk, he is credited with inventing, or at least finessing the purl stitch which revolutionised the hosiery industry in Scotland. Wilson was arrested amid government panic that his supporters were intent on 'capturing' the city of Glasgow. Wilson was charged with treason, found guilty on one count but with a plea from the jury for mercy. Instead he was hanged and beheaded on Glasgow Green, a shocking illustration of the reactionary lengths the authorities would go to to stamp out any resistance. There is a monument to Wilson in the Strathaven cemetery.

It was in this atmosphere of tumultuous change and fraught, often bloodily violent conflict between emerging classes in the Industrial Revolution, that Glenbuck made its steps towards a more lasting presence. The weaving venture was only a temporary one, though some of the actual weavers would continue a cottage industry in a row of houses called 'Stair Row'. Combining this work with farming, weaving in some form lasted in Glenbuck until 1880.

Perhaps more significantly, in the late 18th century textiles provided a base and impetus for the village to grow. Bogs were drained to expand the available farmland and serve seven new holdings. The population grew to 580. Times, though, were still unremittingly hard. Diseases like smallpox, rickets, consumption and scurvy were rife, reflecting the endemic malnourishment and hitting the young and the weak. Still, those with a keen eye for resources and a workforce to exploit sensed opportunity and so in 1786, when significant deposits of iron, coal, and limestone were discovered, developers from far and wide headed up the Ayr valley.

The Cairntable Gas and Coal Company started small-scale iron production, but the venture's name hinted at the resource that was to really spark Glenbuck's development. One of the entrepreneurs tempted by the newly discovered natural bounty was an Englishman, John Rumney from Workington. He founded the Glenbuck Iron Company and obtained a 99-year lease to work the raw materials. A blast furnace, forges and a smithy were constructed.

There is a certain irony that the remains of that furnace are now a scheduled ancient monument, which saved them from destruction when the late 20th- and early 21st-century process of opencast mining obliterated the rest of the village. The mines and pits which initially grew to service the ironworks would play a much more prominent role in Glenbuck's story, yet have not survived in any readily recognisable form.

The workings and the smelting process to extract the iron needed coal, which in turn led to the opening of a number of shallow shafts and pits, accompanied by various water works to power machinery, and pumps and wheels to drain water from the coal workings, such as at the 'Air' pit. This had a shaft '25 fathoms deep'. There were two pits sunk south of Airdsgreen, coal and ironstone was drawn from pits at Gaffhill, and a quarry was set up at the foot of Hareshaw Hill. Industry and coal mining proper had got underway in Glenbuck and was to shape and determine the future of the village for the rest of its days.

By 1796, Glenbuck was a modest hive of iron-making activity. The iron rails for early railways that were produced in Glenbuck were among the first – if not the first – ever cast in Scotland. Five small rows of houses were built to provide accommodation for the new influx of workers that made them, alongside additional lodgings for mine officials, while a general store was opened up. But the relative 'boom' was short-lived.

Transportation of product to markets further away, particularly in Glasgow, was time-consuming and costly. The operation ran into financial trouble and new capital had to be injected to keep it afloat.

Development of another kind came in 1802 with the construction of Glenbuck Loch, reputedly made with the labour of Napoleonic prisoners of war who were certainly in the area at the time. While today, this body of water, 36 feet at its greatest depth, has the pleasing appearance to the eye of a natural feature of the landscape, it is a relatively recent addition to it, and was designed with purely economic motives in mind. The cotton mills at Catrine, 17 miles downstream along the River Ayr, required a dependable source of water to power the wheels and looms.

The mill operators, James Finlay and Company, looked just to the south-east of Glenbuck, where there was a boggy hollow in the ground fed by various streams. By damming it at either end and installing sluices, a reservoir could be formed from which a controlled supply of water could then be released into the Ayr. Workmen were appointed to open the sluices and by the time the water had reached Catrine downriver, it was of a sufficient volume to power the water wheels just as the cotton mills were ready to start work.

It was an impressive feat of precision engineering that typified the vigorous ambition of the age. There were actually two dams located exactly 12 hours' 'flow time' from Catrine. The sluices were opened at 6.00pm and closed at 6.00am, supplying twelve hours' energy at Catrine from six in the morning until six in the evening. The 50ft wheels were the biggest in the UK and produced 500 horsepower.

Meanwhile, as the iron industry's fortunes appeared to pick up, production and the facilities to serve it expanded. More homes were built at Glenbuck, this time in two-story blocks. Associated development followed, with pipes, embryonic railway lines and better roads to service the works.

At the time, Aiton's *Survey of Ayrshire* adopted a highly condemnatory tone when describing conditions in Glenbuck, claiming that the ages of the houses could be estimated by measuring the size of the heaps of manure at each side of the front door, which during wet weather formed 'a pool of brown water in which children and ducks dabbled in equal contentment'.

Defying the adage that where there is such muck, there is brass, questions persisted over Glenbuck's iron industry and its long-term economic viability – a phrase that would resonate through the years – and production was closed down in 1812. This was despite what appeared to be a busy order book. One of the last contracts was for the casting of 70,000 rails, and assorted metals for the first public railway in Scotland, the Kilmarnock & Troon Railway. This venture was owned by the Duke of Portland, one of the major landowners in the area, alongside the Douglases and Sir Wyndham Anstruther.

Behind the scenes, however, the iron company had long been in trouble. The detail of the company's fight for credit and survival makes for fascinating reading, but the list of creditors is salutary. Aside from the investors and speculators, the collapse of Glenbuck Ironworks cut deep.

The master of the village's first school, Thomas Clyde, was one of the 'unpreferred' creditors. So too was John Callan, owner of the village store, and the local St Andrew's Lodge. Inevitably, those who had grafted the hardest, the iron workers themselves, were left severely out of pocket.

It all hit Glenbuck hard. By 1820 a Scottish gazetteer described it as standing, 'in a wild and secluded situation between the mountains... the iron works having been abandoned; the village has fallen into decay. Population 237'.

Not for the first time, Glenbuck was effectively being written off, its people being driven away to find work and homes elsewhere. But, as was often to be the case, its inhabitants refused to be beaten. The growth of the villages along the valley revived, and so too did Glenbuck.

Opportunities for worthwhile employment took time to catch up. Despite more people putting down roots in the village, it was still seen as a depressed area. Like so many places across

Scotland and Britain, it was the railways that kick-started further development.

If the extent of the coal reserves lying beneath the Ayrshire fields and hills was what really made the area ripe for exploitation, it was the railways that truly facilitated it, and a newly laid line east to Coalburn to service the mines had a significant impact. Another line went west via the Grasshill Mineral Line and the main Caledonian Line.

Glenbuck was now better connected than ever, and the development of mining and its associated works and housing followed suit. In the 1840s and then 1850s, John Wilson of Dundyvan and then Bairds from Gartsherrie opened up a series of mines. Shafts were sunk, pits opened and the population grew. By the turn of the 20th century, Glenbuck was home to just over 1,700 people.

There were other key milestones in the village's growth. A church funded by public subscription to the tune of £2,000 was erected in 1881, a new school in 1876, and a branch of the Muirkirk Ironworks Co-Operative Society (which only closed in 1953), plus a public hall was opened in September 1904 by J.G. Baird MP.

Even so, it was still an isolated place. It was not as if the railways provided a commuter service connecting the good folk of Glenbuck with the towns and cities beyond. Train fares were a luxury few could afford. Even though the Muirkirk road was improving, cars would be a distant and very elusive luxury. Travellers had the 'Hobson's Choice' of going by foot, and only if there was a pressing need to venture out from this self-contained little village. In return, few outsiders would have wanted to have made the reverse trip. To be blunt, few of Ayrshire or Glasgow's eminent citizens would have quite felt the urge to have a day out in Glenbuck.

In time, Glenbuck would have all the basic amenities it needed to exist essentially on its own. There was work in the shape of the mines, and housing. Neither were of a standard most people would opt for by choice, but by necessity they provided a bare minimum for the requirements of industry and the people who serviced it. At various times churches, a company store, other shops and a school would follow, along with that essential for civilised living, a pub, the Royal Arms. It is additionally worth noting that the Glenbuck store soon severed the 'company' connection and became a branch of the Scottish Wholesale Co-Operative Society. Company Stores were viewed by the people who had to shop in them as an effective form of monopolistic extortion.

By the last quarter of the 19th century, Glenbuckians thus had a self-contained home of their own. It might not have amounted to much, but it was theirs, and from it was fostered a distinct and highly-localised character, culture, and identity. Glenbuck – mining village, was on the map, and in time the world of football would sit up and take notice.

Chapter 3

King Coal and Community

THE estimable archivist and chronicler of Glenbuck and Muirkirk life, James Taylor, wrote in 2006, "A visit to where the once thriving village of Glenbuck stood can be an experience. One can feel a distinct atmosphere and recollections, however small or distant, come flooding back. One can almost hear the shouts from the football fans at Burnside Park; the clink of metal from the Quoiting Rink; the laughter of the children from the school playground; the singing of praise from the Church and Gospel Hall; the sound of the Stottencleugh Burn running gurgling through the village, the nearby farm animals; even the birds in the air; the distant hissing and 'singing' of the train engine coming towards the station from Muirkirk."

Taylor painted an evocative picture. To a cynic, it might come across as indulgent and sepia-toned nostalgia, romanticising a time and a place that had an altogether different reality for the people who actually lived through it. In conversation, and elsewhere in print, Taylor, the former newspaperman (and no slouch when it comes to casting a sharp reporter's eye over events), readily acknowledges that Glenbuck was no working-class paradise. But, like many of his generation, he sees what the destruction of the village entailed. It might not have been a place of bucolic charm but it meant an awful lot to the people who really knew it. A living, breathing community had been destroyed. Glenbuck *was* once a thriving village, and to the men and women who remember it, lived in it and experienced it, its loss is a deep and heartfelt one.

It was coal and those who worked it that made the village. The mineral had been mined, or to be more accurate, gleaned in Ayrshire since at least the 12th century. As Guthrie Hutton explained in his book *Mining, Ayrshire's Lost Industry*, small-scale farmers and agricultural workers would supplement their earnings by picking coal from the outcrops that lay at the surface. The coal was used for domestic fires, small limekilns, or to boil seawater to extract salt, all cottage industries that pre-dated any significant industrialised mining catering for a specific market.

That changed in 1684 when Sir Robert Cunninghame of Auchenharvie developed Saltcoats harbour in order to export coal to Ireland. Indeed, that country provided a substantial outlet for Ayrshire's coal production and, in return, would supply a considerable part of the labour force that was required to man coal's further exploitation in the late 18th century. Iron production (see Chapter 2) increased demand, and with the coming of the railways, new markets opened up for Ayrshire's high-quality coal.

It was at Glenbuck, alongside Muirkirk, that the first substantial mines began production. Once resources on the surface had been picked clean, mine companies had to open up pits and sink shafts to follow the seams as they split and meandered miles under the hills and valleys. This was not an easy process. Hutton notes how natural fault lines made extraction of the coal difficult and the jobs of the miners that much harder. It contributed to the specific conditions in Glenbuck that in turn influenced the idiosyncratic nature of the community.

Sam Purdie, one of the last surviving residents of Glenbuck and himself a former collier, has made comprehensive studies of mining in the village. "The earliest major remains of the industry in Glenbuck can still be seen south of the village in the evidence of several 'Bell Pits',' Purdie says. "The coal was accessed by miners descending on ladders and brought to the surface by horsepower. Until recently you could still see the traces of the circular paths the horses trod out around the winch system, which raised the coal."

It wasn't just coal that was mined. Ironstone containing the metal ore, limestone, and 'fireclay' used for furnace lining, were also viable resources, to the arguable extent that the pits were not coal mines as such but multi-purpose workings to extract a whole range of raw materials. The Limestone Coal Measures that contained this natural bounty were made up of coal seams ranging in thickness from 30 inches to nine feet. As their riches were exhausted, the mineshafts, tunnels and passageways spread out ever further.

Glenbuck's pits were many and varied. Over a near 100-year period they defined the geography of the village. They were given evocative names like Grasshill, The Lady, Galawhistle, Blaweerie, The Davy, Macdonald, Monkey, Maidenbank and Ponesk. There were plenty more, chiefly those too aged, small, and transient to be given names, formally or colloquially. These pits and workings in turn often gave their names to the rows of terraced housing that accommodated the miners and their invariably large families. It was on streets like 'Grasshill Row', 'Jubilee', 'Spireslack' and 'Auchenstilloch Cottages', nicknamed 'Monkey Row', that the future footballing stars of the village grew up.

As a key component of the Ayrshire mining industry, Glenbuck was at the forefront of innovation, pioneering for example, the use of electrical generation by steam turbine. The increasing use of machinery through the decades changed the nature of mining considerably. But over the course of the life of the Glenbuck pits the basic experience of working underground remained largely the same. Purdie, the last of five family generations to work in the mines, recalls that in his time working in the nearby Kames pit after the Second World War and in an industry nationalised by the Labour government, he operated in a pit that was still of 'the steam age'.

Whether in the 19th or 20th centuries, the work was hard, poorly paid and all-too-frequently lethal. To modern minds, especially those too young to have any real knowledge or opportunity to know about the British coal industry before it effectively died out in the 1980s, the life of a miner seems incredible. Adults and teenagers, and, further back in the industry's history, even younger youths had a working day few now can even begin to identify with. Sent hurtling down into the bowels of the earth in lifts or cages, they would have to trudge often long distances through ever-narrowing tunnels and passages just to reach the coal.

At the face itself, men would have to constrict themselves in unnatural positions for hours on end of back-breaking toil, hammering, cutting, or drilling at the seams and loading the coal into carts, wagons and 'hutches'. They did this in extremes of temperature and noise, often soaked to the skin and covered in grime and muck. They ran everyday risks of roof falls, suffocation, fires, explosions, flooding and serious injury and worse, amid the pounding and clatter of tools and machinery. There were also enormous long-term risks of career-ending injury, and the dreadful diseases endemic to mine work, chiefly via the relentless inhalation of coal dust. This caused fatal conditions such as silicosis and pneumoconiosis that ended thousands of lives prematurely.

Death in the pits themselves came sooner and horrendously often. The litany of fatal accidents and disasters makes for sobering, heart-rending reading. There were a reported 12 fatalities in Glenbuck pits between 1884 and 1928 (see Appendices), though the figure might well be higher. Here and in the wider area, deaths were simply an occupational hazard. Roof collapses accounted for many, but miners died as a consequence of anything from being run over by haulage carts to lift cages plummeting to the ground when chains snapped or winching machinery was poorly operated.

Names of the dead are repeated with a sickening familiarity. On 17 June 1887, father and son John and David Dunbar were killed by a roof fall at the Cairntable Coal Company's Davy pit. Another son, Alexander, was seriously injured. Another Glenbuck family, the Wilsons, suffered a similar fate when first Charles was killed in Douglas in 1899, before his brother William lost his life at the Davy two years later. They were both aged 21. This was not even the worst of it. Back in 1855, one Muirkirk mother, Mrs Gibson, lost two sons to add to another pair killed in previous accidents.

And the redress for such tragedies? From a report in *The Scotsman* of November 1907: 'Sheriff Sharp has issued an interlocutor in an action at Ayr Sheriff Court in which Mary Marshall or Rennie, widow of Thomas Rennie, miner, Garronhill, Muirkirk, sued William Baird & Co. coalmasters, Lugar Ironworks, for £256, 2/-. as compensation for the death of her husband. It appeared from the proof that on 9 February last Thomas Rennie, while at his work in No two Kames Pit, Muirkirk, received a slight wound on the back of his left hand, which had subsequently led to blood-poisoning, pneumonia, and death. The Sheriff finds it proved that Rennie met his death from this injury while in the employment of the defenders, and awards £256, 2/-, the amount claimed, one-third to the pursuer and two-thirds to her three pupil children; and finds her entitled to expenses.'

It was a cruel, unforgiving, often savage world. Yet if the work comes across dependent on sheer brute force and elemental power, and as a consequence unskilled, it was anything but. Miners had to be physically tough and strong, but also clever, and resourceful. Career progression from stone picker to experienced miner was a cherished aim for many, as they sought to earn the relatively superior wages such positions afforded. Many others still had an understandable fear of a life in the pit and would do their utmost to limit their time employed underground, or find some way to avoid working in the industry altogether.

At the pithead the work was scarcely any better. The screening sheds, tool shops, and assorted other works provided innumerable hazards and often awful working conditions. Ian Terris recalled in his memoir *20 Years Down The Mines* a more modern environment in the post-war era, but the themes of mining work had barely altered. Conditions were the epitome of 'Dickensian'. Terris, who would himself escape death in a roof collapse, describes a world in which boys worked seemingly never-ending shifts in gnawing cold. Managers were invariably stern and dictatorial. Old miners still puffed on clay pipes known as 'jaw jammers', and tales of ghosts abounded. 'It was like being in prison,' wrote Terris.

Even for those not directly employed in the pit, it dominated their lives. Hutton notes how in the past wives and children would have to haul to the surface the coal that their husbands and fathers mined, but did so without pay. Even in more enlightened times, family life was determined by the demands of the mine. People lived in houses owned by the mine owners, were forced to buy food and other essentials from company stores to which they were almost always indebted, and were utterly dependent on the pit for their livelihoods. If it failed, the potential consequences were obvious.

As for those early 19th-century homes the people lived in, they plumbed the depths of squalor in a country and period infamous for poor housing. By the 1870s, matters had improved, but Glenbuck's terraced rows were still rudimentary and inadequate. Grasshill Row, for example, comprised single-storey affairs that, at first glance, might have looked reasonably salubrious with their chimneys and slate roofs, but the single-storey abodes were chronically cramped. There was no running water and the drains or 'sheughs' were uncovered. Toilets were, inevitably, located outside in pairs and with no partitions or doors. Sited close to the railway line that ran to Muirkirk, the walls of the terraces were cracked by the weight of the passing trains carrying coal.

Like Terris, Sam Purdie was of a later generation but his own experiences mirrored those of his Glenbuck forebears. Over a near

100-year period, little really altered inside the tiny miners' homes. "We had no electricity, no gas and no water piped into the houses. The houses were, for the most part, miners' rows consisting of two rooms. The living room had the grate – the fireplace where the cooking was done, the clothes were dried, and where the water was heated for the men coming home from the pit to wash in the tin bath in the middle of the living room.

"The living room also had two 'built-in' double beds where the big folk slept; the children slept in the back room. Families of up to ten, sometimes even more, lived, laughed and cried in these rooms, and without much thought of anything better.

"Privacy was impossible and the men went in the bath wearing their working underpants. As the saying went, 'they washed as far down as possible and as far up as possible and possible took care of itself'. When the time came for a summer swim in the river, the young men had to go downstream and get rid of the 'tide-mark' before they put on their swimming trunks." Swims were of course a seasonal treat. Weather for the most part in Glenbuck varied from wet (1,300mm of rain per year in this part of Ayrshire) to savagely cold, with up to four months of snow that often sealed Glenbuck off from the outside world.

The little world of Glenbuck was dominated by the mines in almost every sense, and the effect on the local landscape was transformative. The former Glen of the Buck that used to echo with hunting cries and the thunder of horses' hooves now rang with the din of the pithead. The huge spoil heaps or 'bings' towered over the village, alongside the pit wheels and chimneys that were the skyscrapers of their time and place.

This is not to suggest that Glenbuck at the time was bereft of comfort, physical or spiritual. The families, particularly the women in them, were fiercely house-proud and made the very best of the rudimentary accommodation available, keeping their homes clean and as comfortable as possible for their large broods. Life was a struggle for certain, but away from the privations of the mine, it had both its charms and municipal amenities. Beside the 75 acres of Glenbuck Loch, stocked with Loch Leven trout, was Glenbuck House. It was an imposing home with turrets and towers out of kilter with the rest of the area, providing a vivid physical sign of the differences in social status of the nation in the latter half of the 19th century.

Built in 1879, Glenbuck's grandest property was a baronial-style imitation of a traditional Scots tower house. It was designed by John Murdoch for the man who was effectively laird of the village, Charles Howatson. Born in 1832, Howatson was commonly described as a 'self-made man', but that belied his origins. The scion of a number of prominent Ayrshire farming families, he was a man of considerable wealth and influence. He was also resourceful and industrious, at the age of 15 joining a local mining and iron concern, William Baird and Company.

There, he rose through the ranks to take over Muirkirk ironworks, overseeing a period of sustained growth. He also made his mark in other ways. As a keen advocate of temperance and thrift, he stopped the sale of alcohol at the company store, and paid a bonus to the workmen who abstained. He retired from the management of the works in 1870 at the age of just 38, and went on to pursue twin passions – landowning and rearing sheep.

In 1863 he had leased a farm at Crossflatt, paying ten shillings for each ewe and pig kept on it during the summer. Howatson inherited Crossflatt, while estates and farms at Dornel, Hall, Glenmuir, Auchinlongford, Tardoes, and an old family seat at Duncanziemere were added to his growing portfolio.

The Glenbuck Estate followed suit in 1872, and it was here he was arguably at his most industrious, producing gas coal. But he found his real metier breeding the blackface rams Glenbuck was famous for. He won a Prince of Wales Gold Medal at the Royal Highland Show and never looked back, winning the honour 12 years in a row up to 1903. Howatson's sheep were ideally suited to the testing climate, bred to have thick coats that kept out the worst the punishing winters could throw at them. Of course, there was bounty to be made as well as prizes. As recounted in *Cairntable Echoes*, 'from 1864 to 1875 the average weight of fleece increased from 3¼ to 5½ lbs., and in 1888 it was 6½ lbs., or fully a third more than the average weight of blackface fleeces on similar land in general.'

Howatson wasn't alone in his ambition. Indeed a Glenbuck man, Joe Muir, emigrated to America in 1882, leaving behind his parents who ran the post office, to forge a career as a prolific landowner first in Montana and then New England. "He left home," reported the *Muirkirk Advertiser*, "with the greatest asset a child can inherit, viz., a sound constitution, and the valuable asset of robust health, but with very little in the way of worldly gear."

Such enterprising spirit was employed at home in Glenbuck House, but there is an inescapable sense that Howatson reared animals in a similar way to the way he sought to extract profit from his employees. Consciously or not, in the minds of 19th century industrialists and landowners like Howatson, human beings were a resource. If a sheep had a thicker fleece, its wool was worth more money; if people could be tempted away from the demon drink, they were more productive.

At Glenbuck House, Howatson set about transforming the immediate landscape. *The Scottish Field*'s gushing tribute that compared Howatson's horticultural endeavours to 'Peter the Great's troubles in founding the handsome city of St Petersburg', might have been overblown, but Howatson did make impressive progress. The bleak heath was replaced with softer grassland, woods were planted, and gardens flourished. Howatson was also a prominent patrician in his community. Said to be of 'a genial and homely disposition', he was active in the County Council, the Parochial Board, and the School Board. He founded the Glenbuck Bursary to assist the local students at the universities. He was prominent in the foundation and financing of Glenbuck Church in 1882, and erected Covenanter monuments. Unsurprisingly he stood as a Unionist candidate for South Ayrshire in 1892, but ill health ultimately denied him political office.

Many would mourn his passing in 1918 at the age of 86. Others were more equivocal in weighing up his achievements. Howatson was from the property and mine-owning class, and those whose labour he profited from saw him in a different light. "The kirk [church] was in the middle of the village in an imposing position," says Purdie. "The lectures from the pulpit were specifically aimed at emphasising the virtues of hard work, warning of the dire perils in the hereafter for any dissidence; neglecting to mention that this blood and sweat filled the pockets of the coal owner in his mock baronial mansion."

When it came to religion, the residents of Glenbuck were not an especially evangelical bunch, at least in a formal sense. Faith was practised and expressed in people's homes, including the Shanklys', but while most could notionally be described as Presbyterians, the established Church had only a loose hold over the population. In contrast to the orthodox view of a fundamental and bitter theological divide in the west and south of Scotland between Protestants and Catholics, it seems religion was not an issue Glenbuckians were overly concerned with. As Dave Bowler writes in his excellent book *Shanks: The Authorised Biography of Shankly*, 'while the church might seek to mitigate the awfulness of their circumstances, political engagement was a means of breaking the stranglehold which locked them into that depressing way of life.'

Faith in deities didn't really matter, especially down the pit, where the quality of a man's work and his dependability as a colleague was far more important.

More in tune with the aspirations of the village's inhabitants was the school. Initially, this was a spartan building that served the community during the Glenbuck Ironworks days. It wasn't until 1872 and the Education Act (Scotland) that more comprehensive provision of education was established in the village.

The Act (and its predecessor in England and Wales) was a turning point in British history, and Glenbuck's children were just some of the millions who reaped the benefit. For the first time some form of education was made compulsory for all children aged between 5 and 13. Parish schools were effectively taken over by the state to be managed by locally elected School Boards. The focus was on the three Rs of 'reading, writing, and 'rithmetic'.

Glenbuck's school board was set up in March 1876 and a new school opened a week later under the leadership of headmaster W.S. Bakie. After the pupils were sent home for a week while the building was completed and the paint dried, the initial intake was 106.

For the rest of the school's existence, this roll would rise and fall in direct correlation to the success or otherwise of the mines. If a pit shut down, the number of schoolchildren declined. This was caused either by families leaving the area in search of work, children being taken out by their parents in order to find a job and contribute to the small household income, or simply because the parents could not afford the school fees.

If ever an institution provided an insight into the world of an impoverished mining village, the school was it. Children would often turn up shoeless and hungry; outbreaks of illness and disease would shut the school down completely. As Purdie notes, "The headmaster's manuscript records of the time complained of a great deal of absenteeism ascribed to 'helping at home', 'inclement weather' and 'contagion', though there are good grounds for suspicion that many of these absences were in fact due to the older pupils – still under 12 – being unofficially employed."

By the turn of the 19th century, the school roll almost reached 300. The long reign of the widely respected headmaster John Rodger, which would last until 1927, was in its prime, with the building divided into five classes served by five teachers, and supported by a pupil teacher and a monitor.

While the school served a vital need, it was treated by those who utilised it with the familiar range of feelings common to all children in all contexts and times. Some flourished and made the most of the opportunity. Others muddled along as kids are wont to do, emerging with a basic education that would stand them in good stead for adult life. Others harboured a lifetime's grudge at the strict discipline and control the school exerted, still wincing at the memory of corporal punishment.

But whatever the experience, the school was a visible symbol of Glenbuck's arrival as a proper community. As did, it should be acknowledged, the pub. The Royal Arms "was always a modest inn," recalls Purdie. "At one stage in the village's history three railway lines were under construction and the navvies were regulars. The bar was built at a time when glasses were expensive and pilferage was common. The way round this for the publican was to use round-bottomed glasses which fitted the purpose-carved dimples in the bar top. Years later the navvies and the unstable glasses had long gone but the dimples remained on the bar."

Shops sprang up in the village. As recalled by the late Thomas Findlay in his fine study of the area *Garan 1631 to Muirkirk 1950*, there was Bain's fruit shop, Miss Kerr's bakery, Sanny Hamilton's butchers, the co-op, a fish and chip shop, and a couple of tiny sweet emporiums. The village was populated by characters like 'Slack Jock', Sanny McAlpine, 'Birdie Bone', Sandy McAndy, Jimmy Dalziel and Dugal Burnside. The latter spun the tallest of tales. Though he had never ventured out of Glenbuck in his life, he would regale anyone prepared to listen of his adventures in foreign lands and especially of the day he was attacked by a huge and fearsome bear.

No doubt some of these notable locals would have been habitués of an activity common around the village. Gambling was another vice the likes of Howatson frowned upon, but card games for reasonably high stakes were a common pursuit for many of the men (including Bill Shankly). Games would take place away from prying eyes, usually in secluded corners around the mines or up on the hills and in copses of trees. The village hall was another centre of recreation. Dances were held there, concert parties and political meetings.

Those political gatherings were a reflection of the interest and activism in Glenbuck. It stemmed directly from the experience of work. Mining bred a resolute solidarity, and lasting loyalties. Purdie recalled that Jimmy 'Bowsy' Dalziel was proud to stoke the Grasshill boilers single-handed for twelve and a half pence a day to power the vital pumps, to give steam to the winding engines, "to lower men to the black depths and raise the coal".

In the 1930s, one old Glenbuck miner, M.T. McWhirter, looked back on a time of hard labour but also some fondness to his life down the Maidenbank pit in the late 1880s. He recalled the various jobs from pithead man to 'crawpickers', drivers and pit-bottomers. There were the accidents and injuries, the characters he worked with, and the horses that pulled the wagons of coal between the pits, in particular a Clydesdale breed with the pet name of 'Star' who nobly carried his unceasing burden like some heroic antecedent of George Orwell's Boxer in *Animal Farm*.

McWhirter also wrote of the fun that could be had. 'Cottie' McBride would teach his colleagues how to 'step dance'. Others came to blows over the merits of the famous boxers of the time, John L. Sullivan and Charlie Mitchell.

Political engagement, McWhirter illustrated, was marked, "Piece-time [tea or dinner]," McWhirter wrote, "usually occupied an hour, and sometimes longer if the discussion was keen. Many and varied were the topics that engaged the attention of this pit parliament, and it was at one of the piece-time meetings that one of the miners stated that if the people would return him as their representative in Parliament, the first measure he would endeavour to place in the Statute book would be that all coal miners receive a fortnight's wages every week."

Such camaraderie was infectious. A sense of humour was essential; Terris recalls the necessity of capers and pranks to alleviate the daily grind. It built an *esprit de corps* almost unique in the British workplace. Miners stood their ground and fights were not uncommon, but any disputes among the men tended to be swiftly resolved. The real enmity was saved for the mine owners and bosses.

Glenbuck's politics were inevitably of the socialistic variety. Ayrshire did not lean left to quite the same extent as other places in Scotland, notably 'Red Clyde', and indeed until the 1990s the county town was for many years home to one of the few Conservative MPs north of the border. But in the coalfields and pit villages, the commitment to left-wing politics was marked, and Glenbuck was more militant than most.

The politics of the mining families were forged in the pit and hammered into shape by the everyday experience of life in their small corner of the industrial British Empire. Down amongst the coal the function of and reliance on collective effort was not a philosophical choice but a practical necessity. Everything about mine work needed people to work together. Lives literally depended on it. That had an inescapable influence on the nature and hue of the miners' political outlook.

The experience of pit work drove people to seek representation and to effect change. Not merely in the desire to win the vote for all men and women, nor to alleviate the worst miseries of their condition, but to actively lay the foundations for an entire movement to revolutionise the whole country. Glenbuck, Muirkirk and the surrounding area was a hotbed of early working-class political activity in Britain, and none became more famously active than a little miner from Cumnock whose life and career would resonate around the world.

Keir Hardie (his actual first name was James) was born in Lanarkshire in 1856, but would become a legendary figure in the Ayrshire coalfields. The illegitimate son of a servant, Mary Keir, who later married a ship's carpenter, Hardie witnessed first hand the harsh reality of life for the poor. He started work at eight, became the only wage earner in the family as economic recession took hold, and was first subjected to the frightening conditions of the mines aged just 11.

His was no isolated experience. Many boys of his class and generation went through the same privations. But Hardie's family prided itself on self-improvement and wanted the young Keir to get an education. He was encouraged to learn to read and write but also to think and to challenge. Before he played a critical role in founding and leading what would become the Labour Party, Hardie campaigned vigorously in the area. There are numerous stories of miners in Glenbuck being warned off by owners from inviting him into their homes with threats of cuts in pay or even the sack for any who disobeyed. Purdie's own grandfather recalled the local bigwig Howatson threatening that any Glenbuck family who offered Hardie a bed for the night would be evicted. As a consequence, meetings were often clandestine and held at night.

Hardie was in many respects the antithesis of Howatson. The 'Coal Laird' sought to improve the lot of the mining families but strictly on the mine-owners' terms. Hardie instead strove to empower the miners to liberate themselves. "Why is it," he asked, "that in the richest nation in the world those who produce the wealth should alone be poor?" It was a clarion call the people of Glenbuck readily responded to. When Hardie and his colleagues organised a miners' union in Ayrshire in 1881, and a strike was called to campaign for a 10% rise in wages, the village provided ready support. William Stewart wrote in his 1921 biography of Hardie, 'away up towards Auchinleck they went marching, their numbers increasing with every mile of the road. On through Darnconner, and Cronberry and Lugar and Muirkirk, right on to Glenbuck by Aird's Moss where the Covenanter Martyrs sleep, then down into Cumnock, at least five thousand strong. Never did magic muster such an army of the morning.'

It was not all politics and stirring marches. There were other activities that exercised the minds and the bodies of Glenbuck and other mining folk. Greyhound and pigeon racing were popular pastimes. In common with communities the length and breadth of the country, the new industrial class took to sport with an almost feverish passion. Athletics and team games were hugely popular, and well suited to people whose physical labour made them rudely fit. Football, of course, was the enterprise with which Glenbuck would really make its name but it did have a rival in the shape of quoiting.

Pronounced 'kiteing', the game was an ancient relative to any number of games like bowls and even discus-throwing in Ancient Greece. In 19th-century Scotland it involved competitors on a 21-yard pitch throwing a heavy iron ring – the quoit – rounded on one side and flat at the other, at a metal pin driven flush into the ground or a three-foot square of compressed clay. The objective was to throw the quoit closest to the pin (and not necessarily directly around it) to win a point.

It needed considerable skill and strength, with the steel quoits weighing up to 11 pounds. It became a hugely popular sport, and Glenbuck produced its greatest ever practitioner. Tom Bone was born in 1868 and by the age of 20 was already winning prestigious local competitions. He went on to win the Scottish Championship in 1889, and established himself as one of the country's finest players. His status as the best ever came when he competed for the hampionship of Great Britain, with the English champion James Hood of Liverpool.

This famous match took place at Motherwell in 1908. The man dubbed 'The Glenbuck Marvel' was unbeatable on the day, thrashing Hood 61–27. Bone would go on to win multiple titles and medals, before a mining accident resulted in the loss of sight in one eye. He was never the same man again and died aged just 48.

All Glenbuck mourned his loss, for Tom Bone was from one of Glenbuck's most notable families. Some relatives, however, would burnish the name and become sportsmen in their own right through another sport. This time there would be no clink of steel quoits reverberating through the village but the thump of sturdy boots meeting inflated leather. Football was coming to town.

Chapter 4

The Scottish Football Village

THE game with which Glenbuck made its name has such a long and storied history in Scotland and Britain that it has come to play a huge part in defining national character and identity. Perhaps too much of a part. The omniscient modern popularity of the sport has often made a mockery of its more traditional, less contrived appeal. Until relatively recently, football was a pariah pastime – 'a slum sport played in slum stadiums increasingly watched by slum people, who deter decent folk from turning up' as the *Sunday Times* put it in the aftermath of the Heysel disaster in 1985. Nowadays, expressing a devotion to the game is an essential accoutrement of 21st-century living.

From film stars to minor royals, demonstrating a love for 'footie' has become a curious cultural obsession. Long-standing fans from the 'slum' days can't quite comprehend how their game has changed, bringing with it a hitherto hostile influx of new supporters. The curmudgeonly old guard express bewilderment at seeing people with no previous interest in the game now viewing it as vital to adopt a team and display a conspicuous passion. The phenomenon surely reached its height – or should it be nadir? – when Prime Minister David Cameron, confusing West Ham with Aston Villa in the 2015 election campaign, got himself into an almighty muddle trying to work out which team that plays in claret and blue he is supposed to support.

Quite what the people of Glenbuck would have made of it all is amusing to consider. But if adhering cultural labels based simply on football interests and loyalties can often appear trite today, in the 19th and 20th centuries, the love of and commitment to the sport of football was genuine and powerful. It was etched deep in to the identity and psyche of whole swathes of working-class communities across Britain, and in Scotland took particularly firm root. Those roots were often tangled with England, in what has often been a tortured relationship, but, welcomed by the two football communities or not, football has been a setting in which the two nations have been inextricably intertwined.

Some form of football had of course been played in Scotland deep into the past. The claims for the birthplace of a sport that the *Encyclopedia of British Football* described as 'the game that nobody invented' are perennially, fiercely contested. Some scholars argue that Scotland came relatively late to the party, around the 14th century. But given the wondrous simplicity of football, the innumerable variants around the globe, and the apparently innate desire of human beings to gather together and kick, throw, or propel by some means an inflated bag of some description around a defined area, it's likely that ancient Scots were playing some form of the game far further back in time.

Whatever the true origins, by the medieval period there were proto-football matches taking place in various villages and towns. Rules were either bizarrely arcane or virtually dispensed with altogether, in favour of a prolonged and brutish shoving, kicking and fighting match in which participants were at great risk of serious injury or worse. In common with England, the Scottish authorities frowned upon such activity and there were numerous bans prohibiting the game being played. The common perception is this was due to concerns on the part of the ruling elite that the rural or peasant classes would be distracted from archery practice. In addition, the latent mistrust of large numbers of young men gathering in one place and seemingly threatening disorder pressed the prohibition buttons. Successive King James outlawed football, culminating with James VI (I of England), expressly forbidding his son Henry from indulging in 'the rough and violent exercises at the foot-ball.'

Foot-ball, however, would not be beaten. It surfaced and survived in a number of forms until the 19th century and the period of the great codification of organised sport. The Establishment's view on football undertook something of a transformation. It was imbued with the Victorian thirst for self-improvement and physical fitness, allied to a religious zeal that saw sport as a character-defining, moral imperative that would improve mind, body and soul. Rather than condemning it as an uncivilised activity enjoyed and practised only by the lower orders, it was now seen as a means to an end, ideally suited to an age of rapid industrial growth and colonial expansion.

To put it in blunt economic and political terms, sport built fit, able and broadly dutiful men who would likely make good factory workers and effective empire builders. As an added bonus, team games would also inculcate 'sporting' values and lessons in leadership among the officer class.

In England football developed as an organised sport in two phases: first, in the public schools and universities, and then amid the changing demographics of a newly industrialised country. The age-old enthusiasm for the game among the masses found fresh expression in the formation of clubs representing urban districts and towns, largely in the North and the Midlands. North of the border the picture was slightly different. Here, it was a game that from its inception was based around workplace, church and community.

Patricians still made sure they were involved. Sir Walter Scott was an early champion of preserving the medieval game.

In December 1815 he wrote a ballad about the remarkable 'Carterhaugh ba' match that took place in the Borders, an area that would later be lost to rugby union. The 'ba' was a revival of an ancient fixture, and pitted dozens of men against each other for a rugby-like contest in a woodland pitch on the Duke of Buccleuch Estate. Scott sponsored the Men of Selkirk against the Men of Yarrow, who were in turn provided with backing by Duke Charles at Bowhill House and his brother-in-law, the Earl of Home.

The latter captained a team of shepherds, farmers and tenants. Their opponents were made up of various groups from Hawick, Selkirk and Gala. Whisky was served before play began to the accompaniment of bagpipes and an unfurling of the war banner of the Scotts, a spectacle not seen since 1633. Two thousand spectators saw the teams win a match each, but the organisers decided to forego a decider in favour of a feast, supplemented by more whisky.

Yet for all the nostalgic pageantry, football in Scotland was actually seen as facing a long slow decline, compounded by what Scott described as village games that were 'not always safe', as 'the old clannish spirit is too apt to break out.'

It fell to the people themselves to truly revive the sport and create a social and cultural phenomenon that is so ingrained in Scottish life and identity to this day. In the lowlands and the central belt, particularly in Glasgow, organised games approaching a recognisably modern form took place. In the city's Queen's Park, matches drew in ever-increasing numbers of players. In July 1867, these early footballers – mostly young and middle class, some engaged in skilled trades, others from organisations like the YMCA – decided to form a team, called, predictably enough, Queen's Park.

The side reigned supreme for nearly a decade, later establishing a base at Hampden in the south of the city and winning the first three Scottish FA Cups. Though by the mid-1870s other clubs were challenging, the influence of Queen's Park was such that the club essentially laid down the laws and ran the administration of the game in Scotland.

The growing public clamour for football fuelled the creation of more teams and fixtures, and in November 1870, the first ever international match between Scotland and England took place. The English Football Association had been formed in 1863, formulating in a handwritten notebook what is surely the greatest tome ever written in the English language – *The Rules Of Association Football*. The FA was the pre-eminent governing body in the embryonic game, and its leaders knew it. The FA's secretary Charles Alcock issued a challenge via the letters page of the *Glasgow Herald* and proud Scotsmen heeded it.

At least those proud Scotsmen, well-to-do and connected gentlemen, most of them living in London, who could call on a Scottish family bloodline to qualify to play, that is. Among them was A.F. Kinnaird, who was to become a grandee of the game for the next half-century and would feature in a later connection to Glenbuck (see Chapter 7). Alongside him was W.H. Gladstone, son of the Prime Minister. According to the *Manchester Guardian*, Gladstone jnr., 'the junior lord of the Treasury, did good service on the part of the Scottish team.' The match, played at the Kennington Oval, finished 1–1.

The first international proper, played under the laws of the English FA, took place two years later at the West of Scotland Cricket Ground at Partick. It was preceded that year by a visit from Queen's Park to play in the FA Cup semi-final against the famous Wanderers (Queen's Park would later reach two FA Cup finals, losing both). This early Scottish involvement in England's premier competition was significant. Not only did the Glasgow side contribute a guinea towards the cost of the trophy, but their performance made quite an impression. Though they could not afford to play in a replay, they had shown that the practicality of visiting sides travelling long distances was, at least for one game, feasible. And so, for that first recognisable international, it was a team of nine Queen's Park men and two former players who took on England, the hosts taking to the field in the dark blue shirts of the Glasgow side, and emblazoned with a single lion.

The match ended goalless, despite the innovative style of the Scotsmen. This was a retort to the accepted wisdom of the English footballing oligarchy, who, as pointed out in *Encyclopedia of British Football*, were possessed of a 'patronizing attitude... that England were going north to show the Scots how to play the game.'

Such arrogance was woefully misplaced. Almost from its birth, Scottish football was a team game by definition. In England, value was placed on individualism and physical strength. The seven (sometimes eight) forwards who would line up in the formation of the day would not meld together as a unit, but operated more as a collection of individuals performing their party pieces, chiefly through raw brawn or the art of dribbling. While hacking – kicking an opponent's shins – had been prohibited, the practice of 'backing up' was a key component of the way elite English teams played. Other forwards would support their colleague with a muscular rearguard should any attack break down. It was this that was the rudimentary style that was taught at English public schools and which persisted in the senior ranks.

Scottish sides like Queen's Park had their solo artistes as well, but their players, who tended to weigh significantly less than their English counterparts, operated in a much more structured way. Passing the ball, something that early rules in some formats forbade, was a tactic. For it to work, it required understanding, co-operation and a team ethos, qualities that were readily forged in the workplace and communities where players grew up with each other. It was a philosophy of innovation; a way of playing the game that was tailor-made for places like Glenbuck.

The Scots combined dribbling with passing, both short and on the ground and longer, more lofted passes that encouraged players to head the ball. This expansive style, dubbed 'combination football', was variously praised and denigrated, as related in

Jonathan Wilson's seminal history of football tactics, *Inverting the Pyramid*. Wilson also pinpoints the initial lack of competitive matches for Queen's Park as a pivotal factor in the way they played the game. In the club's early days, there were simply not enough sides to play against, compounded by the variety of rules that saw some opponents wanting to field 16 players. Thus Queen's Park effectively played amongst themselves, instilling a mode of play. It was this 'hot-housing' that again found an echo in the way Glenbuck footballers would develop their particular style.

The Scottish passing game would soon earn dividends. The Queen's Park-dominated Scottish team emerged triumphant from the early exchanges with the English national side, winning seven of the first 11 internationals. The proven value of such tactics bolstered a team-based approach in the wider Scottish game. Clubs came and went; others endured, such as Kilmarnock, Vale of Leven, Dumbarton and until the 1960s, Third Lanark.

Dumbarton and Vale of Leven mark other key staging posts in the evolution of the game in Scotland, and of the people who would play and support it. Situated to the west of Glasgow, and geographically linked to the Highlands, Dunbartonshire and the Vale of Leven were places that drew in migrants from far and wide.

It meant that the people in these areas who formed football teams didn't necessarily come from them. They were compelled by circumstances, often matters of sheer survival, to migrate, from the Highlands, the Western Islands and from Ireland.

As Matthew McDowell notes in his academic paper, *The pit, the pitch and the pub: Scottish soccer players in the north of England, c. 1870-1900*, "within Highland Scotland, there were the Clearances, the collective name for a group of land reorganisation schemes executed to make way for grazing grounds, which eventually became intrinsically linked to emigration. This was coupled with the Highland Famine, striking in 1846, one year later than in Ireland. Both famines pushed migrants into the Scottish central belt, from Glasgow east to the Lothians."

Author and historian Ian Campbell-Whittle has exhaustively researched the nature of the local populations that gave birth to and sustained the early history of football in Scotland, and says: "The potato blight hit Europe – and it was the whole of Europe – in 1844 and persisted until 1852. Its effects were most devastating in countries where potato dependency was greatest. Ireland was the worst example but the Highlands of Scotland were smaller in scale but not far behind in terms of severity. The result was extreme pressure on large numbers of people to move. They had to flee to survive, be it from Ireland to anywhere, and from the Scottish Highlands to the Lowlands and the northern English cities, particularly Liverpool and Newcastle."

The impact on the evolution of football was telling. "In Scotland there is little argument that football started in 1867 with Queen's Park in the newly developing, mainly middle-class suburbs of Glasgow south of the Clyde," says Campbell-Whittle. "As a city Glasgow was drawing people in but was comparatively small – 500,000 and half of what it would officially be 50 years later. Communities outside Glasgow, in Renfrewshire, Lanarkshire and Dunbartonshire... were also at the same time exploding, taking as many people annually as Glasgow itself. It's no coincidence that one such area, the Vale of Leven in Dunbartonshire, was to be one of the hotbeds of football until the early 1890s. The Vale industrialised early, beginning in earnest in the 1840s."

The make-up of the teams that were established reflected the often complex interaction between the various geographical origins of the people who formed, played and supported them. Players for the Vale of Leven were most likely drawn from Highland Scots, for example. The spectre of religion and sectarian division also reared its head earlier here than it would do for football in Glasgow. Of a less divisive and damaging influence was another sport that arguably had a direct bearing on the emerging style of Scottish football. For some players from both Renton and the Vale of Leven also played shinty.

"In 1880 the Vale of Leven club won Scotland's premier shinty competition," explains Campbell-Whittle. "Shinty is a game that is still played widely, as well as in the North but also in Highlands to the north-west of the Vale, and it would have been brought by people as they moved into the Vale."

Campbell-Whittle does not wholly accept the argument that the similarities in formation between shinty and early Scottish football teams was a decisive influence on the way football was played. He also doubts whether Queen's Park were shaped by the other sport, given that few of its founders came from shinty-playing areas. But Campbell-Whittle does consider other links.

"Formation is one thing but style of play another. By the early 1880s England had fully adopted 2:2:6, but were still getting beaten by Scotland. England then adopted 2:3:5, a tactic that came from Wales, but Scotland still won. Scottish clubs were still beating English. Scottish players were in huge demand for their skill and tactical awareness. Formations were initially the same, then different, but the results remained the same. So there was something else; something which seems to have made its difference from the mid-1870s onwards [at] the shinty-playing Vale of Leven clubs.

"The effect of the something-else is fairly easy to identify. It was in attack with Scotland going from matching England goal for goal to scoring two for every England's one. The intimation is that its geographical source was the Vale of Leven, while, in part at least, philosophically it was shinty.

"Shinty is based on a mixture not just of lofted, long passes and some individual dribbling – universal early football tactics – but also quick, short passes stopped, trapped with the feet and passed on along the ground, and of triangles. All were distinctive elements of the Scottish, 'scientific' game before the First World War... It leaves open the possibility of cross-fertilisation in terms of style between shinty and football, with the shinty-playing footballers of the 1870s the conduits."

Campbell-Whittle's research suggests fascinating and highly distinct elements around the gestation of the game in Scotland. Whatever the full impact of these influences, the Scottish game was winning widespread favour. The sport enjoyed a popular boom, with ever-increasing player participation and, significantly, crowds who wanted to watch it. Football was not originally developed as a business proposition, but the growth in spectator appeal presented opportunities and challenges. Fans liked the way Queen's Park played. It was fast, fluent and exciting, and was emulated by other clubs. It also produced good footballers, who inevitably, were coveted by those clubs in northern England who were emerging separately from the hegemony of the public schools, universities and armed forces teams.

These new clubs – like Blackburn, Preston, Burnley and Darwen – were formed out of the factories and cotton mills, local sports clubs and community groups. Swiftly taken over by industrialists and enterprising tradesmen keen to climb up the social ladder, such clubs had a distinctly blue-collar feel and were soon seen as a boost to local civic pride. But they also presented a business opportunity. Spectators needed to be accommodated, to watch teams that strove not just to play the game but to win. All of that necessitated money. Within a virtuous circle of charging spectators in order to pay players to build winning teams that would draw in paying spectators, mass spectator sport and professionalism was born.

The conflict between the amateur game championed by the English elites opposed to new, commercially-aware concerns primarily based in England's industrial north was one of the great schisms in sporting history. It exposed fundamentally different attitudes to the function and purpose of organised sport, not just in football but in cricket and rugby.

Less explicitly noted at the time were the marked hypocrisies on the part of the amateurs, who not only had sufficient private income to indulge their sporting prowess on a full-time basis but collected surreptitious expenses that often dwarfed those claimed by the pros.

Professionalism in football was finally approved in England in 1885, the Football League three years later. The battle was played out in Scotland too. To fulfil their fixtures, English clubs wanted players, and the best ones at that. Many of these were Scottish, who were lured south by the promise not only of a decent job in the mills or factories, but also of being paid to play the game they enjoyed. McDowell wrote that, "One club, Preston North End, and its flamboyant chairman, Major William Sudell, was fairly open about its ability to supply Scots with fictitious jobs while paying their players gate money under the table."

McDowell references Steven Tischler who in his book *Footballers and Businessmen: The Origins of Professional Soccer in England*, stated that, "With regard to soccer, the administrators of sport, typically based within a London-centric, school-oriented circle, used the term 'professional' as a euphemism for 'working-class'; and, as soccer increasingly became an arena where the labouring class sought social mobility, naturally its participants – many of whom worked in industries with insecure futures – would migrate for better opportunities."

It should be noted that professionalism was not solely in the interests of the players. Indeed, it was a situation arguably better suited to the owners. Researcher and historian Andy Boo is creating a 'digital tour' that will take users on a 30-mile circular tour charting 300 years of football history in the north-west of England, finishing with the adoption of professional football. He cites a report in the *Darwen Post* of 3 October 1885, to show why the club owners, or 'committee men', wanted professionalism as much as the players:

'There is no doubt but that committees of the clubs – in this district, at all events – have hailed the passing of the rule with glee, because it places their men at the call of the committee; whereas in seasons gone by the committee were entirely at the mercy of the men. Many instances could be given of *amateur* players in our premier clubs refusing to play in certain important cup ties until such times as they received a certain "sop" which was not always a modest one. The committees were forced to yield, or be defeated in the cup tie. Now, each man is paid a weekly wage, and is registered as a "pro", and cannot play for more than one club without the express permission of the Association; and from what I can learn the Association will not grant such permission unless the man has a "clean" book. It is therefore a serious thing for any player to try any high-handed game with his committee, because they will not stand it, as it depends on them to a great extent to say whether the man shall play football or not. Truly, the tables have been turned.'

Inducements offered by clubs like Preston prompted something of an exodus from Scotland, as the first wave of the so-called 'Anglos' to depart the mother country wore a path many from Glenbuck would later follow. They were by no means welcomed universally in England – indeed there was great hostility in places, and on both sides of the border, albeit compromised. McDowell writes, "The Scottish newspapers railed against the filthy lucre of the English league, but they were not above printing classified advertisements paid for by English soccer clubs looking for a few good men. One unnamed Burton-on-Trent club printed an advert in 24 June 1890's edition of *Scottish Referee*. It read:

"'First-class Centre or Inside-Forward required to undertake management of large Hotel and Spirit Vaults, and play with local team in Midlands. Good Salary. Satisfactory References and Security.'"

The momentum of change was remorseless. In 1886, the Scottish Football Association split from its English counterpart, ending the participation of Scottish clubs in the FA Cup. The Scottish authorities held out against professionalism, but eventually acquiesced to the inevitable in 1893, three years after the Scottish League had been established. By then many of the clubs that persist to this day had been formed, among them two outfits in Glasgow called Celtic and Rangers. "You might as well attempt to stop the flow of Niagara with a kitchen chair as to endeavour to stem the tide of professionalism," said Celtic's J.H. McLaughlin at the SFA meeting that finally voted in favour of turning the game pro. The poisonous religious bigotry that has blighted the great Glasgow football rivalry was to truly manifest itself later. In the early days of the Old Firm power grab, it was more a case of good business.

Queen's Park held out against the tide of change. Once the single superpower of Scottish football, they are still amateur to this day, playing in front of a few hundred spectators. Not just beneath the cavernous stands of the new and latterly re-developed Hampden Park that they moved to in Mount Florida in 1903, but in training and fielding youth teams at the hopelessly charismatic 'Lesser Hampden' sited right next door to the modern monolith. Any football fan who visits both grounds and is not moved by the experience must have the stoniest of hard hearts.

While the intrigues and epochal events surrounding the foundation of the game were being played out in Glasgow and beyond, the citizens of Glenbuck were themselves taking to the sport with considerable enthusiasm. At first it was embraced as an amateur leisure pastime. Later it would offer an escape route out of the pits into the world of the paid professionals. This was a familiar story. As McDowell observes, "The legalisation of professionalism, however much it benefited the position of the major Glasgow clubs, nevertheless did not stop the haemorrhaging of talent south of the border, and did little to stop the collapse of village soccer clubs that, previous to 1890, represented the heartlands of Scottish soccer.

"Dunbartonshire clubs were famed for their dominance of the Scottish game in the 1870s and 1880s. Dumbarton Football Club, a group of players closely associated with the Denny shipbuilding concern, and Vale of Leven and Renton, two village clubs comprised almost exclusively of workers involved in the local, paternalistic calico factories, were the early titans of Scottish soccer. Meanwhile, clubs from coal mining localities in Ayrshire, from places like Kilmarnock, Cumnock, Hurlford and Annbank formed the bulk of new arrivals to Lancashire soccer between 1878 and 1885. Migration and professionalism thus took their toll on such clubs, ensuring that many of them would not be playing in the higher reaches of Scottish soccer by 1900."

Players from another Ayrshire mining community, Glenbuck, would indeed be among those who upped sticks and headed for the professional heartlands of Lancashire and beyond. But the sorry tale of declining village or small town sides was not to be quite the fate that befell the club with which those coveted Glenbuck players originally made their name. This club would eventually fall by the wayside, but as other teams in other mining areas struggled to survive, Glenbuck's provided a sporting sensation.

Chapter 5

The Cherrypickers

IT is not recorded when the first Glenbuckian kicked a ball. Perhaps it was a child of one of those early tenant farmers who picked and prodded the surface for coal, their kids enjoying a rare moment of fun outside the family wooden hovel, and kicking around a ball of rags. Maybe it was one among that more illustrious company which hunted in the area with the Douglases, having a break from chasing down stags. Whoever it was, whenever it was, he or she would be only the first of many, many people to play the game in the village that made the village's name.

Football and Glenbuck was an irresistible, passionate and long-lasting marriage. It produced many offspring, became an intrinsic part of the village's identity, and cooked up a social glue that helped bond the community together. Glenbuck was always a place where the people lived in a productive co-existence. Football cemented that culture of co-operation and mutual dependency, but moreover gave the villagers a joyful expression of belonging and an excitement that work in the mines could not hope to match. The Glenbuck football teams created a sense of civic pride almost unequalled anywhere else.

Coal miners were natural recruits for sporting excellence. The old cliché about shouting down a Yorkshire mineshaft to find a cricketing fast bowler had its counterpart in the Scottish coalfields, which produced an assembly line of competitors seemingly ready-made to excel at playing football. And not only playing it, but managing and coaching the game as well.

Jock Stein and Matt Busby were two of the great triumvirate of Scottish managers from coal-mining backgrounds. It was Bill Shankly who completed that immortal trio, the youngest of the male Shankly clan that included another four footballing brothers. All were Glenbuck born and bred, making it the most prolific footballing family in the most prolific of footballing villages. Yet the great Shanks was just one of many, and among the last that the village would boast.

Michael Walker, author of *Up There*, the superb biography of football in the North East of England, cited in *The Independent* a telling quote about the relationship between the sport and coal from Bob Paisley. Paisley was another ex-miner turned footballer, who did so much to first aid and abet Shankly at Liverpool as part of the Anfield coaching team, before taking the club to even greater heights when he inherited the top job. Describing Hetton-le-Hole, the Durham mining village where he was born and raised, Paisley said: "Coal was king and football was a religion... [to be seen] not just as a recreation, but as a way of life."

That epithet could have been written for Glenbuck. The miners, their sons and families lived and breathed the game. It was an escape, a release, a means of finding fitness in the fresh air, but also purpose and identity. Football gave life to people whose lives were so gruelling.

It all started in Glenbuck, at least on a vaguely organised basis, with the kickabouts and matches played between the residents themselves on any open piece of ground or in the unpaved streets. Such games would develop and grow, ebb and flow, beginning with small-sided encounters involving pairs of players and increasing in number until there were 16, 17, and sometimes even more on each side. Numbers would decline again as younger players headed home for the evening meal, or to bed. The older lads would hang around until dark. Games could therefore last hours, particularly in summer months where at such latitude it was still possible to play at 11 o'clock.

It is a familiar story common to wherever the game has been and still is played. That is part of its beauty – it can be enjoyed virtually anywhere and without the need for expensive or complex equipment. Unlike almost anywhere, however, those impromptu Glenbuck gatherings evolved into more defined contests between actual teams, based on sides representing each pit.

'Fixtures' such as Grasshill versus The Monkey, or Spireslack versus The Davy took on the resemblance of a fervently competitive mini-league within Glenbuck itself. There was no formal table as such, no awarding of grand prizes, but the matches helped to feed a growing fervour for the sport and encouraged more organised participation.

The key word is 'participation'. Glenbuckians loved to play, rather than watch, especially when compared to the lure of the game outside of the village. People from Glenbuck were nominally Rangers fans, but the label should not be stuck too firmly. For certain, Glenbuckians would travel to Ibrox to watch Rangers play, especially when improved rail connections made the journey more viable. But they would also go to Celtic Park to watch the other half of the Old Firm and other teams within reasonable range. The tribal loyalties of modern club football were not quite as rigorous as they would become and indeed still are today, and in common with many of the great hubs of football supporter rivalry – Liverpool, Manchester and London, for example – people would alternate between watching so-called deadly rivals without unduly worrying about any of the forced contemporary strictures of total and exclusive devotion to one cause.

Biographer Stephen F. Kelly points out that Bill Shankly, raised a Protestant, was just one of these 'itinerant' fans: "Once he had started work, he could afford the 1s 6d return train fare. He'd go up there most weekends – one Saturday supporting Rangers, the next supporting Celtic. Given the sectarianism of the west coast of Scotland, it was remarkable that Shankly should divide his allegiances... It says much for his upbringing that his family held none of the bigoted views that divided Glasgow in two.'

That much was true before Shankly's time. Glenbuck's football fans were for the most part just that – fans of football, and took their fancy where it pleased them. Rangers and Celtic were of course increasingly locked into a bitter religious-inspired struggle fought out by great swathes of their support, but Glenbuckians, existing at a relatively comfortable remove of 20 or so miles from the big city, seemed broadly immune from such divisions.

In any case, they were more exercised by playing the sport, as the inter-mines contests showed. Such activity led inexorably to a team being formed to represent the whole village. The first incarnation came swiftly in the early days of organised football in Scotland in the 1870s. Some sources give the foundation as early in the decade, others toward the 1880s. No one is quite sure of the precise date – if any records of a formal foundation exist they have either been lost or are yet to be discovered. What are more certain are the names of the prominent Glenbuck citizens who were the driving forces behind the establishment of a club.

The name 'Bone' runs through the history of the village like one of those seams of coal that did so much to enable Glenbuck's very existence. Some of its progeny, Tom and his younger brother James, would proudly carry the Glenbuck sporting banner through their triumphs in quoiting. It was two other men of the Bone clan, William and Edward, who were at the forefront of establishing the village's football activities.

The club was named Glenbuck Athletic. Its history is told with wonderful relish by a pair of local historian/writers, the Reverend M.H. Faulds and William M. Tweedie Jnr, in their booklet *The Cherrypickers – Glenbuck Nursery Of Footballers*. First published in 1951, it chronicles the rise and fall of the team in its two incarnations and is a charming exercise in celebrating local success. A later edition in 1981 carried a foreword written by Bill Shankly shortly before his death.

'Glenbuck,' wrote Faulds and Tweedie, 'deserves to be remembered, for it holds a worthy place in history – at any rate, in the history of football. For many years it maintained a junior team, which established a great reputation for itself. But the unique distinction of Glenbuck is that it became a famous nursery of footballers. Year after year a succession of Glenbuck lads passed into Senior Football, winning renown for themselves and bringing credit to their native village. The list of Glenbuck lads who made good in the world of football is a long one and contains many notable names. It can be safely claimed that no village of similar size in all Scotland has a record to equal that of Glenbuck. Altogether, the Glenbuck story is a remarkable page in football history.' Faulds and Tweedie relate that history with evident pride.

The strip chosen for that first Athletic side was white shirts and black shorts. Subscriptions were set at a shilling, but each player would provide for his own kit. Such decisions were not at the behest of those with titled positions but were the consequence of democratic vote. Mirroring the wider ethos of the community, the team was to be genuinely run for the village by the villagers. They played for it, manned the organisation, paid for the club's upkeep, and turned out in their droves to support it.

Initially those fans cheered the team on to victory against other local pit teams. There was not a formal league in those early years but cup competitions provided a thrilling opportunity for the players to demonstrate their expertise. Football's early spirit of 'challenge' was also evident. The English FA, it should be noted, described its own cup competition in such terms, and other sides up and down the country also threw down the gauntlet, inviting challengers to individual contests. Glenbuck did the same, placing advertisements in local papers to draw other teams to the village.

Those games were initially played on a patch of field promptly lost when a new pit shaft was sunk on the site. Athletic switched to another pitch on the flank of a nearby hillside, which presented its own obvious problems in not providing a level surface. So a new and more permanent home was found on a flat field close to the main road overlooked by the church. It was not perfect but much better suited to what the team required. Laying close to a stream it was given the name 'Burnside Park'.

With the move, the team prospered. Athletic had a good record on the road, travelling in spartan style in a three-horse brake, or carriage. 'On the cold dark nights of winter,' Faulds and Tweedie wrote, 'the homeward journey was far from comfortable, and the players would often walk a good deal of the distance to ease their cramped limbs.'

At home matches, it was often the opposition that was left feeling sore. Glenbuck Athletic and their fans offered what can be generously described as a robust welcome. If it wasn't the team handing out a physical test on the pitch, the supporters weighed in off it. For all the class consciousness of Scottish miners, and the rigid loyalties the work encouraged, such solidarity would be left in abeyance when it came to a football match. Rivalries were intense. Visiting players, let alone any supporters who might be bold enough to make the trip to Glenbuck, would be pelted with stones as well as a fusillade of insults. The mother figures of the village, who in the week might be a model of domestic Victorian decency and gentle charm, could be transformed into raging touchline warriors ready to take on all and sundry.

Even the presence of a local policeman sitting on the visiting team's carriage did little to dissuade the hail of missiles and jeers. And if haranguing and attacking the opposition didn't sate the hostility enough, there were always the officials to fulfil the role of helpless victim, with some even ending up in a pond or puddle of water blackened by soot and coal dust.

At least, that is the legend as described by Faulds and Tweedie. Yet while they may have applied a degree of artistic licence in describing the atmosphere at Burnside Park, the recollections of relatives, smiling at the memory of what they were told, confirm that Glenbuck was, in the recognisable football parlance, a very tough place to get a result. But it was the way the team played that made a more telling contribution to the side's success. This in turn was down to several significant factors in the village's favour.

Looking at some of the early team line-ups, it seems there was nothing especially revolutionary about Glenbuck tactics. According to Tom Findlay, the team and formation in the late 1880s would look like this:

BONE

BONE   TAIT

MENZIES   WALLACE   DEVLIN

BLYTH   TAIT   MENZIES

MENZIES   TAIT

What looks on paper like a 2:3:5 was more likely a 2:2:6 conventional for the period. Instead the most illustrative feature is the names. There is a near uniformity of groups of relations playing together, with no less than three members each of the Menzies and Tait families, along with a couple of the defensive Bones. It is tempting to say the latter formed the spine of the side.

This was a reflection not just of the clannish nature of Glenbuck's population, but how many people from the same families would play football. These Bones, Menzies or Taits formed the cup-winning side of 1890 (see below) but in various seasons it could be any members of the respective broods – sons, fathers, brothers, uncles, cousins. The key is that this showed that the Glenbuck teams were made up of players who knew each other very well indeed, with all the benefits of mutual understanding, even a preternatural form of telepathy, that successful football teams almost always rely on.

Not only that, but marriage meant that the various surnames were further related in some way – a female Bone would marry a male Wallace and the bonds between relations spread still further. The men also worked together, again fostering that already strong team spirit and bringing a coalface awareness of strengths, weaknesses and characteristics that readily transferred to the football pitch.

And they inevitably trained together a lot. The mass, 17-a-side matches played in the shadows of the pitheads might have appeared to be chaotic kickabouts, but they were a useful tool in establishing a consistent style of Glenbuck play. Everyone was encouraged to know and understand how to play with their team-mates almost as soon as they first kicked a ball. Familiarity bred contentment. A Tait would know that a Menzies liked a ball clipped inside; a Bone would have been aware that a Dalziel was strong in the air.

Never was this cohesion and almost instinctive awareness better exemplified than in the five-a-side format. More so than English clubs, Scottish sides loved five-a-side, and no players loved it more than those of Glenbuck. At fairs, annual country shows and other seasonal events throughout Ayrshire and beyond, the format kept them occupied in the summer months when there were no full-size games to be played, and further honed an 'in-house' Glenbuck style. And given the proliferation of players with the same surname, families were able to field five-a-side teams made up exclusively of relatives.

As Faulds and Tweedie note, under localised 'Ayrshire Rules', the goalkeeper in five-a-side was not allowed to handle the ball, further encouraging a defined way of playing. Competitions would last a whole day, with teams playing for hours on end. At one event in Lanark the five-a-side competition started on a Saturday and did not finish until the following Monday morning.

It bred special teams. The later side of John Hastie, Bob Tait, Jimmy Tait, William Wallace and John Ferguson, was reckoned to be one of the finest but undoubtedly the most famous of these

Glenbuck mini-teams was that of the Knox brothers. Their remarkable exploits around the turn of the century show how successfully Glenbuck players took to the format. Strangely, they did not at first play in a side together, but were split between two already successful Glenbuck teams, until they realised joining forces might be the better option. So it proved. Hugh, Alec, Tom, William and Peter Knox took on all comers and almost always ended up on the winning side. In one season alone they were victorious in 40 of the 41 matches they played. They won prizes, usually clocks or barometers, so often that they ended up giving many away to delighted spectators cheering them on.

Family ties clearly played a big part in the Knox success, enabling them to hone tactics in a close-knit way other teams could not hope to match. A contemporary photo of the Knoxes, each of the brothers sporting moustaches that made them look like members of Wyatt Earp's posse, vividly illustrates how closely they resembled each other, and displays their impressive physiques. But it would be an error to assume their quality was simply down to family ties and physicality. Responding to a suggestion that hard running was key to five-a-side success, Hughie Knox said, "No. The art of the game is to make the ball do the running about."

Knox wasn't the first footballer to make the observation about 'letting the ball do the work' and he certainly will not be the last, but his comment struck at the heart of the way he and his fellow villagers viewed the game. It was not a crude contest of muscle power and lung capacity. Football was a creative art, practised in training, developed through teamwork, and executed on the pitch.

It brought extraordinary success for Glenbuck Athletic. The highlights were a hat-trick of victories in the Ayrshire Junior Challenge Cup, in the inaugural season of 1889/90, and then in 1891 and 1892. 'Junior' football of course, does not denote youth football. It loosely describes the Scottish equivalent of English non-league football and still flourishes today. It has a deserved reputation for high quality and intense competitiveness throughout its various levels, and thus reflects well on those early Glenbuck Athletic sides who achieved so much success in the local Junior competitions.

The settled cup-winning team of 1890–92 reads like a roll call of famous Glenbuck names. The goalkeeper was Thomas Bone, with skipper James Bone and Sandy Tait forming the back line. The half-backs were Joe Menzies, Alex Wallace, and Peter Devlin, while Robert Blyth, James Tait, John Menzies, James Menzies and Richard Tait were the forwards. The team's entry in the *Ayrshire Football Annual* for 1899–1900 read:

'Instituted 1889, Burnside, colours white. President A. Menzies, vice presidents Messrs A. Kerr and A. Millar, treasurer Mr A. Wallace, secretary Mr Thos Bone, Dalziel's Building Glenbuck. Record: played 20 games, won 13, lost 6, drawn 1 scored 62 lost 40.'

This was a team run by the villagers and their families. Some of these players would go on to fame elsewhere but their initial renown was earned through 1890 wins over Ailsa Swifts (13–0), Hurlford Rovers (3–2), and Crosshouse (3–2). Their opponents in the final, Tarbolton, didn't stand a chance and were hammered 9–2.

Cup success became an enduring habit, and one that was to continue when the team changed name around the 1900s. 'Athletic' was dropped in favour of the new moniker – 'The Cherrypickers'. There are several versions of the story behind the new name, with varying degrees of romance and authenticity.

One tale is that it comes from the mining term to denote the practice of separating coal from stones in the screening sheds. The coal – 'cherries' – would be picked out by workers, leading to an obvious connotation with Glenbuck's principal industry. Other writers prefer the roguish larceny of one particular shoplifting caper, when a group of players were caught stealing a box of cherries from Milliken's store in the village.

The final version has a ring of historical truth and a fair grain of logic. The 11th Hussars was a cavalry regiment in the British army with close local ties to the Ayrshire area. It was formed in the 18th century to fight in the Jacobite uprisings and would see active service in theatres of war from Waterloo to the Western Desert in the Second World War. One story has it that during the Duke of Wellington's Peninsular campaign of 1811–13, a group of 11th Hussars arrived in a Spanish village on a burning hot day, desperate to quench their thirst and sate their hunger. Seeing a nearby cherry orchard, the stripped the trees of their fruit, thus earning in the process the nickname 'Cherrypickers' and the adoption of bright red for the colour of their breeches.

East Ayrshire men would have served with the regiment, and so, at the time of the Boer War, the stories of their exploits would have readily circulated around the Muirkirk area. Stephen F. Kelly writes that two of the Menzies brothers would stride around Glenbuck wearing the distinctive 11th Hussars caps. It was a short leap to transfer the nickname of a regiment to a local football team.

Whatever the true derivation, the name stuck and so did the reputation for fine football. The team continued to thrive, winning three trophies in 1906 – the Ayrshire Charity Cup, Cumnock Cup, and the Mauchline Cup. To the haul was added another Ayrshire Charity Cup in 1910, five more Cumnock Cups in 1901, 1903, 1904, 1905, and 1921, and finally, when the Ayrshire Junior Cup was brought home again in 1931.

By this time, the village and the team were in irreversible decline, though sporting activity had continued throughout the preceding tough times. At the 'Glenbuck Coronation Festivities' for example, to mark the crowning of King George V in 1911, the village's schoolchildren showed their prowess in sprints, skipping-rope contests and three-legged races. One 'Lizzie Shankly', Bill's elder sister, came second in the girls' infants' race. Sister Nettie won the older girls' skipping rope. Elsewhere there was the familiar rendition of Bones, Taits and Wallaces to the fore, including Robert Tait who came second in the fancy dress competition for his sensitive portrayal of a nurse. 'After the final of the football tournament,' reported the *Muirkirk Advertiser*, 'the entrants for the costume race cut some high jinks and danced a quadrille on the field... to the great amusement of the company... it was one of the best evening's entertainment the Glenbuck people ever had.'

Such fun was in short supply and understandably cherished. The football team continued to do its bit. In the same year of the Coronation, at the club's AGM the treasurer announced a surplus of £13 1s 7½d. In April, the team beat Ardeer Thistle 5–0 and defeated deadly rivals Muirkirk 3–1 in a Scottish Junior Cup replay. These tussles with the sworn adversaries formed something of an intense and frequently played local derby. Once football resumed after the First World War, Muirkirk Athletic had the upper hand in 1922, winning the first encounter of the season 4–0, their superiority celebrated by a cartoon in the local paper in which a caricature of an imposing Athletic player held a bunch of cherries and declared 'watch me gobble them up!' To the left of the frame a Keir Hardie lookalike warned 'take care – they might choke you.'

The defeat was a sign of things to come. By 1926, the Cherrypickers had to pull out of a Coylton Cup semi-final against New Cumnock due to financial problems. The team disappeared from the fixture lists until a rebirth in 1930. A public meeting was held at – where else – Burnside Park on 30 May 'for considering the resurrection of the local junior football club'. The villagers heeded the call and elected a new committee, which in turn passed around the hat to raise welcome new funds. This led to renewed participation in the 1930/31 season beginning with a rousing 3–2 win over Cronberry Eglinton, but an early second round exit from the Scottish Junior Cup at the hands of Cumnock hinted that the revival was to be short-lived. Defeats in other competitions, including a 5–1 thrashing by Glenafton in the Coylton Cup exposed the lack of talent in a small squad depleted by the village's falling population. With the closure of the last mines in the early 1930s, which in turn resulted in Burnside Park being flooded due to pumping in the pits being halted, the game was assuredly up.

But what a swansong lay in store. Having somehow scratched enough of a team together to reach the Ayrshire Junior Cup Final, the Cherries faced the formidable Lugar. The match at Kilmarnock was tied 3–3, but in the replay at Cumnock, a goal from Duffy (no first name is recorded) was enough to secure a 1–0 win and yet more silverware. The cheers of the Cherrypickers supporters echoed around the River Ayr valley for one last time and then fell silent. The Cherrypickers had played their last ever game.

It was fitting that the club ended on a high, since its success was testament to the consistent quality of the club. The foundation of the Athletic and Cherrypickers sides was that half-century of players who went on to join the professional ranks, a number of whom are considered later in this book. But the lesser-known players who did not transfer to senior football should also be remembered. There were, naturally, more Bones, Crosbies, Blyths, Devlins, Menzies, Wallaces, Taits, and Knoxes. They gloried in such colourful and descriptive nicknames as 'Chuck', 'Pimp', 'Doodles' and 'Silver Toes'. By common consent, Archie McBride was the best to don the Glenbuck colours, while William Wallace was a tenacious and, according to Faulds and Tweedie, 'redoubtable centre-half. A little bandy legged and inclined to crouch, but a difficult man to get past.'

For a namesake of Scotland's legendary warrior who for a while saw off the English, the description was apt, but the chroniclers of the Cherrypickers added that the latter-day William Wallace also 'had a great reputation for clean play.' The praise is important for it reflects well on the manner of Glenbuck's football. It prided skill over brute force, with neat passing, good movement and ball control, and above all, teamwork, honed in the five-a-sides, on the training ground, and in competitive play.

If that sounds redolent of the great Liverpool sides Bill Shankly was to assemble more than 60 years later, it is no accident. Shankly was just one among many who were indoctrinated with the proven value of collective endeavour and excellence. The wisdom of such a philosophy had been hard won in the pit and in day-to-day life in the village. People tended to do better when they worked together. For Burnside Park, read Anfield all those years later.

The Shanklys were a family more aware than most of the value of teamwork. The paternal head of the family, John, was another local who become actively involved in the running of the Glenbuck club. He drew on his experience as a successful athlete, as a middle-distance runner who took on and beat the famous Canty Young over a half-mile. His committed interest in boxing also served the Glenbuck teams well, with his emphasis on clean living and physical conditioning a valuable aid to the overall strengths of the side. Modern football prides itself on meticulous attention to detail, covering every aspect of a player's physical and mental wellbeing, from precise statistical analysis of individual performance to regular dental check-ups in order to identify tooth problems that can have 'butterfly effects' on seemingly unconnected bodily aches and pains. Glenbuck's trainers did not go into quite as exacting detail, but John Shankly brought a different sporting perspective to the benefit of the club.

He was also a fiery competitor with an intense pride in the village, who fitted well with the Cherrypickers' will to win. His great niece, Barbara Alexander, remembered a family story of an encounter with Glenbuck's sworn adversaries, Muirkirk. "One day there was a game against Muirkirk and the referee never turned up, and someone said 'we'll play a friendly.' Johnny was annoyed that someone suggested such a thing and said, 'There will be no friendly game against Muirkirk because they are no friends of ours!'"

Decades later John Shankly's youngest son Bill would talk of creating a 'bastion of invincibility' at Anfield. The ambition found its early incarnation with the Glenbuck sides and his father's own determination to help create a team dedicated to succeed, and one that truly represented the village.

The Glenbuck gene pool might have been limited in numbers, but there was such a rich pool of talent that there was little need to bring in talented outsiders. Contrary to some reports there were a few outsiders that played for Glenbuck, but in an early forerunner of the great Celtic team of 1967 which won the European Cup with a nucleus of players drawn from a Glaswegian radius of just 30 miles, Glenbuck teams were almost exclusively made up of Glenbuck natives, with isolated allowances made for exotic foreigners who might hail from a far-flung place like Muirkirk, or even the wilds of Douglas.

It all helps to explain why so many Glenbuck players did not just go on to carve out professional careers, but became adept coaches, managers and even directors and chairmen of big clubs. Glenbuck gave them an all-encompassing football education and the confidence to put it to productive use.

That productiveness of the Glenbuck nursery cannot be overstated. Over a period of roughly 50 years the village produced four English FA Cup winners, five full internationals, and 50 professionals out of a population that never exceeded 1,700 and which was often much smaller – half or less. To give some idea of just how prolific that figure made Glenbuck, it is worthwhile to draw some comparisons.

At the village's peak population, Glenbuck produced a footballer for every 35 inhabitants – man, woman and child. At the same rate, the city of Liverpool, which had a peak population of 855,000 in 1931, would have turned out around 24,428 players; Glasgow 31,114 from a populace of 1.09 million. London, meanwhile, now enjoying a record population of 8.6 million, would need to be churning out almost a quarter of a million professional footballers – from one non-league club – to keep up with the sporting fecundity of tiny Glenbuck.

Such comparisons, of course, are not like for like, and ignore the very specific circumstances and conditions that existed in Glenbuck between 1870 up to about 1930. But they provide some indication of just how extraordinary this little village was in a footballing context, and why so many of its players went on to often glorious professional careers.

Chapter 6

Blyth's Spirit

IN a team photograph from 1910/11, the players of Portsmouth Football Club are proudly assembled in their white shirts and dark blue shorts, probably relieved at not having to don the original salmon-pink colours. These young footballers are stiff backed and fix the camera with all the confidence that the hope of youth and a new season brings. Skipper Jack Warner, the former favourite of rivals Southampton, sits with the ball at his feet, alongside team-mates with regulation centre partings and stern countenances. There are hints of smiles on a couple of players' faces, but these belie the general mood around the club. Relegated the season before, and facing financial strife, the proud Southern League outfit are finding the challenge of maintaining success in the increasingly competitive world of professional football a tough proposition.

In among their number are a multitude of trainers, officials and directors. Hats tend to delineate the hierarchy: flat caps and straw boaters for team management, more formal headgear for the dignitaries. There is a Reverend E. Cornford on hand, wearing a dog collar and top hat to provide some ecclesiastical pomp. To his right towards the edge of the assembly, his head covered by a more utilitarian straw hat with a broad band, and sporting a moderately old-fashioned wing collar, is a director with his head slightly bowed. His moustached face is concealed in shadow under the brim of his hat as if to indicate an unwillingness to hog the limelight. 'R. Blyth, Esq.' says the caption, identifying the director who had played such a prominent role in the early history of this fine footballing institution. Robert Blyth, that is, formerly of Glenbuck, Ayrshire, Scotland.

Fratton Park is roughly 420 miles from Burnside Park, but the two places might as well be entire worlds apart. Portsmouth is a bustling and famous old dockyard city, self-contained on an island. It has a long and sometimes glorious, often very rough, naval and seafaring past. It also has a well-established pugnacious character among its no-nonsense people, who counter the considerable challenges of life in a port with the gritty self-confidence such a heritage endows. The football club, determinedly clinging to its blue-collar nature, reflects the city, with a sizable and boisterous support staying loyal through all the grim times.

Glenbuck is now a dead place with no human presence. Yet it too was once bustling, and full of bold people intensely proud of their home, mistrusting of outsiders, yet willing to broaden their horizons and seek out new adventures. It was the same kind of mindset that brought Blyth all that way from the Ayrshire coalfields to the English south coast, amid one of the great careers of Glenbuck's footballing sons. Glenbuck and Portsmouth might be at opposite ends of the country, but they share a footballing bond thanks to the spirit of their inhabitants, and Mr Robert Blyth, Esq.

Blyth, of course, was one of those family names that featured prominently in the village's sporting history. This one, Robert, was born in October 1870. He was the son of James Blyth of Douglas and Janet Fleming. The other six children born to the couple included Barbara Blyth who would marry John Shankly and begin a whole new footballing dynasty.

Bob Blyth picked up the nickname of 'Reindeer' in his three years as a Cherrypickers player. The derivation is unclear, perhaps down to a graceful fleet of foot, enduring stamina in the testing Glenbuck winters, or due to a more obscure origin. Whatever the reason, his skills as a footballer were enough to get the scouts calling. There is some dispute as to where he first headed. Some contemporary reports suggest Glasgow Rangers. Others say he was snapped up as a 20-year-old by another Glasgow side, Cowlairs. This was one of the short-lived clubs that briefly flourished in the early days of codified and regulated football.

Founded by railway workers in the Springburn area of the city, it took part in the English FA Cup and was a founder member of the Scottish League, but trod a fine line between amateurism and the still outlawed professional game. Demoted, then elected back into the league, Cowlairs joined the new Second Division before failing to secure re-election to Division One. Beset by financial woes the club shut down in 1896. By then Blyth was long gone. He never played a competitive game for Cowlairs and his brief initial dalliance with Glasgow was effectively a stepping stone to bigger and better things.

Blyth's next club was the grandly named Middlesbrough Ironopolis. This was another ephemeral outfit that made a considerable splash by splitting away from the more conservative Middlesbrough FC in 1889 in a row over turning professional. The ambitious upstarts won the English Northern League three times, before joining the Football League. Costs proved too high though, and the club folded in 1894.

Blyth had already been on the move again, this time back to Scotland and Glasgow, to more certainly join in 1891 one of the emerging forces in the British game, Rangers. At Ibrox he got games and made a mark. From his position as outside-right or wing-half, he scored four goals in 14 games over three seasons. His first game was in a 2–0 home win against Third Lanark at the first Ibrox Park in the Glasgow Cup first round on 19 September 1891. There were seven further appearances that season, and two goals, the first coming in a 2–1 win over Cambuslang in the Scottish League.

For some reason now lost to obscurity, he didn't feature at all the following season but in 1893/94 he made another six appearances and scored another two goals. His final competitive turnout in Rangers blue mirrored his first, against Third Lanark in a 0–3 loss again at Ibrox Park on 23 December 1893.

It was hardly an impact to stun the football world, but it did see him make a goalscoring contributor to Rangers' victorious 1893/94 Scottish Cup run, their first triumph in the competition. Blyth did not play in the final, but his performances had been impressing the talent spotters from further afield. For, like so many Scottish players, Blyth was coveted by English clubs. And the one that secured his services ranked among the finest in the land.

Preston North End enjoyed widespread fame for the quality of their football and their pioneering achievements. They existed as a sporting club playing various games under a number of codes before formally switching to play under the FA laws in 1878, and with great success. 'North End' were among that cluster of clubs from industrious northern and Midlands towns who upset the English footballing establishment, taking over the game with a new style and an ambitious attitude to match. A big part of their strategy was to import Scottish players, a policy begun by the omniscient long-serving club stalwart William Sudell. It brought famous success. They were the first club to win the inaugural league championship, completing a unique double by also lifting the FA Cup in 1888/89. They were undefeated the entire season, earning them the nickname 'The Invincibles', over a century before Arsenal emulated the feat.

Who could resist such a club? Certainly not Bob Blyth. In four years at Deepdale, he played an impressive 124 times, after making an eye-catching debut against Bury. 'Those of us who saw it, well remember the display,' purred 'Abaris' of *The Lancashire Daily Post*. Blyth played in a number of forward positions for Preston before dropping back to midfield. He was not a prolific goalscorer, registering only eight goals, but his confident all-purpose style was well-suited to Preston's mode of play. He was also reliable, and did not miss a single league game between 1895 and 1897. It was this all-round ability and dependability that helped make him ideal captain material, an honour he secured and served with considerable distinction.

The Lancashire Daily Post of February 1899 included a long feature on Blyth to celebrate his qualities and standing in the club. The correspondent 'Abaris' made the telling point that Preston were one of the few clubs who chose their captain by popular vote among the players. Finely balanced between Scots and Englishmen, the ballot showed that Blyth was a players' player, deserving of the highest respect. Abaris noted that to the public's eye, captaincy simply entailed leading the players on to the field and winning the toss. 'But the work of the captain commences when the contest waxes hot,' he wrote.

Deploying the martial analogies much favoured at the time in analysing sport, Abaris continued, 'He is like a commander of military forces, with the difference that whereas the commander fights the enemy [via] his men, the team leader fights with his men against the rival host. His is no abstract theoretical leading, he himself goes strongest into the fight, and while playing his own hand has to keep his brains at work in to direct the operation of his fighting forces... Blyth is a captain in name and captain indeed of his team.'

Football wasn't quite war, but the all-round leadership qualities Blyth demonstrated at Preston clearly impressed. Providing energy and dynamism from midfield he truly led, instilling confidence in his side, whatever the situation. He was an excellent reader of the game, 'with,' Abaris continued, 'the essential faculty for disposing the strength of his team as it best may serve to stave defeat or to press home victory.' In other words, Blyth deployed tactics. In an era when managers were often little more than administrative secretaries, and it was the board of directors who picked the actual team, this was revolutionary stuff. Small wonder Abaris believed

'Robert Fleming Blyth... is one of the best liked and best supported captains in Britain.'

The paper additionally noted Blyth's birthplace of Glenbuck, describing it as 'a kingdom of paramount dignity and influence.' Noting its prolific reputation for producing footballers from a tiny population, the article listed the 'seven [sic] good men and true in England today, turning to account the athletic schooling they had at home.' The report listed Alec McConnell, playing at left full-back for Arsenal; William Muir, keeping goal at Everton; the youthful Ferguson making a great impression at Sheffield Wednesday. Joining Blyth in the Preston ranks were fellow Glenbuckians, full-back Alex Tait and the multi-purpose Peter McIntyre, who ranged over the midfield comfortable in a number of positions. Omitted from the *Lancashire Daily Post*'s class of 1899 was Alex or 'Sandy' Brown, formerly of Preston and that season plying his trade at Portsmouth.

The inference was clear. Across a network of clubs, the Glenbuck nursery was churning out a succession of professional footballers. The Glenbuckian connections being drawn between those aforementioned clubs would crop up again and again as former Cherrypickers team-mates played against and with each other in the leagues, ties strengthened by the bonds of family. 'Scotland could do with more Glenbucks and English football with additions of some such men,' wrote Abaris admiringly. It was clear evidence that within a generation of the Glenbuck Athletic's formation, players from the team and the village were making an impression across the landscape of British football.

The players cited would enjoy varying careers. Alex McConnell's stay in south London with the then Woolwich Arsenal would last just a season. Born in 1875 he initially joined Everton, before moving on to Arsenal in November 1897. He made his debut in a League Division Two match at home to Blackpool playing at left full-back. In all, he made 38 first team appearances, scoring one goal and making another 39 appearances for the club in other competitions. His final game for the Gunners was a United League game away to Tottenham in April 1899. Thereafter he left for Queens Park Rangers in the summer of 1899 and later turned out for Grimsby Town.

It is interesting to note that in Faulds and Tweedie's account of the Cherrypickers, they gave prominent mention to McConnell at the age of 78 (which might clash with his given birth year), but it appears the authors or McConnell were more inclined to talk about his cycling exploits rather than those of his football. He won local races and events in Northern Ireland confirming his reputation as a fine all-round athlete. Of football, McConnell would only say, "I had eleven years as a professional footballer. I was chosen to play left-back for Scotland against England and two days later I signed for Everton; and after that I played for the Arsenal and Grimsby Town, where I finished football. I then took up golf and did fairly well. I won three gold medals. Then I started bowling and did not do too badly at that. I played for Yorkshire in the county matches one year!"

Alec McConnell was indeed chosen to play against England, but having signed for Everton two days later, was deemed an 'Anglo Scot' and thus ineligible.

Signed for £45, Willie 'Gooley' Muir spent five seasons at Everton, and was a dependable goalkeeper for 137 matches, like McConnell making his debut in November 1897, in his case against West Bromwich Albion. Muir also featured for a range of Scottish clubs in a career that lasted nearly 20 years. Born in 1877, he played for Third Lanark, Kilmarnock, and Dumbarton, and most notably for Dundee and Hearts, save for a brief spell with Bradford City. He attained full international status with Scotland, winning a solitary cap for the March 1907 3–0 victory over Northern Ireland. This had come a full 11 years after Muir played, as a Junior international, in the 4–1 defeat of an England XI at Perry Barr in Birmingham. The team was, according to the *Evening Times*, 'considered the best ever to represent Scotland'.

By contrast, Glenbuck's John Ferguson did not in fact play first-team football for Sheffield Wednesday, but instead featured for Hamilton Academical, Cowdenbeath and Dunfermline Athletic over an 11-year period up to 1919. At Hamilton, he joined in 1907 and played as a cultured left-half and initially impressed, but after 43 appearances his form flagged and he was dropped from the team.

Peter McIntyre, described by Faulds and Tweedie as 'in his day, one of the greatest centre-halves in the game', also enjoyed a long career, spanning 19 years at Rangers, Preston, Sheffield United, Portsmouth, Hamilton and Paisley's long-lost 'other' league side Abercorn FC. It was at Hamilton that he became a crowd favourite, becoming the first Accies player to have a caricature immortalised in the sports pages of the *Hamilton Herald*. He played an important part in the Accies winning the Second Division championship in 1904.

In all McIntyre made 164 senior career appearances and scored 16 goals, and testament to his standing in the game was his benefit match on 19 April 1905. Hamilton welcomed the mighty Rangers to Douglas Park for the occasion and won 2–1. McIntyre hung up his boots in 1908 when he had to retire due to injury, having won two Lanarkshire Cup medals.

Of the other Glenbuck pair, the two 'Sandies' Tait and Brown had more famous successes ahead of them. Robert Blyth meanwhile, was at his peak, and the picture of him that emerges is of a genuine all-round football man, not only a very talented player. He could lead and inspire, and manage in the more modern sense of the word, directing how the Preston team played and functioned.

It was straight out of the Glenbuck school, merging the ethos of teamwork with a willingness to take on responsibility and gain improvement, rather than simply be accepting of one's place, either in a football team or the wider world. Blyth was clearly ambitious and the range of skills he learned as a player enabled him to make the natural step into management. This came with the move to Portsmouth and the role of captain, and soon after his appointment as player-manager.

He joined Portsmouth for the 1899/1900 season and became the club's first captain. Another of those Pompey team photos, this time from the eve of that campaign, shows the players kitted out in the original salmon pink. Blyth is there with the bearing of a senior pro, the handlebar moustache and deep-set eyes presenting a slightly brooding look, as, unlike his team-mates, he gazes away from the camera. Perhaps his mind was wandering, for within two years he was managing the club.

He was part of a tumultuous time for the city's football fans. The club had been formed just a season before his arrival out of the wreckage of amateur side Royal Artillery. Led by a local brewer John Brickwood, a group of businessmen raised the necessary capital to resurrect the sport in the city, buying land formerly used for grazing on which they laid out a pitch and erected a basic stadium.

Success came instantly. Under the management of Frank Brettell, Portsmouth finished as runners-up in their debut 1899/1900 Southern League campaign to Tottenham. Brettell was something of a cross between Harry Redknapp and a 'super agent' in the turn-of-the-century game, a go-to man when a variety of jobs needed doing. He had made his name as player-secretary-manager of Liverpool side St Domingo, was a prime mover in the foundation of Everton, and worked as a reporter for the *Liverpool Mercury*.

He lasted a year at Bolton Wanderers as secretary before taking a number of Bolton players with him when he became the first recognised manager of Spurs in 1898. Once again it was a brief stay and less than a year later he was at Portsmouth to become their first manager in May 1899. The ambitious Pompey board had offered to double Brettell's wages and he willingly obliged.

Astute in the transfer market, Brettell brought in a number of players from the old Royal Artillery side and recruited others from the North. Blyth was one of his key signings, arriving as a ready-made experienced pro who knew how to get a team organised. He joined a team on a phenomenal run – 20 wins from 28 games in that debut season – and played a significant part in maintaining the standard. Portsmouth went three years unbeaten at home, leading Brettell to pronounce, "Nothing in the history of football can compare with the phenomenal rise and extraordinary performances of the club." And with that, he was off, supposedly after a dispute with the board of directors and most likely in a disagreement over money.

Portsmouth turned to the man who had proved he was a leader of men and named Blyth as their new player-manager a month later in July 1901. The change worked. Still fighting fit at 5ft 9in and weighing 12 stone, Blyth took charge for three seasons, until 1904.

In his first season in charge, he went one better than Brettell, steering Pompey to the coveted Southern League championship. The title was built on the recruitment of England internationals Arthur Chadwick from Southampton and Steve Smith from Aston Villa, allied to Blyth's clever management. He and Portsmouth continued to think big.

The next season they signed another England cap, Fred Wheldon, who was joined by one of Blyth's old Glenbuck and Preston team-mates, the returning Sandy Brown from Spurs. The Southern League title was not retained, but the mood at the club and in the city was heady.

It was an eventful, topsy-turvy time. To the Southern League triumph was added the Western League, alongside the Portsmouth Cup. It completed a triple haul of trophies, including the enormous Southern League shield, modestly showed off by Blyth to the Fratton Park crowd in a photo that placed him, uncharacteristically, centre stage.

But it was also a period of busy activity in player arrivals and departures and frequent off-field upheaval. An incident in one match seemed to sum up the club during the period. Goalkeeper George Harris was kicked in the eye during a game against QPR and crashed into a post. Carried into the dressing room, a doctor in attendance feared at one stage Harris might die, but he made a miraculous recovery and by the final whistle was up on his feet again.

Blyth himself was caught up in the turmoil, complicated by the complex rivalries and tensions between the various leagues and governing bodies. In 1903, Southern League Portsmouth were found guilty of offering 'financial inducements' to transfer three players from Liverpool who played in Division One of the Football League. The players, Sam Raybould, William Goldie and John Glover, were banned by the Football Association for seven months, their absence widely seen as the reason why Liverpool were relegated that season. Portsmouth were fined £100 and Blyth was also sanctioned, suspended without wages until January 1904.

Robbed of the gainful employment football had provided for him for the previous 14 years, Blyth became landlord of the Pompey Hotel, which adjoined Fratton Park. On his return to the role of manager he was running a pub and running a football team. Yet within five months he was quitting the manager's job for good. The official reason given was that he could not combine the two roles. There were rumours about a power struggle at board level, given some credence by director Richard Bonney's accession to the post of team manager, but the eventual outcome was that Blyth handed in his resignation in May 1904.

'The announcement that Mr Robert Blyth had resigned the managership of the Portsmouth Football Club was made yesterday, and created quite a sensation in local sporting circles,' wrote the *Evening Telegraph*. '... much of the success of the organisation has been due to him. In recognition of his services it was decided to apply to the Football Association for permission to give him a benefit match, and in probability the first home Western League match of the season will be allotted him.'

After 168 appearances and half a dozen goals for the club, Bob Blyth's playing and managerial career at Fratton Park had come to an abrupt end. His fall was not an isolated fate. Football at the time was a burgeoning but murky new industry, regulated in an uncertain and inconsistent way and ripe for exploitation by those with a sharp eye for a main chance and a quick profit. There was a favour here, a favour there. Rumours of bribes and underhand payments were rife, along with bitter disputes and tales of behind-closed-doors skulduggery. If it sometimes had the appearance of the Wild West or a Gold Rush, it was no coincidence. There were fortunes to be found in them thar football hills and it invited all kinds of prospectors and dubious operators.

Blyth negotiated and survived the pitfalls better than most and he and Portsmouth were not quite done with each other just yet. His appointment as a director in 1909 was followed by a vice-chairmanship in 1920 and election as chairman in 1924. It meant he had served the club at every level.

In the meantime he had reacquainted himself with what would become that most familiar of employment for former players by becoming a publican, this time at the Travellers Joy in nearby Milton Road. He lived out his life in his adopted city until 7 February 1941 when he died at the age of 71. He was buried in Milton cemetery, a few hundred yards from Fratton Park.

The Blyth stamp on Portsmouth was not confined to Bob's career. His brother Willie also made the familiar Scottish footballer journey to play as a pro in England. The family connection undoubtedly played a part in bringing him to Portsmouth for two seasons between 1903–05, where he played 28 Southern League games and 16 Western League games, and scored a solitary goal. He moved on to Preston for a short spell before ending up at Carlisle where he too was elevated to the boardroom, and where he would play an important part in the Glenbuck story a generation later.

'R. Blyth' reappeared on a Portsmouth team sheet with the signing of Robert's son, the expansively named Robert Roberts

Taylor Blyth. Born in Muirkirk in June 1900, that den of iniquity to Glenbuck eyes, he nonetheless had something of the old Cherrypickers fire, scoring two goals in just ten starts at Pompey, before switching to rivals Southampton.

The family's playing presence at Pompey had thus drawn to a close but there was and still is a more physical reminder of the lineage's great contribution to the city's footballing cause. Under the South Stand at Fratton Park there is a plaque that prominently features Robert Blyth's name alongside his fellow board members. It was unveiled in commemoration of the opening of the new stand in 1925. Designed by another great Scot, the famous stadium architect Archibald Leitch, who did so much to define the built landscape of pre-war British football, it sets in bricks-and-mortar permanence the debt Portsmouth owed to their very own son of Glenbuck.

Robert Blyth had carried the Glenbuck name with great distinction as one of the first footballers to leave the village side and make a go of things in the world of the paid professionals. He was witness to and an active participant in some of the great developments, good and bad, of the sport that was captivating Britain – its inspiring episodes and its murky, closed-door machinations. There were however two contemporaries, compatriots, team-mates and village neighbours who would make an even bigger on-field impact, and their efforts would play a major part in securing what was then the biggest prize of them all.

Chapter 7

Scottish Flowers of the South

THERE'S a story from the very early days of Tottenham Hotspur that illustrates something about the nature of the north Londoners and their 133-year-old footballing institution. In 1887, five years after the club had been formed under a streetlamp by a group of Tottenham schoolboys aided by the pastoral care of a local cleric, John Ripsher, the team made a trip to Luton. In Spurs' pre-leagues era, every match was billed as a friendly, but the encounter with their Bedfordshire hosts would have been as hotly contested as any of the clashes the big guns of English and Scottish football were then engaged in.

As the two captains headed for the centre circle pre kick-off, the Luton skipper is said to have sniggered and remarked to his team-mates about how small in stature their youthful Tottenham counterparts were. According to the *Tottenham and Edmonton Weekly Herald*, the visiting captain John 'Jack' Jull, a survivor from the first-ever Spurs team, replied, "Wait till after the match, old man, before you say any more; schoolboys or not, we can beat you!"

That at least is the sanitised version. It's probable a few choicer words were exchanged in more colourful and industrial language, but the sentiment was the same. This bunch of small lads were made of determined stuff and refused to be cowed by supposedly stronger, bigger opponents. Spurs won 2–1.

The tale is emblematic of Tottenham's history and identity. From the outset, this was a club of upstart suburban Londoners who didn't take kindly to being lorded over by anyone, whether in the shape of complacent Luton players or the Oxbridge patricians who ran the game. In short order Tottenham would thrillingly challenge the northern powerhouses that had themselves partially overthrown the old guard and professionalised the sport. The success would present Spurs with a chance to become a dominant force in the newly configured game. Instead, frustrated by a combination of official obstruction and their own inertia, they failed to fully exploit the opportunity. Spurs have always thought big, and bold, though the outcomes have never quite matched the ambition.

Flash, cocky, exotic, pioneering, occasionally glorious, often arrogant, are just a few of the descriptions that have been applied through the decades to the boys from White Hart Lane. Bill Shankly had his own witty and rather cutting view of the club. 'Drury Lane fan dancers,' he once dubbed them, pursuing the showbiz metaphor by dismissing yet another free-flowing but fragile Spurs side as 'Cockney tap dancers' – entertainers who flattered to deceive. Indeed, that Luton win in 1887 was oh-so-typical of those 133 years. The victory was part of a run of eight wins out of ten games unbeaten that came to a clanking halt south of the river the following February when Tottenham were stuffed 6–2 by 'Royal Arsenal'.

This then was the club and situation that provided the environment for the next chapter of Glenbuck's considerable contribution to the fabric of British football. It would see two former Cherrypickers play in the grandest game of all, win honours and international acclaim, and draw in unprecedented spectator interest. It is a story of triumph, tragedy, an *Escape To*

Victory style game played in a First World War internment camp, and the earliest incarnation of some of the game's most cherished traditions and customs. Plus, an awful lot of Bath buns.

One of its leading characters was yet another Scotsman from Ayrshire making substantial waves in English football. John Cameron was born in 1872. A bright boy, he was educated at the local Ayr Grammar School and excelled at sport and especially football, earning a call-up from the local Ayr Parkhouse side before moving on to the citadel of the early Scottish game, Queen's Park. Cameron won a solitary Scotland cap in 1896 playing in a 3–3 draw with Ireland, which earned the Scots the British Home Championship.

Still an amateur, he headed south at the age of 24 to Everton. At the lavish, recently-built Goodison he won glowing reviews for his performances as an inside-right but could not quite establish himself in the Toffees' team. To earn his keep he was also working for the Cunard shipping line in Liverpool, and as a sports journalist. It was while he was at Everton that Cameron also took on the role of secretary to the forerunner of the PFA, the Association Footballers' Union. It had been formed in February 1898 to oppose the Football League's new rules that any professional who wanted to move to another club could only do so with the permission of his present club. This practice, the infamous 'retain and transfer' system, would survive as an archaic and highly restrictive rule well into the 1960s. In the 1890s, players were further angered by a plan by the clubs to impose a maximum wage of £4 a week. Cameron was still an amateur but stuck up for his fellow players, saying that the union, "wanted any negotiations regarding transfers to be between the interested club and the player concerned – not between club and club with the player excluded".

For the men who ran league football at the time it was radical, even dangerous talk. Norman Giller, Fleet Street legend and a wise chronicler of Tottenham's varying fortunes over the years, suggested in his study of the club's managers *Tottenham: The*

Managing Game that Cameron was virtually blacklisted by the northern clubs. Dissatisfied with his failure to nail down a place and angered by the impositions placed on men trying to make a living out of the game they excelled at, Cameron was tempted by Frank Brettell (who in the near future would link up with former Glenbuck players at Portsmouth) to join the more welcoming Southern League. Cameron duly signed for Spurs in May 1898, turning professional in the process, and found a club attuned to his ambitions and philosophy – not just in how the game should be played but in the way it was seeking to progress as a whole.

"Cameron comes in as such an important person in the club's history, because of the football the team were playing, and what kind of club it was," says Martin Cloake, journalist, co-chair of the Tottenham Supporters' Trust, author of a number of books about the club, and proud north Londoner. "The first thing to bear in mind about Spurs was that they were a team from the south. The game was developing, and the early big clubs had been those from the industrial north and Midlands. It wasn't only that Spurs weren't from the north; they weren't even from one of the more industrialised areas of the south like West Ham, which was formed at Thames Ironworks, or even Arsenal, who were formed at a munitions factory in Woolwich. Tottenham was a club of the suburbs."

There is a persistent narrative of British football that only the madding hordes of the inner cities gave birth and succour to the club game. The stereotype is a Lowry painting – all back-to-back houses, grimy industrial settings and terraces packed with swaying, rattle-twirling multitudes. The stadiums rise up from streets where small boys kick bundles of rags before being plucked to play for their hometown or local club, invariably owned and run by the neighbourhood factory owner, Justice of the Peace or an avuncular brewer.

There is some truth to this portrait but there is another depiction – one of aspiring, upwardly-mobile young-ish men from down south and in particular London. Men imbued with a hunger for the sport and possessing an entrepreneurial eye on the commercial possibilities of its embryonic clubs in growing urban areas. Tottenham in the 1890s was one of those places; Spurs one of those clubs.

"The growth of the suburbs is a big story in Victorian and Edwardian times in terms of how populations in the cities were growing and the wider story of the development of urban Britain," Cloake says. "Tottenham was a team being embraced by that newly confident and slightly better-off suburban working class. There had also been that divide between the professional and the amateur."

The perpetual conflict over professionalism had at least been slightly resolved with its sanctioning by the English FA in 1885 and the formation of the Football League three years later. But as Cloake says, there was still a view in the south that, "being paid to play football wasn't really the done thing. Which is all very well if you've got independent income. Within the English football establishment the northern clubs were perceived as cheats for paying their players. It wasn't the kind of thing 'gentlemen' did; it was what 'tradesmen' did. So that old class divide was in there.

"The rise of clubs in the south and the Southern League was being checked. Originally the Football League wouldn't let the southern clubs join. Potentially there were two different codes developing, as there was in rugby league and union. There was therefore a whole background in how sport and society was changing and how those fairly deep-seated class differences lay behind the Spurs run in the Cup in 1901. Spurs had already established themselves as effective, playing quite attractive football, which is where Cameron comes in – the idea of the team playing in a certain way and attracting an audience. They won the Southern League. Then it was a case of could they go on?"

Tottenham was a club and place in the process of swift and dynamic change. The area was for centuries a rural spot of marshland, farms and country estates where the London-based nobility would spend their leisure. The coming of the railways and the development of the River Lea and New River waterways spurred urban development. Population and housing grew, but as late as the 1890s, it was still an underdeveloped place where new terraced streets of brick-built houses were sited besides market gardens.

Spurs developed quickly from a team of friends, some of whom attended a local Scottish Presbyterian school, into a club attracting increasing support. A row over supposed financial impropriety in the 1893/94 season had pushed the club towards professionalism and becoming a limited company. Known as the 'Payne's Boots' affair, it centred on Ernie Payne, who was on Fulham's books but rarely played. Switching to Spurs as amateur rules allowed, he arrived in north London for a game but without any kit. Spurs gave him 10 shillings to buy a pair of boots, a trivial detail subsequently ruled as 'unfair inducement' by the staunchly traditionalist and vehemently anti-professional London FA, which suspended Spurs for two weeks.

It enraged the club and won them widespread sympathy and publicity. A wealthy local businessman, John Oliver, came on to the committee that ran the club to provide funding, business acumen and good jobs in his carpet factory for the players. Joining him as adviser was Charles Roberts, a born entrepreneur who was reputed to have been a baseball pitcher with the Brooklyn Dodgers, and a man who knew how to put on a show. Within two years the pair had steered the club to a new stadium (the current White Hart Lane) on a former market garden, gained membership of the Southern League, and engaged Brettell as secretary-manager. Spurs were on the up and meaning business.

It was achieved with Scottish playing talent. No less than nine of the 1897/98 team were from north of the border. Foremost among them, Cameron was one of Brettell's first signings, and the Ayrshire man made an immediate impact. He was top scorer with

24 goals in 53 appearances in his debut season and added a touch of class to Tottenham's play. At a fraction under six foot, he was tall for the time and blessed with a fine all-round game, with neat passing and quick interplay his forte.

With Brettell lasting a solitary season, the project Roberts and Oliver had embarked on looked in danger of stalling before it had got underway. They need not have worried. Turning to the 26-year-old Cameron, in February 1899 they appointed a forward-thinking player-manager who brought a sense of purpose, strategy and determination to succeed. Progress was rapid and it was the signing of key players, among them two from Glenbuck, which propelled Spurs into the big time.

Football then as now was a game of contacts and connections as well as, maybe even more than, on-pitch action. Cameron's work with the nascent players' union helped him to find leads and make the necessary approaches to bring in new blood. Whether his Ayrshire contacts would have been needed to tip him off about Alex Tait and Sandy Brown is doubtful, since he would have been aware of their qualities from their displays at Preston. But he would certainly have known about Glenbuck's reputation for producing footballers with good technique, who were comfortable with the ball at their feet and had an ability to read the game. Tait and Brown fitted the bill.

Both made a dramatic impression at Spurs, but it was Alexander Tait, the defensive fulcrum of the Ayrshire Junior Cup-winning Glenbuck side, who was the more enduring. A remarkable character as a well as a wonderful player, he would become one of Tottenham's earliest and foremost legends. He was born in December 1871, making him slightly younger than Bob Blyth, but he grew up fast. One of 13 children, Tait began work in the mines as a youngster, driving the pit ponies to earn a vital wage for the large Tait household.

Football was his release and one at which he excelled. Early on he forged a reputation as a tough, uncompromising defender with a fearsome tackle. But he was also fair and no mean player, well drilled in the Glenbuck principles of pass and move. His talent was clearly good enough to earn a senior call-up and he was signed first by Ayr.

He would not make a senior appearance for the local senior club, nor at his next port of call, Lanarkshire side Royal Albert, the coalfield-based club named after a boat owned by the local mine owner, Captain Johns. A loan spell for Tait at Rangers proved more fulfilling. He made seven consecutive appearances for the 'Gers in the 1891/92 season. His debut was in a 6–1 win over Vale of Leven at Millburn Park while he was also present for Bob Blyth's Rangers debut later that September. Tait's final game for Rangers was in a 5–1 defeat to Clyde at Ibrox Park on 24 October. He featured more at Motherwell, making 17 appearances at the then Dalziel Park ground the following year.

It was a peripatetic early career, but stability came with a move to Preston North End in 1894. Brought in as part of the club's tradition of signing Scottish players, he became a firm favourite at Deepdale, his tenacity and aggression earning him the nickname 'Terrible Tait'. The reputation was only partly deserved. Tait was straight out of the no-nonsense late 19th century school of all-out commitment, but he was a much more rounded player than the name suggests. He was adaptable, able to play either on the left or the right side of defence. He even went in goal when keeper John Wright was injured in a game against Small Heath.

It was not all plaudits and success at Preston. Tait was not a guaranteed starter, as the club struggled to maintain the incredibly high standards of the late 1880s. In truth 'The Invincibles' were on the wane. They had been the trailblazers for professional and league football, exploiting the opportunity provided by the early introduction in the unionised north of a half-working day on Saturday that freed up a ready pool of potential support. But the practice and the competition, particularly Aston Villa, had caught up. Sudell, one of the first Mr Fixits of football, left the club the season Tait joined after a failed share issue, and would later be jailed for embezzlement.

North End were still a big name and would continue to be a considerable draw for an ambitious player, but after 79 appearances in cup and league, at 27 years old Tait needed a move. He headed south, to Tottenham.

The Preston link was apposite. Spurs loved Preston. They took their strip of white shirts and dark blue shorts, and the nickname of 'The Lilywhites'. They also signed players and emulated something of the Lancashire side's success. At Spurs, Tait was installed at left-back and never looked back. He and Cameron were a perfect fit. The defender thrived in a side playing high energy and fluent football, while the young player-manager knew he could rely on his fellow Scot.

In his book *Association Football and How to Play It* written in 1910, Cameron reflected on his career and the distilled experience and wisdom he had picked up along the way. It is a treasure trove of early football training, management and leadership, from the advice that players should eat 'a substantial meal' two hours before a match, and groundbreaking warnings of the dangers of smoking, especially at half-time, alongside adverts for football knickers ('cost: one shilling and fourpence') and Bovril: 'For warding off the colds and chills to which the spectators are susceptible, BOVRIL has been found invaluable.'

'There are a good many people who think that the office of captain is not very important,' Cameron wrote, 'but my idea is that the judicious choice of a skipper is very great indeed. I have heard it said that the office is an empty honour in a professional club, but I am sure that this is a great mistake, and in an ordinary club as much depends on the leader as all the rest put together. The best players in the world are sacrificed if placed under an inefficient general, but on the other hand a leader of ability and energy has often made a strong club out of what seemed to be very unpromising material. So the best all-round player should be skipper.'

Cameron singled out his old club's skipper, who by 1910 had moved to neighbours Leyton: 'Alexander Tait and Walter Bull, when they were leaders of the 'Spurs, were examples of ability and experience going hand in hand, and they naturally commanded respect. Tait, of Leyton, was ever quiet as a captain, no shouting on the field of play, but a friendly "tip" during the interval.'

The tribute illustrates Tait's qualities and negates the popular image of 'Terrible Tait' rampaging around the pitches of England striking fear into quivering opponents. Tait was tough and looked the part with an intense stare, and was another player with a bushy moustache that seemed to convey an almost Old Testament-promise of diabolical retribution for any winger that dared to try and go past him. But he was not remotely just some simplistic battering ram and vehicle for meting out bodily harm to the opposition.

"He was a motivational player," says Giller. "He was made of granite and tackled like a tank but delivered slide-rule passes, much in the mould of a future great Spurs Scot called Dave Mackay." As Tottenham author and historian Bob Goodwin relates, 'Many a commentator openly regarded [Tait] as the best left-back in the country.' He could tackle, of that there was no doubt, but his all-round game made him a fine all-round player. His one arguable weakness, a lack of pace, was compensated for by his timing, anticipation, and awareness. If a team-mate went on the attack and was out of position defensively, Tait provided cover. It was innovative, forward-thinking football that required intelligent players, not just athletes, and Tait was the exemplar.

He did not miss a single game for the triumphant Southern League campaign of 1899/1900, his dependability endearing him further to the home support. The title had been keenly contested with Brettell's new club Portsmouth, entailing that Tait and Blyth, Glenbuck team-mates just a few years before, were battling against each other for southern-England supremacy. The outcome was decided on the last day of the season. Spurs travelled to Kent on

28 April needing a result against New Brompton, whose players were on the promise of a bonus – from Portsmouth – if they could do the Hampshire side a favour.

It appeared early on in the match that the New Brompton players would be celebrating with bulging wallets that night as they took a surprise lead, but Spurs came back through goals from Cameron and Tait – one of his only ten goals in nine years for the club – to win 2–1, and with it the Southern League. The match is notable, not just for the importance of the win, but the support it attracted.

Huge numbers of Spurs fans had made the trip south to the club that in 1913 would become Gillingham. The Medway towns had been invaded. "The place was absolutely flooded with thousands of Spurs fans who went down there to watch their team play," as Cloake observes.

On their return to north London they joined tens of thousands more thronging the streets in celebration. When the players arrived back, the Tottenham Town Band led them and a trail of supporters up to White Hart Lane. It prompted feverish reporting in the London papers, which acclaimed Spurs as the 'Flower of the South'. The *Tottenham and Edmonton Herald* even printed a celebratory verse referencing the background of the Boer War and the Dreyfus Affair in France:

> *What care I of things South African,*
> *Or whether the Boers will fight,*
> *Or that France has ceased to know the way,*
> *Between what is wrong and right?*
> *I care not for things political,*
> *Or which party's out or in,*
> *The only thing I care about,*
> *Is will Tottenham Hotspurs win?*

The unforgivable use of an errant 's' appended to 'Hotspur' aside, the poem reflected the feverish excitement surrounding Spurs in the region. Twenty years on, the *Tottenham and Edmonton Herald* produced an early history of the club, titled *A Romance of Football*. There was indeed something poetic about the club, but there was also a hard-nosed desire for success, which the local populace were most keen to buy into.

"This was the new order, if you like," says Cloake. "A pretentious term, perhaps, but people knew it. If you're trying to work out your identity, to make sense of your place in the world, to make something of yourself, things like football can symbolise what you're doing. So, for a lot of Spurs fans it was a case of 'that's people like us'.

"Ironically, there were no Londoners in the side. But people indentified with the club – the whole 'flower of the south' thing, a style of football that was both successful and entertaining, and it brought the crowds in. It was quite a rowdy crowd, as well. Suburbs then meant something different now – it wasn't all quinoa and fancy coffee. The ground was closed a couple of times and the club fined because of the behaviour of the support."

John Cameron had words of advice for fans, writing in 1910, 'Just a word or two to the spectators. They should not judge quickly or harshly, and should always recognise that it is one man that must decide, rightly or wrongly.' He was talking about the treatment of referees, whom Spurs fans were notorious for barracking, alongside incidents in which visiting players were reportedly attacked. Teams from east London in particular appeared to be singled out for special treatment and would, reported the *Herald,* be 'pelted with mud, rotten turnips and other vegetable refuse.' Tottenham was, just like Glenbuck, not a place for faint hearts.

"But I think people embraced Spurs," adds Cloake, "partly because they were trying to make sense of their own place in the world. There's always been a strong strain of regionalism in Britain, which can manifest itself in negative ways but it can also be manifested in very positive ways. In a place as big as London, you have to chop it down a bit. Spurs were marking out that little part of London, but also, spreading into the Home Counties to the north and east of the capital.

"People like Tait, Brown, and Cameron made it happen. The guy was a visionary. He built this club that was essentially formed by a group of kids and a local vicar and turned it into a sporting institution. He wasn't the only one; it was an age of great ambition, but Cameron established a legacy that carried on with Peter McWilliam, Arthur Rowe, Bill Nicholson, Keith Burkinshaw, possibly on to Harry Redknapp – about Spurs playing quick attacking, successful football."

Another comparison, that of Cameron with Bill Shankly, is irresistible – a fellow Ayrshire man who rolled up at an English club and transformed it with almost revolutionary ideas. In 1901, Cameron's side was packing fans in at the new White Hart Lane ground, with people clamouring to become part of this exciting experience called mass spectator sport, and keen to hitch their fealty to a club on the up. With the Southern League win, Tottenham had loudly announced their arrival as one of the emerging forces in the game, carrying the banner as the strongest club the region had to offer.

The question now, was could they take on the northern giants in the FA Cup?

Cameron's team-building continued in pursuit of the objective, but with the addition of only one player. To the ranks of three Englishmen, two Welshmen, an Irishman and the large contingent of Scots, was added Sandy Brown, another former Preston player who the season previously had scored 29 goals to propel Portsmouth to the runners-up place in the Southern League. None of his new team-mates had played for Spurs for more than four seasons, so any feelings of being isolated as the new arrival would have been tempered by others in the dressing room for whom a move to London was also a new experience. But if Brown was the freshest recruit, he had no trouble slotting in to the side.

Brown was a Glenbuck Athletic player but one of the few supposedly not actually from the village. The details of his birth are commonly given as Beith, on 7 April 1879, but these are misleading. Findings by Andy Mitchell of the Scottish Sports History website, reveal a different story and one highly illustrative of society at the time. "I did some research into his background (helped by contributors to the scottishleague.net message board). It had long been thought Sandy was born in 1879, but a careful analysis of records in Glenbuck showed that his date of birth was in fact 21 December 1877 and his mother Margaret White was not married. However, six months later she married the father, William Brown.

"So Sandy Brown was born to Margaret, a domestic servant, at Glenbuck. Then on 21 June 1878 William Brown, a labourer, married Margaret White in Glenbuck. And the following year, on 6 August 1879, a brother to Sandy, Thomas Brown, was born at New Rows, Glenbuck."

Over his life, Sandy Brown comes across as a more reserved figure than Tait, reflective perhaps of his family past. Being born out of wedlock still carried great social stigma in the early 20th century, and it would have been understandable for Brown not to want people prying into his private life too much – maybe even leaving factual inaccuracies about his birthplace and date unchecked. It is worth noting that in that 1911 fancy dress competition that entertained the people of Glenbuck and saw Tait's relative Robert as runner-up dressed as a nurse, the contest was won by an entrant billed as a 'swell darkie'. The past really is a different country.

The Brown brothers Sandy and Tommy began their footballing careers young with Glenbuck Athletic. The elder sibling turned pro with Scottish Cup holders St Bernard's in Edinburgh in 1896, just after his 18th birthday, and was an immediate success, scoring eight goals in 15 league matches with the now defunct club that played its home matches at the evocatively named Royal Patent

Gymnasium Grounds. Such talent led to the familiar move south and three seasons at Preston. This was arguably the most stable period in Brown's career. It was one subsequently punctuated by frequent moves with Brown as a goalscoring gun for hire, firstly at Portsmouth, then Spurs, to Portsmouth again and then on to Middlesbrough, before a more settled spell at Luton Town. The frequent moves can be partly explained by Brown's capabilities as a striker. He was not an especially refined footballer, but his physicality and eye for a chance made him a coveted asset. A report of a performance for Middlesbrough in the *Daily Mail* of 19 September 1904 describes how Brown 'nearly brought down the rigging with a terrific shot.'

It was a spectacle that would have been familiar to Spurs fans. Though he was on the club's books for only two seasons, he scored 100 goals in 113 competitive and 'friendly' matches, a genuinely prodigious strike rate. Like many of the most prolific goalscorers, Brown did little else. Bob Goodwin goes as far as to describe him as looking lazy and disinterested at times. Neither, according to some views, was there that much finesse to his game. Brown was not tall or particularly big, but used his strength well, allied to an unerring nose for a chance. 'One part of his game that could never be questioned was his bravery,' wrote Goodwin.

His signing by Spurs was clearly regarded as a major coup. The club's official handbook of 1900 marked him out as 'every inch a footballer, and is undoubtedly a capture to the club. He hails from Glenbuck, a small mining village away in the wilds of Ayrshire… Proud Preston induced him to cross the border [where] he developed from a raw youth to a player of the first water… The 'Spurs were lucky to sign him, as several First League clubs were after him.'

Money no doubt played a part in the fortune of the move, but the chance to rejoin Alex Tait, and be managed by Cameron, were also irresistible temptations. Brown's arrival turned the Southern League champions into a more potent force. While form in the league dipped, compounded by a number of injuries, the side and in particular Brown really clicked in the FA Cup.

From the first round, delayed by the death of Queen Victoria, the cup run had the feel of destiny about it, not least because Spurs were drawn against the team that had inspired them so much, Preston North End. It took a replay but Brown's hat-trick in that 4–2 win at Deepdale established momentum. In the next round, Spurs faced the holders Bury. This was to be a true test, but a Brown brace saw the Lancashire side off. Suddenly, people not just in the south, but across the country were sitting up and taking notice. The *Manchester Guardian* wrote of 'a great triumph… Tottenham Hotspur [is a team] that plays with spasmodic fluctuations. They gave the great crowd they had to cheer them on a succession of expectant thrills.'

Expectation duly rose for the quarter-final at Reading. Spurs' hopes were very nearly dashed by the Royals, but luck was on Tottenham's side, when the referee failed to see Tait handle on the line and thus deny the hosts a clear penalty. Two more goals from Brown underpinned a 3–0 win in the replay, putting Spurs through to face Football League founder members West Brom. Despite playing virtually on home soil, the Midlanders could not contain Brown who ran amok, scoring all four unanswered goals.

So Spurs were in the FA Cup Final against northern giants Sheffield United. The excitement in the capital and beyond was unprecedented. No southern team had come close to lifting a trophy monopolised by Football League clubs, Southampton having been thrashed 4–0 by Bury the season before. It would be stretching a point to say the Scottish- and northern-player-dominated Spurs team enjoyed universal support in the south, but the broad goodwill was tangible.

On the day the scale of more committed support was breathtaking. The tie was played at Crystal Palace, with an official attendance of 114,815 – a then world record and still the third largest crowd ever in England. Even this number does not convey the true scale. These were spectators formally admitted to the stadium. Gathered on overlooking vantage points and not counted among the official attendance were tens of thousands more.

"Spurs getting to the final against Sheff Utd was a meeting of two worlds – the north versus the south, the old order versus the new," says Martin Cloake. "There was real anticipation – who was going to come out best, were the old order going to put the upstarts in their place? There's a tremendous description in the book *A Century of Great Soccer Drama* by John Cottrell, which has a fantastic quote about this bright spring morning breaking over London and this enormous movement of people. It was reckoned over 250,000 people went to Crystal Palace Park.

"Cottrell talks about the main rail terminals of London full of the 'northern men with their flat caps and the cockneys with their bowler hats'. People were wearing colours and hand-made rosettes and even in those early days, that old tradition of dressing up for the Cup Final had begun. It was by far the largest crowd that had ever watched a game of football anywhere in the world up to that time." Cottrell's 1972 tome also unearthed a gem about the catering laid on for the vast crowd, including 55,250 portions of cake, 20,000 French pastries, 6,000 pork pies, 200 rumps of beef, 250 chines of mutton, 40 whole lambs, 22,400lbs of potatoes and 10,000 Bath buns.

The Spurs fans among those delighting in the fare might soon have had indigestion, so tense was the match. United were clear favourites, with recent league titles and FA Cup wins to their name. They boasted a roster of talent including George Hedley, Ernest Needham, Walter Bennett and, most imposingly, famous goalkeeper William 'Fatty' Foulke. Weighing in at 20 stones and standing 6ft 4in he was a giant of a man. To see him take the field at Crystal Palace towering over team-mates and opponents conjured up memories of that 1887 game against Luton when the Spurs players were mocked for their diminutive size.

Ultimately the outcome of the 1901 final would be the same, but not before two matches and no little controversy. The 'Cutlers' took the lead through Fred Priest after ten minutes. It seemed as if the big occasion might get to the Londoners, but Brown settled nerves with a 23rd-minute equaliser before putting his team 2–1 up six minutes into the second half with a thumping drive. It was said that Brown's brace so enraged Foulke that he picked the Spurs man up and swung him through the air. The lead was gone after just a minute and in dramatic circumstances. Fred Lipsham's shot was kept out by Spurs keeper George Clawley and then turned away as Bennett lurked to pounce on the rebound. Corner kick. Not, however, according to the referee Arthur Kingscott, who to the astonishment of the players and anyone in the vast crowd who had a reasonable view, gave a goal to United. The game descended into a battle of attrition and Spurs were grateful for Tait's cool head at the back.

Sadly for Mr Kingscott, but to the enormous entertainment of much of the rest of the nation, his remarkable error was captured for posterity by the fledgling newsreels. Seeing the opportunity for a genuine sensation, the distributors rushed out copies and the film was shown around the country. The surviving footage is beautifully nostalgic. It shows Foulke striding his domain like a colossus; there are grainy, jerky shots of 'Terrible' Tait nonchalantly taking to the field, with top-hatted dignitaries trying to get a piece of the action. And it shows that Lipsham's goal was not a goal.

Cloake says, "As far as I've been able to research, it's the first game when a referee's decision has been examined by moving pictures and caused controversy. At the time, cinema was emerging as a new art form and it was a novelty. There were a group of cameramen going round Britain filming major events, they would work that into a basic film and it would be shown at the cinema. It would be film of a circus or people punting on the river at Cambridge, couples walking in Hyde Park on a Sunday – just things happening in moving pictures. People loved it, it didn't matter what it was, it was just put it up on a screen. Nothing's changed, really."

Spurs had themselves enjoyed good fortune earlier in the competition when Tait's handball at Reading went unnoticed by the ref. But there was a perception this was something on a different scale. At the time, Cameron instructed his players not to complain. Years later, he revealed how he seethed at the injustice, writing, 'I have never been so furious on a football pitch.' The usually diffident reports of the period could not avoid the controversy, with *The Times'* correspondent observing, 'much was said by the spectators as to the wisdom of the referee.' While highlighting the tension that negated against an entertaining game, *The Times* concluded Spurs had been the better side, though there was a sniffy aside about 'the commonplace character' of the play, due, naturally, to professionalism making it 'such a necessity to consider the exchequer of the club.'

The result deprived esteemed guests like Sir Redvers Buller VC, and veteran of the Zulu War, of the chance to present the trophy and medals. Instead, he addressed the crowd, saying to laughter and cheers, "There are many things that interest a soldier in the game of football, and essentially it is a game in which, as a rule, the side wins which is best practised at shooting." Lord Kinnaird, President of the FA, former captain of Old Etonians and veteran of those first England v Scotland internationals 30 years before, beamed his approval.

There would be greater fun in store for the grandee of the amateur game.

The replay was set for the following Saturday at Goodison, but as Liverpool had a fixture that day, the venue was switched to Bolton's Burnden Park. The problem was the town's railway station was being rebuilt and the Lancashire and Yorkshire Railway Company refused to offer cheap fares. It meant the crowd was a fraction of the original game – just 20,470 supporters, leading to a glut of unsold food and the nickname of the 'Pork Pie Final'.

The game itself was a better contest. Again Sheffield took the lead through Fred Priest, and again put Spurs under the cosh but this time, the Londoners were able eventually to establish their own rhythm and play their way to victory. They narrowed the middle of the park and found space between the United midfield and defence with neat threaded passes. It was a Cameron tactical masterpiece and it was fitting that he should score one of Tottenham's three goals, the others coming from Tom Morris and, inevitably, Sandy Brown who sealed the win with a fine header.

After another long pre-amble about the evils of professionalism, and veiled references to the satisfaction that at least a southern team had claimed the trophy from the dominant northern sides, *The Times* analysis considered Spurs deserving winners, while reporting that, 'The success of the Tottenham eleven aroused great enthusiasm in the suburbs of Tottenham and Hornsey.' This was a classic piece of understatement. London had not seen such an outpouring of joy and celebration since, it was claimed, the relief of Mafeking in the Boer War a year earlier. Tens of thousands thronged the streets, and would stay to welcome the returning victors home early the next morning.

They were having quite a journey. On the train back from Bolton, one Spurs fan, a bricklayer by trade, asked if he could hold the trophy. As soon as it was in his grasp, he filled it with something suitably invigorating and it was passed around for everyone to drink – including Lord Kinnaird, usually a notable abstainer. 'These incidents show that the duke's son and the cook's son have been numbered amongst the Spurs well-wishers', cheered *The Herald*.

When this party of fans mildly overcoming class barriers finally arrived at South Tottenham station bearing the famous trophy, it was bedecked with ribbons in the club colours. They had been tied on by Mrs Cadman, wife of one of the directors, thereby establishing a tradition that lasts to this day, as well as the less reliable 'fact' that Spurs always win a trophy when the year ends in '1'. In 1901, days of celebration followed. Fireworks were set off and a brass band played *Hail The Conquering Heroes Come*. Later at the ground a 'kinematograph' showed highlights from the final. It all helped Spurs produce an account £2,554 in the black by the season's end.

The story does not quite end there. Rumours have long circulated that Tait and Brown were allowed to take the trophy to Glenbuck. It was reputed to have been placed in the window of Barr's shop for all the village to see, but definitive proof of this Scottish sojourn for the priceless silverware is hard to find. The *Ayrshire Post* focused on the management of Cameron and all but ignored the Glenbuck element to the story. The FA has no record in its archives of the trophy's journey north. Similarly Spurs cannot find evidence that confirms the event. It could simply be that the club allowed their Scottish heroes to briefly take the cup north on a nod and a wink.

It had been quite an adventure for Tait and especially Brown. In all he scored 15 goals in that season's competition, four fewer than those notched by Preston's Jimmy Ross for his 1887/88 season record, but a memorable achievement nonetheless. Brown also scored in every round, and is still a member of an elite group of just 12 players who have achieved the feat in the FA Cup's 143-year history.

Mat Snow, journalist, author, Spurs fan and former editor of *FourFourTwo* magazine says of the 1901 team's Scottish core, "Bill Shankly once said 'If you've got three Scots in your side, you've got a chance of winning something. If you've got any more, you're in trouble.' Spurs had five Scots in the side, two from Glenbuck alone – and they won something: the FA Cup, the only non-league club ever to do so.

"In the final and its replay, Glenbuck man Sandy Brown scored three goals, while Sandy Tait was critical in keeping a physical, verging on brutal, Sheffield United strike force at bay. Brown was the hero of the FA Cup campaign but Tait the enduring Spurs legend, still remembered over 60 years later. Our best left-back ever? Double-winner Ron Henry has to be a rival; Gareth Bale too – but only when he was moved up the pitch."

Future fortunes for the three main Scottish protagonists of the 1901 Cup win, and of their club were mixed. Tottenham's victory did not herald an overthrow of the old northern order. No other southern club won the FA Cup again until Spurs 20 years later. It wasn't until the 1930s that Arsenal under the inspired managership of Herbert Chapman, presented a serious challenge to the northern and Midlands elite, while Spurs would have to wait until after the Second World War to win the Football League title.

Cameron stayed in charge at Tottenham for another six years, but, frustrated by the struggles of the club to gain membership of the Football League, and amid 'differences with the directorate' he resigned in 1907, after 139 goals in 293 appearances. Returning to journalism, he later coached in Germany at Dresdner SC, and was interred at Ruhleben, near Berlin when the First World War broke out. Here he was joined by 5,000 other detainees, including a group of former England internationals led by the famous Steve Bloomer. Cameron became secretary of the Ruhleben Football Association, which organised cup competitions and matches, including remarkable fixtures between English and 'World' XIs.

It was however a far cry from Crystal Palace. After three years Cameron was repatriated. He had by his own admission been lucky to avoid the bloodbath of combat, but his health had suffered and he was never the same man again. He managed Ayr United in 1918 before dropping out of frontline football, and died in 1935, aged 63.

For his Ayrshire compatriots, their lives and careers would take different turns. And all the while, others among the Glenbuck progeny were making their presence felt far and wide.

Chapter 8

Glenbuck Highs and Lows

WHEN the earnest bishops, reverends and assorted clerics of the 19th century saw the light and began to embrace the idea that sport might be generally regarded as A Good Thing, they had spiritual as well as practical motives. The theory was that organised, competitive exercise would encourage a new breed among the lower orders, giving them strong limbs but also decent morals. The men of the cloth wanted to rear young men – and it was most definitely men – who would play hard but fair, resist the evils of drink and carnal lusts, and learn how to take orders. As Thomas Arnold, deacon and headmaster of Rugby School put it, sport was a "formidable vehicle for character building".

Quite what Arnold would have made of the nature of professional football 60 years after his death is a wonder to behold. Not only were huge crowds being drawn to watch the game and thus, it was feared, being tempted away from church, but those young men who excelled at the game were being *paid* to play it.

The Reverend T.C. Ceilings was one of those expressing concern. Thankfully, it was billiards that saved the day. Mat Snow quoted in his chapters in *The Spurs Opus* a wonderful extract from the Rev. Ceilings's article in *The World Of Billiards* in 1907: 'The paid player may only have one match a week; he trains daily, but the actual work certainly does not average one hour, and he is a law unto himself for the rest of the 24. Now, on some grounds, the men are expected to be there from nine to 12 and two to five, and often with only a cattle shed to shelter in. They have no bar, and smoke and loaf the time away… There they must stick, or run the risk of fine or suspension.

'It demoralises a man, and the result was that very early in their history the directors of clubs like Aston Villa, Sheffield United, Fulham, Tottenham Hotspur, Southampton, and Chelsea saw that if they were going to preserve the morale of the teams they must do something, and so they established social clubs, which have capital billiard saloons.'

One of the most prodigious patrons of that Spurs social club and its billiard saloons was none other than Alex Tait. It aroused no little attention in the press, turning him into unlikely front-page material. But if 'Terrible' Tait was hardly the David Beckham of his day, the coverage was recognition of his esteemed standing in the game.

Tait lasted nine seasons at Tottenham. Added to the spells at Rangers, Motherwell, Preston, Leyton, and finally Croydon Common, it completed a 20-year career as a professional player. He never won a full Scotland cap – suspicions about the latent resentment on the part of the Scottish FA to selecting 'Anglos' who had taken the English club shilling saw to that – but Tait's standing in the game was among the most high-profile and respected in early-20th century sport. Not bad for a former pit boy from the 'wilds' of Ayrshire.

He had maintained his own high standards and consistency after the FA Cup win, even if his club did not, becoming captain in 1904 and a personality readily identified with White Hart Lane. In September 1905 he had star billing on the front page of the *Daily Mirror*. The paper was little more than a year old and represented a new kind of mass media, originally published to cater for a largely middle-class female market. Only in later years would it become the best-selling paper of the working class, so it says something for Tait's celebrity (and the club's proximity to the paper's offices) that he was deemed suitable for a dedicated feature.

With accompanying photos showing Tait hard at work, leisure and play he was described thus: 'That the game of football is not all fun, as so many people think, may be learned from the photographs. They depict Mr Tait, the captain of the 'Spurs, who takes his benefit on October 21; golf, a Scot's relaxation; a fast fifty yards for the wind; skipping, another footballers' exercise; keeping the eye in form on the ball; and after the day's training, pleasure at the billiard table.' The benefit match mentioned was played against New Brompton, who had provided the opposition when Tait and Spurs won the Southern League.

The *Mirror* was quite enamoured with Mr Tait. In another article, sub-headed 'How a Professional Player Keeps Fit' it countered a negative view of the craft: 'There are few better living men than the average professional footballer. It has become the fashion to describe him as a hooligan in magazine articles written by people who know nothing about the truth.' After revealing the truth, including training, yet more billiards, a visit to the theatre, travelling to matches, 'discipline stricter than a soldier' and no more than £208 a year in earnings, the article held up Tait as the model pro.

'Tait has rarely or never played a bad game, and has never been known to show the least sign of spitefulness in his play... he was born in Glenbuck, a little Ayrshire town which has turned out more famous players perhaps than any other its size in the "Land of Cakes."' As Julie Welch, dame of Fleet Street football journalism, wrote of Tait's popularity, 'Not the most twinkle-toed of players, Tait had everything else: positional sense, intelligent distribution, and a willingness to cover for team-mates. At White Hart Lane he aroused the same kind of deep, enduring, unconditional passion in the hearts of the fans that Graham Roberts would do in later times. He might have been a hard bastard, but he was their hard bastard.'

Rev. Ceilings might not have approved of the profanity but he would have welcomed the billiards. In his homily to the virtues of the game in keeping footballers on the straight and narrow, he wrote 'Just outside White Hart Lane station on the Great Eastern Railway is situated the first of the London Football Social Clubs. And here you find from 10.30 in the morning till the same hour at night the players congregated and the tables in full use. If it be a wet day and Captain Sandy Tait feels the need of exercise, he will challenge his friend Walter Bull to a game or games, for they will play perhaps a couple of hours, and they tell you that the amount of walking involved makes them, at any rate, feel healthily tired.'

It was in the social club that Tait would occasionally attend to the coal business he ran as a sideline. He was becoming an all-round man of many means as well as a fine footballer. Hailing from the Ayrshire coalfields, it was natural for him to venture into that trade, but he was also developing as a coach, an official (he acted as a linesman for the Spurs v Cambridge University match in November 1905) and as a writer, or at least a ghosted one. It was Tait's byline that appeared beside the *Daily Mail*'s report on Tottenham's 2–0 win over Burnley in round one of the FA Cup in January 1906. 'We were the best team and I think if the ground had been in good condition we should have asserted our superiority much better,' Tait wrote.

The admirable playing career finally wound down in November 1908 when he played for Leyton against Millwall. The *Daily Mail* reported he would move into management after 'a good innings'. For all his fearsome reputation he had never been booked, and he brought a degree of professional calm to his management roles, though they were not nearly as successful as his playing ones.

For one season, 1910/11, he managed at The Nest, home of Croydon Common, and the south London borough's first professional football club before Crystal Palace. Alan Futter, who has studied and written about the club's history says, "Prior to the First World War, the club played in the Southern League along with many of the household names of today; West Ham United, Norwich City, Southampton, QPR and Millwall. Indeed, 19 of the 20 clubs in Division One of the Southern League at the outbreak of war in 1914 later became long-term members of the Football League. The only one not to do so was Croydon Common."

Tait arrived at Croydon to find the directors had scheduled no less than 80 matches and bequeathed a squad desperately short of manpower. He brought in fresh personnel and some old Croydon faces, including club favourite Percy Barnfeather, but missed out on the tantalising prospect of signing superstar Steve Bloomer, then in the twilight days of his career but still a huge draw. It appears raising the necessary finances to pay fees and wages did for Tait's time at the club.

The fate of Croydon Common seems reflective of Tait's management career, but his renown did not abate. Alex Jackson from the National Football Museum at Preston unearthed a moving story from the First World War involving Tait, his sons, and even a reference to the Crystal Palace grounds where Tait senior had burnished his football fame. *The Sporting Chronicle* newspaper in 1918 reported:

'Last Friday the paper's London correspondent visited "The Nest" – James Tait, son of Alexander Tait to be found there and to be the new groundsman – for some time a gardener at the Crystal Palace.

'Young Tait, who was born at Preston when his father was assisting the North End, has been before the Medical Board on three occasions, but he has failed to pass owing to a tubercular knee, which has left the limb stiff. His younger brother, who was a clerk at the FA offices, joined up at 17, and went to France with the First Football Battalion. But the youngster only arrived there a month in advance of his gallant father, who has now been three years on the active service with a labour battalion in the R.E. Father and son have met upon three or four occasions, and last Christmas the lad walked nearly twenty miles to see him.

'"Sandy" had a quaint experience out there. He was in a village in France when a "Tommy," who was happened to be passing, got down from his horse, and approached the old full-back with a smile of greeting. Then he turned aside with a half-apology, thinking he had made a mistake, and was heard to say, "Well, I'm damned. I thought it was Sandy Tait." He passed on, and Tait had no opportunity to reassure him.'

Tait's reluctance to proclaim his celebrity spoke volumes. It was reflective of his values, a code of behaviour instilled in him in Glenbuck where inflated egos were either mocked or given short shrift. Yet Tait's famous reputation would endure. In September 1922 he was temporarily appointed as trainer-coach of 'Corinthians and Casuals... This engagement of a famous professional as coach should strengthen Corinthians,' the *Daily Mirror* claimed. In the same paper in 1934, in an article headlined 'When Footballers Were More Than Human', Arthur T. Rich lamented the changing ways of the game and harked back to an age when a fan would, apparently, 'quite willingly have laid down his life for the Spurs... Was not the name of Sandy Tait one to conjure with? The men who kicked the ball on the playing field were very gods to schoolboy eyes. Sandy Tait was not of common clay.'

Later still, when his old club wished to illustrate the qualities of the players in another Spurs team, the all-conquering Double side of 1960/61, an enterprising lyricist scripted a verse for the club anthem *And the Spurs Go Marching On!*:

> *Ron Henry's seen at full-back on the left hand of his mate*
> *He's quick to make a tackle, Ron, he doesn't hesitate*
> *When Ron goes in to tackle we remember Sandy Tait...*

It was testimony to Tait's ageless appeal. The family's sporting connections continued not north of the river but in south London, with son Sandy becoming a much-loved figure at the Oval for Surrey County Cricket Club where he was a masseur. His dad, equally cherished, and he too a remarkable character, passed away in Croydon in April 1949.

He survived his old Spurs team-mate and fellow Glenbuckian Sandy Brown by five years. The two players provide an interesting contrast. One became a club stalwart, the other more of a drifter whose talent was arguably never fully realised. 'The Glenbuck Goalgetter' was an outstanding striker, of that there was little doubt. But life experiences appear to have clouded his story, and understandably so.

He hailed from another venerated Glenbuck footballing family, which was closely involved with the formation of Glenbuck Athletic. Sandy Brown was nicknamed 'Towey' while at Burnside Park, where he was a gifted teenager, able to more than hold his own with the brawny men of Ayrshire Junior football. His rise through the ranks of Scottish and English clubs was testament to his qualities, but it was when he was set to earn recognition at the ultimate level that his career appeared to stall.

On 5 April 1902, Scotland met England for the 27th time. The venue was Ibrox. It accommodated 68,114 spectators, a large number of which had been gathered on the West terrace, extended just a month before. Designed by Archibald Leitch, this end comprised wooden planks fixed on to an iron and steel framework embedded in concrete. In the weeks beforehand, some fans had reported that the terracing felt unsafe, but the warnings went unheeded. In the first half, a section of the terracing collapsed, sending 25 people (some reports cite 26) plummeting up to 50 feet to their deaths. Over 500 more were injured, some horrifically.

The game was halted, but only temporarily. Even more astonishingly, spectators re-gathered precariously around the gaping hole to continue watching the action, the roars of the crowd mingled with the agonised screams of the injured and dying. Amid this dreadful scene, Sandy Brown was playing – and scoring – for

Scotland in a 1–1 draw. It is even said that the goal was key to the tragedy. Bobby Templeton had embarked on a run down the wing and the crowd swayed forward to keep him in view. Instead of crossing, he cut inside and passed to Brown who slotted home, the action precipitating massed movement on the terrace seconds before the dreadful sounds of splintering wood were heard and the floorboards gave way.

The players were of course, blameless. Culpability for the disaster was eventually laid at the door of the contractor who was said to have supplied 'inferior' timber for the terracing.

Brown had played in a 'Home versus Anglos' trial match a month before and looked set for repeated senior call-ups, but the Ibrox match was declared void and his name thus removed from official records. He would have to wait until April 1904 when he was a Middlesbrough player for his solitary Scottish cap, earned in a 1–0 defeat to England at Celtic Park.

Thereafter the life and career of Brown was an unsettled one. Luton Town provided some stability and in each of three seasons he was top scorer for the Hatters. Indeed he was top marksman for seven of the 12 senior campaigns he played in, registering 142 goals in 283 matches in Scotland and England, not counting the 25 goals he notched in the FA Cup alone. He was, by any measure, a great player, but there is a nagging undercurrent of not quite fulfilling his talent to the full.

Tottenham would hold mixed memories for him. Aside from the 1901 FA Cup win, he was feted by the home crowd when he returned alongside eight of his old cup-winning team-mates in 1907 for a benefit match for trainer Sam Mountford, a laconic old Spurs character who had once said with evident pride that the side was the 'least exercised' in football. Thereafter a spell at Kettering provided the end to Brown's playing days.

He became landlord of a pub in Luton, the Dew Drop Inn, in tandem with his wife for whom the brewing trade was a family affair. At the age of 23 'Towey' had wedded Winifred Gilboy in

October 1901. She was the daughter of a well-known Tottenham publican, W.F. Gilboy, who ran the White Hart pub immediately in front of the main entrance to White Hart Lane stadium (another Spurs player, goalkeeper George Clawley, also married a Gilboy sister). The pub is still there to this day, though is set for demolition as Spurs look to build their glitzy new ground, but it was a spit-and-sawdust boozer built on more solid foundations than the Browns' relationship. The marriage was troubled, to the extent that 'marital difficulties', as a headline ran in the *Luton Times* of 1909, contributed to the pair having to forego running the Dew Drop Inn.

Brown had by this time returned to live in Tottenham. He later went back to Glenbuck and the prospect of working in the mines. But the coal industry in East Ayrshire was already in terminal decline and by the autumn of 1922 and reconciled with Winifred, he was off on his travels again, this time to the opposite end of the Earth. New Zealand would provide a new home for the couple, who ran a hotel in Auckland. Living a whole world away, Brown slipped out of public profile in Britain until he died in the town of Granity on 6 March 1944.

The fates of his brother Thomas were almost as gilded but also had their fair share of disappointments. By the time he was born in August 1879, the Brown family were more settled, but he appeared to have the same wandering instincts of Sandy as well as his strengths as a centre-forward. It was markedly different to the Glenbuck Taits, Sandy and his younger brother Robert, who were models of stability. Little is know about the career of Robert Tait other than its dependability – 133 appearances and 22 goals at inside-left over three years at Motherwell and ten at Cowdenbeath. By contrast the younger Brown sibling was frequently on the move.

After a non-playing stint with Third Lanark, he travelled south in August 1899 to play for Leicester Fosse, the forerunner of Leicester City. Fosse were another ambitious club formed by boys from a religious background, and had joined the Football League five years before. Brown, nicknamed 'Bogey', made a great start with a goal on his debut in the match against Woolwich Arsenal and looked well set for a successful career in the East Midlands. Indeed he was top goalscorer for Leicester for three seasons, returning a very healthy strike rate of 41 goals in 77 appearances.

This was not uninterrupted success, however. After less than two years he was effectively sacked for 'training indiscipline' and spent a year at Chesterfield. The move was supposed to be permanent, but the Derbyshire side could not afford the fee and Brown was despatched back to Leicester. This was again short-lived; a year later he was off to Portsmouth, almost as a direct replacement for brother Sandy, but just four games and three goals later, in 1904 he was heading north to Dundee.

He stayed at Dens Park for two seasons, scoring seven goals in 14 games – once again a decent ratio. But his stay ended with yet more disappointment. He was unfit and overweight for the start of the 1905/06 season. Even a regime of Turkish baths couldn't make much of an inroad on his 13 stones, and in January he was sacked.

The story of 'Bogey' Brown was an indication that not all of the graduates from the Glenbuck academy would find the professional game to their liking. It was a hard, demanding, and unforgiving place. For all the image of the likes of Sandy Tait enjoying their billiards-saloon leisure, the game then as now was ultra-competitive. Most promising young players did not make it. Unlike today, the rejects or the ones who couldn't make the breakthrough into the Scottish or English elite did not have the safety net of one lucrative contract to set them up for life. Serious injury could ruin careers and lives, and rejection result in a similar fate.

The pay was not that great, set by the supposedly free-market loving club owners and league officials at a maximum £4 a week in 1901/02. Transfer fees hovered around the £400 mark with a maximum £10 signing-on fee for the player. Underhand payments were rife, and a number of clubs were punished for breaking the rules. The players were bitterly opposed to the restrictive conditions they worked under, later prompting the establishment of the players' union proper under Billy Meredith. At a time when the average skilled workman earned £2–£3 a week, being a pro footballer was not a bad living and immeasurably preferable to a working lifetime down the pit. But the notion that Glenbuck's travelling superstars were living high on the hog was false.

Never was this better illustrated than in the case of Joe Wallace. He was one of four Wallaces to wear Glenbuck colours and make the grade in senior football, and among the smallest. Standing just 5ft 4in he was a pocket dynamo of a forward, drawn to Tyneside in January 1891 and the club that would become Newcastle United. East End was one of a number of early clubs in the city and its outlying areas. Yet the intense popularity of the game that has been such a feature of the North East was not initially so conspicuous. Paying crowds were relatively low. Those early clubs competing for the limited support, like Newcastle Rangers, Stanley and Rosewood were part of a local scene in which a variety of clubs and teams came and went, before a series of mergers narrowed down the choices available for locals to follow.

Paul Brown, author of *All With Smiling Faces: How Newcastle Became United* says: "A large number of clubs emerged on Tyneside throughout the 1880s, but in the beginning there was no real structure around them. To give a modern day comparison, it would be a bit like having a load of Sunday League clubs but without the league. So you've got lots of football clubs, affiliated to cricket clubs, churches, pubs and workplaces, arranging occasional friendly matches against each other, and playing very occasional cup matches. Because there was no league, there was no regular and reliable income stream. So as well as a natural ebb and flow of interest, clubs regularly went out of business because they weren't making any money."

The development of club football in Newcastle was like a series of streams and brooks, some petering out to oblivion, others forming tributaries that eventually fed into a single river. Two of the main branches were East End (born out of Stanley) and West End. In 1886, West End took over the lease of a ground at St James' Park. The two clubs vied for supremacy in who would forge the main course of the game in the city. Both were founding members of the inaugural Northern League, both fielded a mix of amateur and paid players. It could have been that Newcastle developed two major clubs, thus creating a very different environment to the 'one-club-town' situation that has both helped and arguably hindered Newcastle in the modern era.

"By the late 1890s," Brown says, "when the Football League, and in the North East the Northern League, had formed, two leading clubs had emerged on Tyneside. They both played in front of similar crowds, around 2,000, but up to 5,000 for the biggest matches, and they were pretty evenly matched on the pitch. In 1892, with East End beginning to dominate on the pitch, West End went bust and folded. A deal was made for East End to take over the lease on West End's ground, St James' Park. The move aggrieved both sets of supporters, and East End tried to appease them by changing its name to Newcastle United."

Crowds at the time were simply not big enough to sustain two clubs with professional ambitions. "That's true," says Brown. "Most clubs at the time could only hope to attract crowds in the low thousands.

"It's worth remembering that association football was a new attraction, so there was no underlying devotion to the game. Even FA Cup finals were only getting crowds of 5,000 or so in the early 1880s. It wasn't until the 1890s that football really boomed in popularity.

"Another factor is that clubs were ultra-localised, by which I mean spectators would watch matches in their own neighbourhoods, rather than go further afield. This changed slightly once the Football League came along, and they began to shift allegiance to league clubs in order to watch a better standard [at] matches."

If the city with a then population of around 145,000 was to make a real impression on the fast-growing sport, it required the backing of the whole of Newcastle. United by name, united by nature, meant the club had a broad appeal in a place on the up. As Brown adds, "Newcastle was booming, largely due to industry based on the river, not just shipbuilding but everything from coal to chemicals. A lot of migrants did arrive for work, many from Scotland. Lots of them took up residence in the East End, where East End, obviously, was formed. East End was actually formed in 1881 by a group of teenagers. They were all local to the Byker and Heaton areas, and were mixed blue- and white-collar working class, including teachers and shipbuilders.

"I think football in Newcastle then was community-based rather than specific to an industry, which probably reflected the diverse occupations of the founders. When East End issued shares in 1890, they were sold in local pubs for 10s each, payable in instalments, with the specific intention of making them accessible to the working classes. Records show that the majority of shareholders were manual workers or clerks."

The new club, relatively more democratic and accountable than many of its contemporaries that were becoming the fiefdoms of business elites, joined the Second Division of the Football League for the 1893/94 season. Wallace would be a star of the opening campaign. He was one of no less than 13 Scotsmen who made up half of the club's squad. Yet again, a club looking to prosper in the early years of organised professional English football was looking to do so with Scottish playing talent. Foreign imports in the English game are nothing new.

'Wee Wallace' as the local press dubbed him was a revelation at St James' Park, playing across the front line, on either wing, as an inside-forward or operating as a central striker. From any position he scored goals – six in his and the club's first six games in the Football League in 1893/94 and 17 in total, making him United's top goalscorer.

Thereafter the games and goals started to dry up and within two seasons he was largely out of the first-team picture. Unlike the Glenbuck Browns and many other footballers, he did not take the option of packing his bags and hitting the road. It seems 'Wee Wallace' had put down roots in the area. He stayed on Tyneside when he moved to Rendel and worked as a labourer on the shipyards.

"Wallace was one of a handful of players who made the step up from East End in the Northern League to Newcastle United in the Football League," says Paul Brown. "As is the case when any club steps up a division, there are some players who don't have the ability to go with them. To be fair to Wallace, he did play more games for Newcastle in the Football League than in the Northern League, so he did manage to make the step up for a couple of seasons.

"Another point to mention is the influence of East End secretary (and effectively manager) Tom Watson on bringing Scottish players to England. He pioneered the 'poaching' of talented Scots, offering them jobs in Newcastle factories to entice them down. He went on to manage Sunderland and Liverpool, winning the league at both with teams made up largely of Scottish players. He didn't sign Wallace, but did set the template the club followed for many years."

Wallace's kin would follow in Glenbuck's propensity to send footballers out to bigger clubs in Scotland and England. Alec Wallace made a modest impression at Lanarkshire side Airdrie (where the world's first penalty was taken by Royal Albert's James McCluggage in 1891), but it was a later pair of Wallaces who enjoyed longer and more eventful careers.

Robert, 'Bob' or 'Bert' Wallace kicked a ball too late to feature for a Glenbuck team but did the next best thing and donned Muirkirk colours in the Junior leagues. An outside-left, he was physically well-built and strong, attributes that led to regional senior clubs making offers. In 1923, another venerable name in

Lanarkshire and Scottish football, Hamilton Academical, won the chase, bringing Bob Wallace to where John Ferguson had gained his first opportunity in the pro game. Wallace did not make much headway at Douglas Park, featuring in just four games, though he did score in the Lanarkshire Cup game against Hamilton Garrison. He was soon loaned out to Bathgate, and by the summer of 1924, he was off once more, but on what would have been one of the longest of Glenbuck's footballing journeys, even greater than Bob Blyth's odyssey to Portsmouth.

At just 19, Bob Wallace pitched up at Plymouth Argyle. He had two fellow 'Accies' to keep him company, Fred Craig and Paddy Corcoran, but it was still an impressive undertaking for such a young player. His spell with the Pilgrims was again transient, with just a single appearance for the Devon side – but what an appearance.

Joining the club for a four-week tour of South America, which included an impressive 4–0 win over future world champions Uruguay, Wallace played against Buenos Aires's Boca Juniors. Sea travel did not agree with him. According to the *Western Morning News* the club's Scottish manager Bob Jack (who had first managed the club in 1905, when he took over from none other than Frank Brettell) reported that 'Everybody is fit excepting Wallace who is intermittently upset by the sway of the ship. He has had very few comfortable days, and it will take a week or more on land to put him right.'

Wallace did indeed look slightly peaky in a photo of the party en route to Argentina on the RMSP *Avon*. Any queasiness or disorientation would hardly have been helped by the game in which he did play. It was some encounter. The Boca fans celebrated their side's opening goal so enthusiastically, carrying all 11 players on their shoulders around the pitch, that the game was delayed for half an hour, with the visitors seeking refuge in the dressing room.

Eventually, when play restarted, Argyle were awarded a spot kick by Plymouth referee Fred Reeve who had travelled with the group. Again, Boca fans invaded the pitch, and again the Argyle players had to run for cover. It was agreed in the dressing room that, in the interests of life and limb, Pilgrims' winger Corcoran would take the kick and deliberately miss. But team-mate Moses Russell was having none of it, scored and prompted another pitch invasion that forced the game to be abandoned.

Anything after that would have been a comedown, but a two-year spell in the Plymouth reserves added to Wallace's frustrations. He only featured in one senior game, an away fixture at Southend United. In search of first-team action he moved to Devon neighbours Torquay United, in the summer of 1926, though that too was problematic. Illness entailed a long lay-off, and it was not until 1928 that he was fit to play again, but by this time what had looked to be a promising professional career had eluded him.

There were better times for another later Glenbuck Wallace, John, who became a mainstay of Partick Thistle. The son of a Cherrypicker, George Wallace, he was a nephew of another, Willie Wallace and, in a further sign of the close inter-relationships between Glenbuck's families, also a nephew of Sandy 'Towey' Brown. This later Wallace was born in Glenbuck on 3 September 1916. He signed for Partick in November 1935 from Cumnock Juniors. By coincidence with the Glenbuck Blyths, his home address while at Partick was listed as Blyth Buildings.

At peak fitness Wallace was 5ft 10in and weighed 11st, and he stayed in Glasgow for 11 years, making 154 appearances and scoring 102 goals, a highly impressive strike rate. It would have been more but for the interruption of the Second World War, but was reflective of the centre-forward's reliability and the stability he benefitted from at Firhill.

His antecedent Joseph would no doubt have loved such a dependable environment. He had made such an impact with the early incarnation of one of the great clubs of the English game, but drifted out of the limelight and into the harsh realities of life on that dreaded destination where no player wants to go, the football 'scrapheap'. Newcastle United's club records show that in 1933, in the grip of the Great Depression that ruined so many lives, 'Wee' Joe Wallace was destitute, forced to accept handouts of money and clothes from the big club looming over the Tyne at St James' Park. It was a long, long way from north London billiard saloons.

A line-up of the famous Glenbuck Athletic football club, later to become the Cherrypickers. This side included members of the village families who played for and ran the club over its roughly 50-year existence. A number went on to play professionally.

A present-day view of the site of Burnside Park, looking west. The Blackface sheep for which the area was famous are running across what would have been the pitch, near the intersection of the halfway line and the touchline.

A contemporary photo of Burnside Park when it was still in active use. The line of the wall running along the centre is where fans would cheer the village team on (and abuse the opposition).

ERECTED 1925
DIRECTORS
R. BLYTH (CHAIRMAN)
A. E. HOOPER, T.C. (VICE-CHAIRMAN)
S. CRIBB   G. LEWIN OLIVER
WM. C. KILN   H. PANNELL, M.C.
S. B. LEVERETT   J. POOLE
    G. F. PRESTON, FIN.-SECY.
JNO. McCARTNEY, SECY.-MANAGER

The plaque at Portsmouth's Fratton Park that commemorates the chairmanship of Bob Blyth, Pompey's former player and manager. It was unveiled on the opening of the new stand in 1925.
© Colin Farmery

A page from John Davidson's contract (right) that he signed in 1922 with Coventry - £7 a week (plus bonuses) and a £10 signing-on fee.

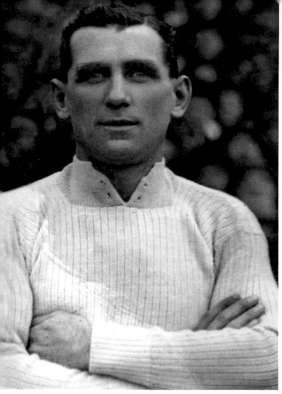

George Halley, Glenbuck's third man to win the English FA Cup, with Burnley in 1914. He was a crowd favourite at Turf Moor and one of the best half-backs in the country.

Darling of St Andrew's, Johnny Crosbie. Known as 'Peerless', he was a dashing, skilful player, well-suited to picture portraits.

Halley (first left, front row) in the FA Cup-winning Burnley team of 1914.

Spurs players celebrate one of Brown's goals in the first match of the 1901 FA Cup Final, in front of the then world-record crowd at Crystal Palace. Note the penalty-area pitch markings of the period.

Alexander 'Sandy' Brown - the man known as 'The Glenbuck Goalgetter'. His 15 strikes in the 1900/01 FA Cup campaign underpinned Tottenham's triumph as the first and only non-league side to win the trophy.

Alex 'Terrible' Tait, living up to his fearsome nickname with an intense stare for the portrait photographer. The image is misleading; Tait was a tough tackler, but a fair and accomplished player.

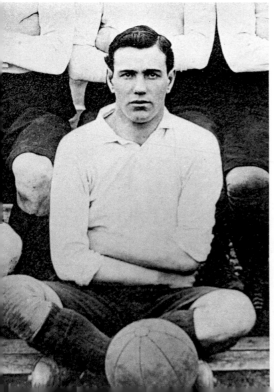

Brothers Bob (right) and Bill Shankly inspect the washing line at Third Lanark. This was the club Bob managed after leaving Falkirk. Third Lanark's Cathkin Park was once one of the great stadiums of Glasgow football, but now stands empty and overgrown after the club folded in 1967.

Jimmy Shankly at Barrow. He was the second of the Shankly brothers to make it into the pro ranks.

Bob Shankly stands behind his good friend and footballing soulmate Jock Stein.

Shankly talking football with a group of his young admirers. Author and journalist Tony Evans said, "He never patronised you. He talked to us as equals."

The King of the Kop in communion with his people.

Ian Callaghan, at home with his record collection. Liverpool's record-appearance holder said of Bill Shankly, "He promised my mum and dad he'd look after me, which he did. I had 14 wonderful seasons with him."

Bill Shankly, the determined young footballer, at Preston North End.

In later life, sister Liz showed a picture of her younger brother Bill in his Scotland strip. The pair shared a close bond and a remarkable likeness.

Ian St John scoring the winning goal in the 1965 FA Cup Final.

Glenbuck then and now. Two views of the village taken from almost the same spot. (Above) showing the main road as it would have been in the early 20th century. (Below) shows what has been left behind in 2015 following the end of mining and the destruction of the village.

The next generation: Lewis Standley of The Shankly Family Foundation FC receives the Shankly Cup at Douglas in June 2015 from Bill, Bob, Jimmy, Alec and John's niece, Barbara Alexander.

Chapter 9

Glenbuck Near and Far

THE first flourishing of Glenbuck players had seen their presence spread across Britain to the furthest reaches of southern England and, in a couple of cases, even further afield. They were part of the great Scottish diaspora that took hundreds of thousands away from their homeland to escape persecution and poverty, or simply in the hope of better lives. Many took their footballs with them, and seeded the game in foreign climes. But for those enterprising young men of the Glenbuck pitheads, there was also opportunity closer to home, and many readily took it.

Kilmarnock loomed large over the history of East Ayrshire football. As the main town in the area it had an in-built draw, the logical place for local players to make the step up to the paid ranks or to use as a stepping stone to bigger and better things. Steeped in the poetry of Burns and churning out Johnnie Walker whisky by the barrel, the town was a relative home from home for Glenbuck natives otherwise deeply suspicious of outsiders.

The town's football club was a modest but veritable body. As early as 1919 it could reflect in biographical form on a half-century of existence. *50 Years of the Kilmarnock Football Club* was penned by 'an old player'. The anonymous scribe need not have been shy, for it is a tome of great charm. Its writer showed how the club arose from familiar origins. Just as in north London and Tottenham, a group of Kilmarnock cricket players wanted some sporting activity to keep them occupied in the winter. They laid down fledgling roots at Rugby Park and at first took up the rival code, before settling on football in 1873. This required a more suitable field and the players asked the farmer for permission. 'Hoot aye, lads, play awa'. I think the grass is a' the better of being trampit a bit,' he apparently replied. The move was a success, but when the team returned for another match the farmer this time sounded less like Rob Roy and more like a landowning baron, and wanted £8 for his trouble.

After a series of rent disputes and the setting up of rival teams, the club coalesced into a recognisable Kilmarnock FC. They were an irascible bunch, goalkeeper 'Old' Bob Rankin among them, who in one game pushed the boundaries of Victorian sportsmanship to the limit. As darkness descended during one game, the opposition launched into a break with the Killie defence nowhere. Rankin hit upon the idea of moving away from his goal to stand between the post and the touchline, loudly shouting at his defenders to cover. The opposition, unable to see the goal in the dark, used the cries as a kind of location device and shot in the direction Rankin's shouts were coming from, sending the ball harmlessly away from the Kilmarnock goal.

A tall tale, but Glenbuck players would have enjoyed the joke and the shrewdness in preventing the concession of a goal. They would also have been thrilled by the club's daring innovation in hosting one of the first ever floodlit matches in 1878. The game was well attended, but not wholly successful. Portland defeated the home side 3–1, and the electric light was so dim that two players received bad injuries including Bailie Miller who was 'permanently disabled as far as football was concerned.'

The club fared better in local football circles, winning Ayrshire cups and entertaining the likes of Hibernian, Renton and Preston

North End, in between major team overhauls, as players departed for elsewhere in Scotland or south to England. In a prime example of the recruitment food chain in action, Killie turned towards Junior football, raiding local clubs for talent that helped Kilmarnock progress through the newly professionalised game and into the Scottish League.

The unnamed writer of *50 Years of the Kilmarnock Football Club* glossed over many of these – 'It would be useless going into details of the doings of the club... for these must be fresh in the memories of present followers' – but he did make special mention of two such players with the strongest of Glenbuck connections, Willie Banks and George Halley.

Banks was a versatile player but performed best at left-half. He was signed from Glenbuck in 1904 as one of that rarer breed: non-native born, hailing instead from Riccarton, now a suburb of Kilmarnock. His performances for the Junior side tempted Kilmarnock into giving him a contract, and after making his Scottish League debut against Dundee, he spent three seasons as a mainstay of the Killies midfield.

He was described by author Bill Donnachie as 'on the small side, but a tireless and unsparing worker and the engine of the side.' In all he made 64 appearances and scored three goals at Rugby Park, but his was in the main another of those wandering careers – a season with non-league Atherton; a brief spell at Portsmouth after an equally short stint at Hurlford. It was at Manchester City where he was to reach the highest level. Sold for a Kilmarnock record-setting fee of £450 in 1905, he spent two seasons at City's then Hyde Road ground, playing 26 times and scoring a solitary goal, and helping City to fifth place in the 1905/06 season. It was to be his professional high-water mark. By 1913, Banks was winding down his career at Nithsdale Wanderers. Halley by contrast was stepping out on to the greatest football stage of them all.

'Kilmarnock have signed George Halley from Glenbuck Athletic,' reported the *Dundee Evening Telegraph* on 28 November

1907. 'He plays outside-right and made a good show in Kilmarnock's reserve XI on Saturday.' Halley would go on to make many more good shows, and not just for Kilmarnock. Following the course set by Tait and Brown, he became an English FA Cup winner with Burnley, and in the closing days of his career, went further in making a substantial contribution to the Lancashire side's first league title.

Halley was another Cherrypicker 'outsider'. Born in Cronberry on 29 October 1887, he was a player of considerable dynamism and whole-hearted effort. He was skilful, attack-minded and benefitted from a fast turn of speed. He could score goals and get back to protect his defence. It is tempting to describe him as the all-purpose, box-to-box midfielder in the Steven Gerrard mould, though the nature of formations and tactics at the time dissuades such a comparison.

The more certain truth is that Halley quickly outgrew Junior football and moved on to Kilmarnock. He made his professional debut at the age of 20 against Clyde in the Scottish League Division One. In contrast to a number of other Glenbuck players, Halley did not then make a rapid transition to the English league. He stuck at Rugby Park for four years, learning his trade and honing his midfield craft, growing up as a man and as a footballer so that by the time the big English clubs did come calling he was arguably more mature and better equipped to establish himself, unlike for example, Tommy Brown.

There had been a form of international recognition of his growing quality, too. Halley had featured in a Football League versus Scottish League match in February 1910, the visitors beating their English counterparts 3–2 at Ewood Park. Halley also played in an SFA-organised trial match for the 'Anglo-Scots XI', hinting again at the attitudes by the governing body towards those 'exiled' in England. There was to be further international disappointment much later in Halley's life. But far greater career satisfaction would come in domestic English football.

It was that grand old name of league football, Bradford Park Avenue, who took the plunge in signing Halley, bringing him to West Yorkshire in May 1911. The club would lose their league status in 1970, but for many years were a sizable draw for ambitious players, and in the 1910s they had their eyes on promotion to the top flight. Park Avenue needed someone of Halley's mettle. He arrived with a reputation for fine play but also feisty commitment. Halley had been up before the SFA's delightfully named 'Rough Play Committee' in 1911 and would later be called up by the English equivalent for other on-field transgressions.

They were illustrative of a strident will to win fostered in those ultra-competitive matches at Burnside Park. But there was much more to his game than gung-ho physical effort. Halley could play, and his impressive displays, notably in Bradford PA's shock 2–1 defeat of Sheffield Wednesday in the FA Cup third round of 1913, led to another move just a month later, this time across the Pennines to Burnley.

Halley was joining a team on the up and a region competing for the highest honours. Lancashire or Manchester sides won three out of four league titles between 1911–14, and Burnley were keen to join in with the success. The club had evolved from a rugby team in 1881, and had played at Turf Moor, still their home today, since 1882.

Manager John Haworth was the prime instigator of Burnley's rise. He changed not just the club colours to claret and blue but the mindset, removing the 'almost but not quite' attitude to one that demanded success. Halley was a player who would buy into it eagerly. On his arrival the *Manchester Courier* hinted obliquely at an eyebrow-raising transfer fee of 'four figures'; according to some reports it was £1,200, not a record sum for the time but befitting a player described by the *Dundee Courier* as 'one of the fastest wing-halves playing.'

He made a successful debut in the 3–1 win over local rivals Bury on 15 March 1913 and was thrust right into an exciting FA Cup campaign. Victory in the semi-final eluded Burnley, but, added to promotion to Division One, it prepared the ground for a more momentous campaign the next season.

Halley was at the heart of it, driving the team on to a respectable 12th place in the league and further still in the FA Cup. Wins over South Shields, Derby, Bolton and Sunderland took the Clarets to another semi-final but this time victory over Sheffield after a replay.

It resulted in a final of firsts – debut appearances in the fixture for Burnley and opponents Liverpool, and the first sighting of a British monarch at football's then most prestigious occasion. King George V added the royal seal of approval to a clash between two of northern professional football's most aspirational clubs.

The match was played at Crystal Palace, hosting its last ever FA Cup Final. There was, according to the *Hull Daily Mail* a 'big invasion from Lancashire', bracketing the travelling Liverpool supporters with their Burnley counterparts among the 74,093 crowd. The paper previewed the game and drew attention to 'Halley: 5ft 8in, 11st 8lbs, one of a splendid half-back line.' He was, uncharacteristically for English teams of the era, one of only two Scotsmen in the Burnley line-up, facing a Liverpool side dominated by players from his homeland.

The sight of seven Scots in the Liverpool ranks would have horrified the letter writer to the *Bootle Times* of October 1887 who lambasted the local club for a similar recruitment strategy: 'Bootle Football Club, indeed! Absurd isn't it, to term a company of football players, who are foreigners to the town the Bootle team?… A club which is supposed to be local, but is no more local than would be the gentlemen's team, were they to play here – is simply worked by a few outsiders.'

Welcomed or not, those outsiders had been crucial to English football, and Halley was just one of many who proved their worth. He needed to be on his game in the 1914 final and duly lived up to Burnley hopes and expectations, and did his country and old village team proud.

Industrious and adventurous throughout, he hit the bar from a chance created by a corner kick, but it was his defensive qualities that really shone as he chased, tackled and corralled his team-mates into seeing off a stern Liverpool reply to Bert Freeman's second-half goal. It proved to be the winner. 'When Burnley scored the only goal of the game 12 minutes after the re-start,' reported the *Aberdeen Journal*, with conspicuous deference to royalty, 'the deafening cheers were followed by another outburst of applause obviously directed at the King, whose face was wreathed in smiles.'

Those regal smiles were not nearly as broad as the grins of the ecstatic Burnley fans and players. They had won the FA Cup and looked set to build on the success with Halley playing a prominent role. But those hopes were curtailed by looming global conflict. Though football was played for another full season, with Burnley finishing fourth in the League, and the 'Khaki Cup Final' was contested at Old Trafford, the sport belatedly called a halt to competitive games following intense public and political pressure.

Having temporarily hung up his boots, Halley duly picked up a rifle, becoming the first from the club to enlist in May 1915 almost as soon as the shutters had come down on football grounds around Britain. He was one of 32 current or former Burnley players who served in the First World War. Seven never came home.

Mercifully, Halley would return safely, but not until after two-and-a-half years of overseas service in Mesopotamia and India. He was, as the *Burnley News* proudly proclaimed, 'the first to join up, but the last to return.' The local paper reported that Halley had maintained his fitness by 'before-breakfast training on ship' and playing in a six-a-side competition with the army. He was made captain for a single game to honour his service, and looked set to pick up where he and Burnley had left off as football resumed in August 1919.

It did not quite work out as planned. While Burnley made further strides on the pitch as runners-up in the league to West Brom, albeit by a distant nine points, there were off-field problems for Halley to contend with. In November of 1919, Halley was 32 and a concerned father, who was summoned to a local police court in breach of the Vaccination Act. Halley had apparently failed to have his child vaccinated but, according to the *Lancashire Evening Post*, was able to produce proof that his child was unfit to be vaccinated at the time and that, as a former serviceman, he was a firm 'believer in vaccination'.

The incident came at a time of grave concern over health issues and immense loss of life due to the flu pandemic that swept across Europe. Having survived four years of conflict, Halley would have been naturally cautious as to the well-being of his growing family, but it would be he himself to suffer from life-threatening illness. 'A serious report is to hand this morning,' wrote the *Lancashire Evening Post* on 15 February 1921. It revealed an 'unfortunate coincidence' for Halley 'that the right-half, on the day of his selection to play for Scotland for the first time, should have developed pneumonia.'

The disease was a potential killer even for fit athletes like Halley. It effectively ended his season and dashed his hopes of a long-awaited senior international call-up, due to come in a tie against Ireland. But there was a happy ending. Having overcome the illness, he recuperated in Blackpool and by the middle of March was having a 'walk out' as reported in the *Burnley News*. After an unbeaten run of 30 games, his side in turn overcame some late stumbles and won the title on St George's Day, 23 April.

Halley had been a key player in the club's success. The *Burnley News* paid tribute to him as a 'big influence in the working of the right wing. Speedy and certain in his tackle, he was also a rare feeder of the right wing. And much of the credit for the effectiveness of that department belonged to him.'

He thus went out on a title-winning high. After 160 appearances for Burnley, he moved to Southend in November 1922 before a final run out for non-league Bacup Borough, which drew to a close in 1926. He became a plasterer by trade, providing for a family of two sons and four daughters, settling down to quiet anonymity at number 12, Haven Street. Halley died on 18 December 1941 at the age of 54 in Burnley's Victoria Hospital. The *Burnley Express* spoke for many Burnley fans when it paid tribute, describing him as a 'stylish player, [who] formed one of a middle line which was regarded as being without superior in the League.'

Glenbuck had produced its third FA Cup winner and its first Football League champion – an astonishing achievement by any measure. In the meantime it had still been turning out a succession of less storied players manning the professional clubs of England. Back in Scotland, another pair had been delivered to Kilmarnock.

John Anderson was an import for Glenbuck Cherrypickers, coming from Muirkirk Thistle in 1915 before his switch to Killie. There he made 11 appearances and scored a solitary goal. He was a promising inside-left but his career, like so many others, was swiftly interrupted by war, and he joined up early in 1916. John McConnell fared better in football terms, playing 14 games for Kilmarnock after being signed from Glenbuck in July 1902. The brother of former Arsenal man, Alex McConnell, John was born in Mossend near Motherwell in 1881. He grew up to be a fine defender – firm in the tackle, and a player team-mates could depend on. He went on to have two spells with Grimsby Town, split by a season at Brentford, and then a tour through a number of Junior clubs as his playing days drew to an end in 1912.

Brief though the duo's Killie careers may have been, they were evidence of the club's continued willingness to recruit from Glenbuck. They were not the only senior club in the area to see the isolated little village as fertile territory for signings. Another natural destination for an ambitious footballer was Ayr United. Six Glenbuck-born or connected players headed west to the county capital, and would feature in connection with Ayr FC or its successor Ayr United.

The town had, according to the *Ayr Football and Athletic Club Official Guide Book* of 1901, 'always been looked upon as the strongest athletic provincial centre – in fact, no town in Scotland with half-a-dozen times the population could compete with the "Auld Toon" for class and quantity.'

John Bishop was one of those who tried to live up to such exacting sporting standards, but is not recorded as playing a single game, a similar fate for Sandy Tait back with Ayr in 1889. William Barr fared better. Though he only had six games in 1916 to test his mettle, it led to him playing in a variety of positions, and being party to a number of Glenbuck connections and coincidences, as Ayr historian Duncan Carmichael has unravelled. In August, Ayr United played Rangers at Beresford Park in a match to raise funds for the Red Cross. The Ayr inside-left was John Davidson (see Chapter 10), formerly of the Cherrypickers, but not formally signed to Ayr. Barr's first team debut was in a 2–1 loss away to Dundee in January 1917. The Ayr team that day thus fielded no less than three ex-Glenbuck Cherrypickers: Barr was at centre-half, Johnny Crosbie at inside-right and Alec Shankly inside-left. Later in 1919 the links continued: Ayr signed Billy Crosbie, cousin of Glenbuck's Johnny Crosbie and the relatives briefly formed a right-wing partnership.

Alec Shankly, the senior member of the famous footballing clan, would stay at Ayr for a while longer. His story is told later, alongside another member of the Glenbuck/Ayr alumni, John Crosbie. It was a later recruit, James Nisbet, another cousin of the Crosbies, who served United longest, playing at Somerset Park for six years.

Nisbet was not a Cherrypicker. He was born in Glenbuck in August 1904 and could have appeared for his home village side, but started his career instead with Cumnock. In 1926 at the age of 22, Ayr United signed him and it was a mutually successful pairing. He joined just as Ayr had been relegated to the Second Division, but played a leading part in the promotion back to the First in 1928. In addition to the 139 first-team appearances and 31 goals scored from an outside-right berth, he was selected three times for Scotland, becoming Ayr's most capped Scottish player in the process.

The international games came in quick succession for the winger, renowned for his dribbling and adept passing. It was on an unbeaten 1929 summer tour of the continent that Nisbet played against Norway, Germany and the Netherlands, and he excelled in a happy trip by scoring twice in a 7–3 victory over the Norwegians.

It was not only Ayr competing with Kilmarnock for such talent from Glenbuck. Hamilton were another club who sought a ready supply of players from across the Lanarkshire–Ayrshire border, and one man the club readily welcomed was Archie Garrett. He came from Coalburn but impressed with Glenbuck, before joining the Accies in 1907. It was the beginning of an 11-year association, interspersed with trips down south to play for that most defiantly proletarian of London clubs, Millwall.

The Londoners have long been presumed to have a strong Scottish streak running through the club. A number of Scots worked in the Isle of Dogs factories and docks that gave birth to the original Millwall Rovers, though the notion that Millwall was a club formed by Scots is a false one. At any rate, Garrett's stays in London were stopgaps during his long association with Hamilton, comprising 113 games and three goals and a range of positions for an adaptable, dependable player.

The same could not have been said of a fellow Glenbuckian, Tom Knox – not that he was unreliable but more that he never got the chance to disprove it. Coming from the famous Knox family who had trounced all-comers in five-a-side competitions could not quite bridge the gap between small-side and Junior football with that of the senior game. The wing-half played three games for the Accies between 1904–09, scoring twice, but was unable to dislodge Alex Scholes and Hugh Kilday from the club's midfield engine room. As for his siblings, William Knox was recorded as registered with Merseyside's twin powers, Everton and Liverpool, but did not play a senior game for either, though there is some evidence of outings with the reserves. Hugh Knox played for Greenock Morton in 1901/02 before moving to Sunderland, though again, not to feature in first-team action. The *Edinburgh Evening News* of August 1901 reported that 'H. Knox, 20, discovered in Glenbuck' was one of Sunderland's new signings and the *Sheffield Daily Telegraph* was similarly intrigued, saying of Knox that he had been unearthed 'in the wilds of Ayrshire'. But such mild exoticism did not lead to anything amounting to meaningful action on Wearside.

Indeed it was another Knox, Peter, who was to enjoy a more colourful career, despite not actually turning pro. He did accept an invitation from Rangers to join them for one of their tours, but he continued to thrive in Junior football, while forging an off-field career as a registrar and welfare officer. He was also imbued with a sense of civic duty serving as a senior member of the Justice of the Peace Court, president of the Miners' Welfare Institute and the local nursing association, and as a director of the Co-operative Society. His own son Peter would later play for Clyde.

And what of those other Glenbuck clans that dominated village life for decades and did so much in the cause of the village's football team? The Taits had been well represented chiefly through English cup-winner Sandy. As for the Bones, their contribution to professional football was more ephemeral.

A 'Johnnie Bone' is recorded as playing for Everton in 1901/02 at inside-left. He played in two matches, a 2–0 defeat at home to Blackburn and another home loss, 1–0 to Grimsby. The first, according to the *Liverpool Courier*, was 'played in weather of the most uninviting description.' Bone did his best amid the tempest, going close with a 'swift low shot'. In similar desultory conditions against Grimsby he had a good effort and 'tested Whittaker with a fine shot, which the custodian scooped out at the expense of an abortive corner.' Whatever the quality of his overall play, it was not enough to enable Bone to make more of a mark on Merseyside.

Even more obscure is the Aston Villa career of Jock Bone. It appears that the claims for professional status for the Bone brothers rings less certain than the famous quoiting exploits of their relative Tom Bone.

There was another Glenbuck family waiting in the wings whose football lives were decidedly more high-profile. They would have made a formidable five-a-side team to take on the Knoxes, had the two broods been playing at the same time. And it is a safe bet as to who would have been the most vociferous player on the field. For the Shankly boys were coming to football, and football would never be quite the same again.

Chapter 10

The Brothers Shankly

ASHOWER of drenching rain stops. The sun breaks through swirling grey cloud on a late July day in 2015 and, viewed through the trees that ring the shoreline, Glenbuck Loch positively sparkles. The body of clear water is transformed into a brightly lit paradise. Swans gently cruise the surface, hawks hover over a densely wooded little island, and in the distance, the Lowther Hills look ruggedly handsome. It is beautiful, a place of peace, tranquillity, and utter quiet.

But that is part of the problem. It's too quiet. Glenbuck Dam, as the locals rightly insist on naming what is, after all, not a natural loch but a man-made industrial relic, is severely lacking in people. East Ayrshire needs jobs and fishing tourism might provide a few. The water here at Glenbuck is packed with trout. Angling licences are among the cheapest in the area, and it could be easily reached from the nearby A70. Instead, there is not one fisherman on the shoreline and there's just a single boat on the water.

The craft's ancient engine splutters into life and the boat chugs slowly towards the shore. Two men have been clearing weeds, and as the vessel approaches they proffer greetings. The boat gently bumps up alongside a small wooden jetty and the men secure the craft with ropes. At its prow, written in bright red paint, is its name: 'Cherrypicker'.

"Aye, the Glenbuck Cherrypickers, you ken what that means?" asks one. The authors nod in agreement and Sam Purdie, down from Perth on a trip to his birthplace, sets off on lively conversation and reminiscences with the two men. They are Stewart Burns and Bobby Ward, who look after the fishing facilities and keep the lake maintained in hopeful anticipation of the anglers who still might come and cast their lines into the cold waters. Burns and Ward hail from Muirkirk but have close family ties to Glenbuck. Like Sam, Stewart was born in the village. And he knows a thing or two about those Shanklys.

"I knew Jimmy," Stewart says, recalling the second son of the prodigious footballing clan. "They were a wonderful family and Jimmy was a nice guy – very pleasant. He had a sister who lived in Glenbuck [Liz] and another who lived in Muirkirk [Bel]. I'd say Jim was in his 50s, when I first knew him. We thought of them as old men. Jim, his family, other people from that time, they were all characters."

So here is a kind-of contemporary of one of the famous Shanklys, the family that lived and breathed football and had an unquenchable passion for playing and talking about the game. Well, not quite. "He didn't talk about football, never mentioned it," says Stewart, himself an avowed non-football fan. "I didn't know about the Cherrypickers till I was in my teens, and I've never seen a senior game of football in my life, I watched Juniors, but this is my interest." He smiles ruefully and wafts a hand towards Glenbuck Dam and its shores full of fish, but empty of fishermen.

Burns knows all about Glenbuck and something of the many footballers it produced, but is not one to wallow in any nostalgia for the place. He remembers with a shudder what the conditions were like, and what it meant to live in a dying village suffering from woeful neglect and casual indifference from people who had the means and power to make a difference, but conspicuously did not.

"It's terrible. I've taken people up to have a look at what's there now," Burns says, "but I left Glenbuck when I was 10 or 11 when all the work had gone – there was plenty of work in Muirkirk at that time, you could pick your job. Put it this way. We lived on White's Row, some of the old mining cottages. When we went to Muirkirk we had a toilet and running water inside. We didn't have that at Glenbuck."

As if to confirm the reality of living conditions and precisely why there should be no romance attached to them, Stewart talked about one of Jimmy Shankly's jobs after his football career had wound down. "He was a council worker. Driver of the bucket lorry, they cleaned out what they called middens." That work for the council was about as essential as any public service work could be. In the days before proper sanitation in isolated villages like Glenbuck, people would have to use outside toilets, sometimes called middens.

The waste would be deposited in pits or large metal barrels into which ashes from household fires had been thrown. The toilets were placed on top. At some point, someone had to come along with the unenviable task of clearing the pits out. One of them was Jimmy Shankly and his bucket-lorry crew.

It is a common complaint that today's young football apprentices do not have to do the menial tasks of cleaning boots or scrubbing floors that footballers of previous generations had to. The thought of cosseted and lavishly rewarded young superstars having to even contemplate a post-playing career in removing sewage has comedy value. But for men like Jimmy Shankly, it was no laughing matter.

It was an utterly different world, and Glenbuck during his family's time was different further still to many of the places Britain's then aspiring footballers were being nurtured in. Mining was never an especially dependable source of employment, but back at the turn of the 19th century, the pits in the village were vulnerable to temporary or even permanent closure. People started to leave – sons and daughters at first, but then whole families, looking for some kind of stability and job security.

By the time Jimmy and the boys of the Shankly family were first running out on to Burnside Park or the streets to play football, the population had slumped to around 700. It would rise and fall as mining fortunes improved or declined, but the trend was downward. Bringing up a family of ten children in such an unpromising situation would have tested the most resilient of families, but the Shanklys were made of redoubtable stuff – the parents, and their ten children, including the youngest, Bill.

"I just cannot tell you how nice a person he was," says Barbara Alexander. "It was a Shankly trait. They were all like that." Bill Shankly's niece, and daughter of his beloved sister Liz, is sitting in her immaculate living room in Cumnock, just a few miles from the vanished village in which she herself was born. Over cups of tea she shares her memories of her famous uncle and the extended Shankly clan. Photos are handed round, showing Bill, his relatives and friends back in Glenbuck's humble streets.

A family tree lays out the connections and often bewildering repetition of names – 'William', 'Robert', 'Barbara', and others appear frequently across the generations. And that's not counting the extended family of non-blood relations and friends, especially the matriarchs and women who were given the affectionate title of 'auntie'. Together they give credence to that old maxim about it taking a village to raise a child. Because Bill Shankly and his siblings were proud products of their home environment, instilled with Glenbuck's unique values, and those of a huge family circle.

The story of the Shankly presence in Glenbuck begins with one couple making the opposite journey to those established village families heading for the exit route. Glenbuck and the sport of football were to be in that couple's debt for their determination to make a living and raise a family.

John Shankly hailed from Douglas and had married Barbara Blyth. Though Muirkirk-raised she came from a well-known family with strong Glenbuck connections, and was one of seven children, born to James Blyth of Douglas and Janet Fleming, two of whom would play and administrate in professional football (see Chapter 6).

The Shankly children's father John was, perhaps surprisingly given the family's obsession with the game, a reluctant footballer. While his all-round sporting and organisational skills had come in handy for the Cherrypickers, it appeared he had been a decent Junior, but opted for athletics as his preferred discipline.

In truth, there wasn't so much time to pursue sporting interests. John and Barbara had their work cut out raising ten children. The father figure was a disciplinarian who unquestionably ruled the home, but he was much loved by his family. John would become a batman for an officer during the First World War and worked as a postman, but stopped delivering letters to become a tailor. He fitted the men of Glenbuck in their Sunday best and did running repairs on the meagre clothing that most families had to make last. A shirt or a dress needed to have a serviceable lifetime longer than that of just one individual's childhood. John's alterations and stitching skills were in constant, though hardly well remunerated, demand. Bill Shankly said in his autobiography that customers would frequently not have the two shillings to pay for his father's work. "Just pay me when you can," John Shankly would say, knowing full well the customer never could.

Poverty ensured that, and the Shanklys were no exception. Even the sons and daughters of a skilled tailor needed hand-me-downs and handouts to stay clothed. "I don't know how they ever survived, especially with such a big family," says Barbara. She remembers how her mother Elizabeth worked in service and drew on the generosity of employers to help clothe her siblings. "Before she got married my mum was in service in Cambuslang. My mother went to do the housework for the Hurrell family, and she was given pass-me-down clothes for the family in Glenbuck."

Barbara Shankly gave birth in a remarkable gender pattern to alternate sons and daughters – five girls, five boys. The unplanned arrangement had a fortuitous outcome. Each succeeding child would be brought up not just by his or her parents but their preceding female sibling. "When my uncle Sandy was born, my auntie Net was next and she would help to bring up my uncles Jimmy and John, then my mum [Elizabeth] would help bring up the next of them," says Barbara Alexander. "The older siblings would bring up the younger ones – they had to. My granny never worked and there were no jobs in Glenbuck for her and other mothers. But she worked hard cooking, washing, bringing up kids – it was a full time job."

This rather traditional division of labour made a lasting impression on all the Shankly boys including Bill. It was that ethic of teamwork again – the clear lesson that individuals functioned better when working together. Liverpool FC's renowned organisation that ran like clockwork across Europe had an unlikely genesis in the suffocating confines of a two-room Ayrshire cottage.

It was No. 2 Auchenstilloch Cottages, but better known locally as 'Miners Row' or 'Monkey Row' to reflect the same nickname for one of the nearby pits. "Auchenstilloch was too big to spell or say for the miners so they called it 'Monkey Row'," according to Tom Hazle, whose family were neighbours of the Shanklys and later lived right next door.

And No. 2 was certainly crowded. Though the Shanklys were later able to live in two cottages with the dividing wall knocked through, the parents and their many children somehow squeezed into the rudimentary abode. There was no kitchen as such but the permanently lit stove provided valuable complementary heat to the coal fire keeping out the gnawing winter cold. "They used to have wheelie beds – beds that went under another bed," says Barbara. "On the Monkey Row, they were all very, very poor.

"Between the room and the kitchen they had a swing. Yes, a swing! It was bound to be a madhouse and my mum used to say, 'You would swing somebody and they would shout out "touching the ceiling ma, touching the ceiling!"' You can just imagine it."

Out of this ever-lively place sprang five footballers. The first was Alec, or 'Sandy'. Born in 1893, he operated as a forward, mostly in the inside-left position. Bill Shankly claimed his oldest brother signed for Ayr United before the outbreak of the First World War, but officially at least, he did not register pro forms until 1916.

Unlike in England, league football continued. Shorter travel distances were cited as a main reason for the difference, but Scottish clubs were shorn of playing talent just as much as their English counterparts.

Alec Shankly played 29 games for Ayr, his debut coming in a 5–0 league defeat away to Celtic on 9 December, before he joined up for military service with the Royal Scottish Fusiliers. After the war he returned to Ayr and then moved on to Junior side Nithsdale Wanderers. It is also possible he was the 'A. Shankly' who played for Solway Star in the 1927/28 Qualifying Cup.

Solway were another of those short-lived clubs briefly active in the Scottish game. Based in Annan not far from Gretna and the border with England, Solway were formed in 1911 and were members of the Scottish Third Division for the three years of their existence. William Bain was another Glenbuck player who featured at the club's Kimmerton Park, as were John Davidson and Hugh Smith.

Davidson, born on 31 January 1894 in the village, would go on to join Coventry City for the 1922/23 season. The writer of the club's opening-day programme for that campaign was impressed with the new man's dedication. 'Davidson, the inside-right from Glenbuck, who signed up for City after his first trial game, was working down an Ayrshire pit on the Thursday night before he appeared at Highfield Road on the Saturday.'

Sadly, as Coventry historian Jim Brown notes, "he apparently was very keen but according to contemporary reports 'lacked the necessary quality'". Davidson played just four games for City. As a consequence his career was largely another of those in which he moved frequently in search of the right club, at the right time.

Arguably neither ever came. He left Coventry in July 1923 and played once for Kilmarnock. In November 1923 he joined Nithsdale Wanderers before two months later signing on at Thornhill, and eventually went back to Annan and two seasons with Solway Star before the club, at least temporarily, went out of business.

Alec Shankly's career had in truth been similarly frustrating. A long-term sciatica condition put paid to both his playing days and effectively his working life. Long before this the Shankly family had reached its peak of ten children. With all those mouths to feed it was imperative that others were bringing in a wage. Mining provided some kind of opportunity for the boys, domestic service for the females. It was second son Jimmy who turned football provider with a career that took him around Britain. He traded his skills as a centre-forward from the Cherrypickers to Portsmouth, Halifax, Coventry, Carlisle, Sheffield United, Barrow, and Southend.

Some of these stays were relatively long. He played at Bramall Lane for a full season and scored a hat-trick for the Blades in a match against Burnley in March 1927. Other appointments were a case of blink and you'll miss it, signing for Halifax only to be immediately loaned out to Luton, before heading back north just as swiftly ('loan' in this sense is a loose term; the practice was not formalised until the 1960s.)

Jimmy's five years at Southend proved to be an important spell. For a former miner who had come out with his brother John and Alec during the punishing strike of 1921, gainful employment was precious. Earning £8 a week in the season and £6 in the summer, he sent money back home from the Essex seaside to supplement the Shankly family's income.

Brother Bill reckoned that at 5ft 11in and 13-and-a-half stone and blessed with two good feet and power in the air, Jimmy could have been one of the finest centre-forwards ever born, but he had his place in the Sheffield team blocked by other, top-class players. He was more of a success at Southend, then in the Third Division South, and was regularly top scorer.

Jimmy bagged a round century of goals for the Shrimpers over 152 games. He notched no less than 35 in the 1928/29 season, a club record that stood for 29 years, and was a serial collector of hat-tricks. He had lulls in form and potency, however, which led to barracking from some sections of the Roots Hall crowd.

Before the switch to Barrow, there was one notable match in which Jimmy featured, making him the first Glenbuckian to play at Wembley. In 1930, Clapton Orient had been forced to find an alternative home venue while their ground was closed for modification. A Torquay player had been badly injured due to the close proximity of the stand wall to the touchline. While that was being remedied, Orient temporarily used Wembley, and played two matches at the relatively new national stadium. One of these was on 6 December, against Southend. A crowd of just 1,916 turned up to see the Os win 3–1 and Shankly twice strike the crossbar.

When Jimmy eventually retired back to Scotland with his Yorkshire wife, his grateful family helped him set up a coal business, and he lived out his days close to his Glenbuck home. For brother John, it was another story of 'have boots, will travel', but, after a period with Portsmouth and then Luton Town, he roamed chiefly around clubs close to Ayrshire. Alloa and Greenock Morton were his main employers, as he spent three seasons at Recreation Park plying his craft as an outside-right at either end of his six-year career, sandwiching three seasons at Morton's Cappielow Park. There was a very brief four-month sojourn to Blackpool in 1930/31 that cost the Seasiders a £1,000 transfer fee. A cumulative Scottish total of 125 appearances and 33 goals indicate a broadly fulfilling life as a professional. But John had his fair share of frustrations.

Two of his contracts were cancelled, stemming from a heart condition that ultimately did for his playing career and prematurely ended his life. John was physically the slightest of the Shankly brothers, at just 5ft 6in tall. He was a fine player as his decent goalscoring record at Luton testified, but he found the rigours of the game hard to cope with. Bill recalled that 'training was too much for him... he suffered an overstrained heart muscle'.

That led ultimately to the end of his playing days at the age of 33 but he could not avoid a return down to the pits. Not only was the graft hard, he had to travel to Muirkirk to find it. Labouring away on the afternoon shift, he would not get home until 11 at night, where his mother Barbara would be expectantly waiting for him, ready to serve up his late evening meal. It was a poignant relationship, with Barbara, the ever-caring, gentle soul who her children all adored, looking after her slightly vulnerable middle son.

John never married and ended his own days in a football setting. He was one among the vast 127,000 Hampden Park crowd for the famous 1960 European Cup Final in which Real Madrid thrashed Eintracht Frankfurt 7–3. John, the deft outside-right, would have been as thrilled as any to see Puskas, Di Stefano, and Gento wow the crowd with their fulminating skill. Perhaps too excited, for John's heart gave up during the game. He was taken to Glasgow's Victoria Hospital where he died that night.

It was a reminder, if the Shankly children in their adulthood needed any, that life was short and needed to be enjoyed and fulfilled as much as possible. For the next brother, Bob, it was a principle he adhered to in a career that took the story of his family and of Glenbuck's footballers on to another level.

Bob was three years older than Bill and a few inches taller. The pair otherwise bore a striking resemblance to each other and their father John. They were pictured with their brothers and mother Barbara in a fascinating little feature by 'The Sentinel' in *The Weekly News* of 1 July 1933. Headlined 'Scotland's Unique Football Family', the report detailed the careers and connections of the clan and the extended relatives. Father John was pictured in sergeant's stripes during his war days with the Royal Scots Fusiliers, his clipped moustache giving him a neat and confident bearing.

There were family photos of the boys as children with their mother, who by the time the report was written looked every one of her 50-odd years, worn out by constant child rearing. Uncle Billy Blyth, of Carlisle directorship fame, was also pictured, emphasising the family's spread through the professional game.

Bob in the 1933 picture stood out in the centre background, a mop of hair adding to his stature. He was 23 by then, and coming to the end of his three-year spell with Alloa Athletic after earlier stints with Auchinleck Talbot, and Kent non-league side Tunbridge Wells Rangers. He was effectively unemployed. The Sentinel wrote, 'Alloa had £200 against his name, but at a recent meeting of the Scottish League, the figure was reduced by half. Bob is on the look out for a club.'

The club that would benefit from his reacquaintance with professional football was Falkirk. Bob Shankly played at Brockville for 14 seasons. It was a spell interrupted by war but one in which he excelled at centre-half, his calm authority underpinning the side nicknamed 'the Bairns'. The club crest featured an image of the town's steeple clock reading three o'clock and the motto of 'Touch 'ane, touch a'', a defiant, all-for-one-and-one-for-all credo a Glenbuck lad would be enthused by. Falkirk and Bob Shankly served each other very well.

The playing career had got off to a promising start. In 1929 Bob featured in two pre-season trial matches for Ayr United but he wasn't signed owing to competition from other clubs for his services.

Fresh out of the mines and eager to impress, and living next door to Jim Nisbet in Glenbuck, Bob then scored on his Alloa debut along with brother John in a Penman Cup victory over Dundee. Sixteen years later, by the time boots were hung up in 1946, Bob had played 334 games and scored 21 goals. Like a couple of other former Cherrypickers, Bob is also listed as one of those who won Scottish international honours. This is not quite correct. He did play for a representative side in a match against the Irish

League in September 1937. Instead, more glittering honour was to come his way as a club manager.

"I look for character. I want lads with guts and go, who won't crumple when things don't go their way." This was the Bob Shankly template for what he wanted in a player. It was, naturally, a characteristic of Glenbuck teams, and Bob distilled its essence in the clubs he managed. He took over first at his second home, Falkirk, and led them for seven years and bequeathed a team that won the Scottish Cup in 1957.

His next stop was in south Glasgow and Third Lanark. This venerable name of Scottish football, founded by members of Third Lanarkshire Rifle Volunteers and now sadly no more as a professional concern, played at Cathkin Park, a ground purchased from Queen's Park when they moved to the new Hampden. Today, Cathkin Park provides haunting reminders of its once gilded past. Nestling in the middle of a housing estate and with glorious views into Glasgow city centre, the pitch is now a council-owned field, but, emerging in and out of the trees, the substantial terraces and banking can still be seen, now overgrown with moss but giving an indication of what a major club Third Lanark was.

The team's trophy-winning days were behind them when Shankly was installed, though again he left a team capable of competing for silverware, as the Thirds reached the Scottish League Cup Final the year of his departure in 1959. There was also said to be an interested spectator who watched some of Third Lanark's matches under Bob Shankly. Jock Stein was forging his own managerial career and would call on Bob for advice and wisdom.

The merits of that intelligence and experience were manifested in Bob's next appointment. When Willie Thornton resigned at Dens Park, Bob put in an application. There was a rival for the post, a certain W. Shankly, then manager of Huddersfield Town, but Bob's calm authority had convinced the Dundee board to opt for the older of the two Shanklys.

"Bob Shankly is a legendary figure at Dundee," says Kenny Ross, author and historian of the club, and chronicler of the club's and Shankly's finest hours. The reasons are obvious. "He managed them to the Scottish League championship for the only time in their history in 1962 and then to the European Cup semi-final in 1963. They knocked out the likes of Cologne, Sporting Lisbon and Anderlecht en route before losing to AC Milan in the semi despite a 1–0 home leg win."

Memories of that European Cup run can still reduce gnarled old Dundee fans to tears. It had everything – wonderful football, goals, drama, feverish excitement and raw emotion. Shankly's maxim about the need for his players to fight and never give up came in handy for a tempestuous away leg at Cologne, in which the intervention of some soldiers of the British Army of the Rhine helped the Dundee players to survive a near-riot at the final whistle. But at the centre of it all throughout the campaign, Shankly was the resolute, reassuring heart.

That European campaign was a glorious failure. Shankly's Dundee side were a joy to watch, scoring freely as Bob brought the best out of rare talents like Alan Gilzean, Ian Ure, Alex Hamilton, Gordon Smith and Alan Cousin. In the season when the side reached the Scottish Cup Final in 1964, they scored an astonishing 141 goals. The insatiable hunger for them came as a consequence of Shankly's reasoned demands. "No one could argue with his philosophy or how he moulded his team into winners," says Ross. "He let his players express themselves but earned their utmost respect and they rewarded him with the greatest days in the club's history."

The run towards the league title in 1962 is the stuff of Dundee legend. Rangers were seen off 5–1. The incredible comeback to beat Raith 5–4 after being 4–2 down with less than half an hour to go, was described by Bob as "surely among the greatest feats recorded all season."

Sounds familiar? Like another Shankly not averse to a piece of tongue-in-cheek hyperbole? There were similarities between the two brothers but also clear distinctions. Bob was a measured man and usually unfussed by great football drama. He was a fine tactician, an effective communicator, and a smart man-manager, as Ross confirms.

"There's a story that when Dundee played Highland League Inverness Thistle in the Scottish Cup in 1963 Shankly was worried the game was going to be [frozen] off. His players were concerned as some had been involved in a shock defeat to Fraserburgh four years previously so he sneaked out of the hotel at midnight, went to Thistle's ground, climbed over the wall, and saw the pitch was going to be good enough for the game. He got the players some continental rubber boots to wear and was able to reassure them at breakfast. Dundee won 5–1."

After two seasons of bedding in his way of working, Shankly brought home the silverware. He had a reputation for honesty with his players and a hands-on, no-nonsense approach on the touchline, but also a dry sense of humour. He was an old-fashioned boss in a rolled-up-sleeves sense, but in addition a forward thinker. They named a stand after him at Dens Park in 1999, a decision reached by popular vote among the fans.

After 130 wins in 259 games in the Dundee dugout, the loss of players like Gilzean, Ure and Charlie Cooke prompted Shankly's own departure, to Hibs, to replace Jock Stein on the Celtic legend's recommendation. Shankly struggled at first, courting unpopularity by selling crowd favourite Willie Hamilton before steering the side through a period that included some thrilling European ties. The problem of players being sold reared again and led to Shankly leaving for Stirling Albion, where he became a director. He nearly lost his life in 1975 after being involved in a bad car accident with his friend Stein, but recovered. Like his brothers John and Bill, it was a heart attack that finally took him, at an SFA meeting in May 1982 at the age of 72.

Bill had pre-deceased him by a year. Coincidentally, the two Glenbuck Shanklys who made such a mark as managers had died around the same time as another of their village's stellar footballing products.

Johnny Crosbie had followed what many of his Glenbuck peers had achieved in carving out what looked like a modest but commendable life as a footballer. Born in the Gorbals on 3 June 1896, raised in Glenbuck, and benefitting from both schools of hard knocks, he was a determined individual who turned out for the Cherrypickers, made the brave switch to Muirkirk Juniors, and then did the hard yards of pro service with Ayr United, Clyde and Ayr again, with war service intervening. Two of his Ayr club-mates, John Bellringer and Bob Capperauld, lost their lives. Crosbie, who had been among the first to sign up, prompting Ayr to pay him half his football wages while he was in the forces, emerged broadly intact and looked to resume his career with no great expectations. He played 165 games for Ayr, and scored 45 goals. So far, so reasonably good.

But football had more in store for Johnny Crosbie. The Ayr directors had their eyes on improving the standing of their club by purchasing Somerset Park. Looking at their assets, Crosbie was young enough and good enough to be sold for a decent sum. Newcastle were interested in the inside-forward and offered £3,000. The Ayr board were cock-a-hoop but happier still when Birmingham City came in with a bigger bid, worth a club record £3,700.

It was also a great deal for Crosbie. Success had eluded Birmingham despite their early conversion to professionalism in 1885 and their status in the nation's 'second city'. There has always been something of the frustrated about the club, with success often tantalisingly out of reach compounded by an element of self-destruction – the club failed to take part in the 1920/21 FA Cup because secretary Sam Richards forgot to send the right forms in.

But the club anthem 'Keep Right On', still roared with great gusto by the team's loyal and fervent support, sums up the story of the Blues. The club was and still is defiantly urban, situated in what was the heartland of Midlands industry with factory and railway smoke swirling around St Andrew's, and drop forges rattling the terraces and stands. Crosbie might have come from rural Glenbuck but as a boy of the mines he knew the character of his adopted home and its people well, and thrived.

A good-looking man, he was celebrated in cigarette card form and idolised on the terraces. Known as 'Peerless', he was a flair player, who could liven up the dullest game with his sparkling skills. With his considerable assistance, the club won promotion to Division One in 1921. Silverware was still a stranger to the St Andrew's trophy cabinet, but life in Division One was eventful, long-lasting and fun. That elusive trophy so nearly came when Birmingham reached the FA Cup Final in 1931. Crosbie, stepping out on to the Wembley turf five months after Jimmy Shankly had trodden it, set up the Blues' goal, but the 2–1 defeat to neighbours West Brom denied his team winners' medals. As author Tony Matthews noted, the Cup Final programme said that he was 'The mastermind of the Birmingham attack... for Crosbie is a real star.'

Crosbie left Birmingham in 1932 after 72 goals in 432 appearances. Such was his popularity that he had been granted two testimonials. He moved to Chesterfield and in retirement, settled in the Midlands. It had been a wonderful career, topped off with international call-ups. He played against Ireland in April 1919, Wales in February the next year and followed in the path of Sandy Brown by taking on the Auld Enemy in a 1–0 win at Villa Park. There were also four representative games for Scottish XIs between March 1920 and March 1923.

Towards the end of his life, Crosbie returned to Ayr and made a non-matchday pilgrimage to the Somerset Park his transfer had paid for. At the grand old age of 85 he died in February 1982, just a few months after the youngest of the footballing Shankly brothers had himself passed away. He had quite an eventful life in football, too.

Chapter 11

Shanks

A GROUP of young lads are hanging around on a street corner, passing time and setting their particular world to rights. They range in age from those still in short trousers to some nearing adulthood, but despite the generational gaps they are at ease in each other's company. They talk about the things all young males have always talked about – friends, girls, what entertainments are on offer, their conversation peppered with grand boasts and white lies that kids are prone to tell.

One among the number sees a familiar figure approaching. "That's me off," the complainant mutters, and slouches away. A couple of others follow him, but most of the rest stay. The young man walking purposefully towards them is never short of a few words, and even if he is not everyone's cup of tea, he's usually worth listening to. He may be definably one of them, but there's something different about him, too. Small in size, but a person who carries himself very well. He is butcher's-dog fit and, as befits a son of a tailor, looks the part in one of the neat suits he invariably wears. He is the embodiment of confidence, and for the rest of the darkening evening he will hold his audience in thrall – whether they like it or not.

"I maybe shouldn't say this," says Tom Hazle, one of the last surviving Glenbuckians, and who would remember those street-corner gatherings so well, "but if someone said 'oh here's Wullie Shankly' a few would have walked away. Wullie could talk for sure and it was interesting, but he would have taken over the conversation. He liked to be the centre of attention."

Tom is nearing 90 and still getting around on his bicycle. They bred them to last in Glenbuck, and his mental recall is as hardwearing as his physical fitness. Tom's memories of the disappeared village extend back nine decades and are expressed with a glint in the eye when it comes to Glenbuck's most renowned offspring.

Sitting in a Muirkirk pub in the winter of 2014, surrounded by the noise of lunchtime drinkers seeking refuge from the cold, with a jukebox incongruously blaring out Cliff Richard's 'Summer Holiday', Tom expresses a clear and abiding impression of one of British football's most famous sons. Hazle is one of the few who can claim with credibility that he knew Bill Shankly before he found fame.

"I was brought up next to him and I ken his mother and father and all his sisters. He was quite a few years older than me. I was about 11, then the war intervened and Wullie was away in the air force. But I remember him well. It was at the Union Butts where we stood on the corner at Dunblair. It's not there no more, obviously, but I can see it now. Wullie would come along, and a couple of them went away because he took over the conversation. It was good conversation, but he took over!"

Note the use of 'Willie' or 'Wullie', rather than 'Bill'. Shankly may be known to the wider world that took him to their hearts by the latter of those first names, but to those from Glenbuck he was and always will be 'Willie'.

It's this ever-so-slight contrariness that informs a more nuanced and rounded view of Shankly. It paints a picture of the real man behind the legend: who he was, where he came from, and how he was made. It makes a flesh-and-bone human being out of second-hand imaginations.

The sportswriter Matt Vallance, whose parents were born in Glenbuck, concurs with Tom's assessment of Shankly's reputation in the village. He points out how the miners of Glenbuck were interested in all sorts of matters, from the institutes, to their various clubs and associations. Sam Purdie chips in: "If you stood on the corner for ten minutes the whole problems of the world were solved."

"That's because they were into their philosophy – their free thinking," Matt continues, "and Shankly was too intense for some of them. That was the impression I got from my father and uncles." Billy Ward, one of the last of the Glenbuck-connected footballers who played for Queen of the South in the early 1970s, sits alongside Tom, Matt, and Sam, and remembers being told similar stories about the great man whose life they are all considering. "He would just talk about football," says Billy. "Well, a bit on billiards as well."

Billy, reluctant like Tom to even moderately question the Shankly legend and provide a slightly different take on his character, is careful not to claim absolute certainty. "See, it's not for me to say, but I heard that when he was young, Shankly was a reserved type of boy. Just an opinion, I'm not saying he kept himself to himself but he was different. Though he couldn't have been that reserved."

Tom nods in agreement and says with evident understatement, "Well. He was a big talker."

Bill Shankly could certainly talk a good game but he could deliver on it too. The young man who would become a professional footballer, an international, a successful manager and eventually a football demi-god attaining an almost mythic status within the sport, showed early on the characteristics for which he would become renowned. And Glenbuck demonstrably made him the superstar he would become.

Shankly's hard work, determination and commitment came to the fore in those early days on the street nicknamed Monkey

Row. His absolute belief in the values of teamwork and collective endeavour were forged out of the mines and the shared struggle for survival. The philosophy of not just how to play the game, but live the life, sprang from the doorstep of the tiny cramped house in which he grew up. Liverpool FC in particular and the game in general reaped the benefits.

As a neighbour, Tom Hazle knew full well what the cottages were like to live in, but his own family and then some of the Shanklys were able to move out when Ayrshire Council built new houses in the 1920s. "There was hot and cold water, an inside toilet, a bath. Wullie would have been about 14, I guess, when they moved in. He would later talk about not seeing a proper bath before then."

The Weekly News's profile of what it erroneously called the 'Shankley family' of 1933 gave the address as 5 New Houses. The move from the hopelessly inadequate terraced rows owned by the mining companies into the more spacious and modern council accommodation improved the lot of the Glenbuck families able to move into them. For all the economic woes and the village's fortunes ebbing and flowing according to the success or otherwise of the pits, it was still a "wee thriving little place", insists Barbara Alexander.

At the time of her uncle Willie's youth there were several shops: the butcher's run by the Hamilton family for generations; Annie Bain's general store that sold a bit of everything, including the sweets and chocolate that would provide rare but precious treats for the village kids; there was a post office, and, as cars made a tentative inroad into the community, a garage.

"It's funny," says Tom Hazle, "but my sister phoned me recently and said 'Tom, I've a question for you. When we were in Glenbuck, were we middle class?' 'What made you think that, Betty?' I asked. 'Well,' she said, 'we had a car and no one else had one just then.'"

Tom and Betty's father Alex, or 'AV' was a member of the Glenbuck aristocracy. He ran the Co-operative store and was later the manager of the Royal Arms pub. Set in a mining community and close to all sorts of industrial workings, including at one time three intersecting railway lines under construction or maintenance, the pub served the needs of thirsty men and was invariably busy. It was close to the Stottencleugh Burn, so when that flooded so did the pub. Not that this inconvenience would get in the way of the serious business of drinking, as Sam Purdie notes. "It was forever flooding. The water would run off into the burn, and then inundate the pub, but it wouldn't stop them drinking. They would just stand on crates at the bar – a bar that had dimples on it from all the elbows leaning on it."

He was being mischievously wistful: as previously noted, those recesses were carved by the pub owners to stop drinkers pilfering the round-bottomed glasses.

Bill Shankly, however, was not one of those who would add to any erosion of the wooden bar. A teetotaller, he would play cards, but was also well read, with the works of local hero Robert Burns among his favourites. Like so many of his generation and class, Shankly was highly intelligent, even if formal education did not best suit him. Young Willie had attended the same Glenbuck schoolhouse as generations of Glenbuckians had before him, in one of the 30-strong, mixed-age classes in which discipline was absolute.

"The teachers were a load of crabby old bastards," is Tom's blunt assessment. "Very tough. They didn't use the cane; they had the belt, the strap. You could get it for talking in the class, just carrying on." Bill was no model pupil and on one occasion earned the ire of the fearsome head Mr Rodger. Shankly had once been caught climbing a ladder to move the classroom clock forward by half an hour. By way of punishment he was made to stay at the top of the ladder for another hour.

This was a moment of humour amid schooldays that would often reflect the harsh nature of the world outside the classroom. Attendance generally was poor. During the miners' strikes of

BIBLIOGRAPHY

The Killies Who's Who – Bill Donnachie; Mainstream 1989

Newcastle United: The Ultimate Who's Who by Paul Joannou; N Publishing 2014

The Black-and-White Alphabet – Paul Joannou; Polar, 1996

50 Years of the Kilmarnock Football Club – Anonymous, Standard Printing Works, 1919

Ayr Football and Athletic Club Official Guide Book , 1901

Scotland Who's Who – Paul Smith; Pitch 2013

All With Smiling Faces: How Newcastle Became United – Paul Brown; Goal-Post, 2014

A Century United: The Centenary History of Southend United – Peter Miles and David Goody; Shrimper Publishing, 2007

Dundee Legends – Kenny Ross; Yore 2010

Dundee Champions of Scotland- Kenny Ross; Desert Island Books, 2012

In Search of Alan Gilzean – James Morgan; Back Page Press 2010

There Is A Bonnie Fitba Team: Fifty years on the Hibee Highway – Ted Brack; Black & White Publishing, 2009

Birmingham City The Complete Record – Tony Matthews, DB publishing, 2010

Scottish League Players Records Division One 1890/1 – 1938/39 – Steve Emms and Richard Wells; Soccerdata/Tony Brown 2007

Football League Players Records 1888-1939 – Michael Joyce; Soccerdata/Tony Brown 2012

A Record of Pre-War Scottish League Players; published by PM Publications, Willie Maley the Man Who Made Celtic – David W Potter; Tempus Publishing

Association Football and the Men Who Made It – Alfred Gibson and William Pickford; Caxton Publishing Company, 1910

Academic papers

The pit, the pitch and the pub: Scottish soccer players in the north of England, c. 1870-1900. Presented at the North American Conference on British Studies, 14 November 2010 Baltimore, Maryland USA – Matthew L. McDowell

The Fatalities of the Ibrox Disaster of 1902 – Robert Shiels; The Sports Historian vol. 18, The British society of Sports History, 1998

Websites

Bbc.co.uk

Abandonedcommunities.co.uk

Jardine's Book of Martyrs – https://drmarkjardine.wordpress.com/

http://www.scottishmining.co.uk

creativescotland.com

National Army Museum – nam.ac.uk

Glasgow FA – glasgow.co.uk

Hamilton Academical Memory Bank – www.acciesmemorybank.co.uk

www.scottishsporthistory.com

Scottishfa.co.uk

Englandfootballonline

Foxestalk (Leicester City)

lfchistory.net (Liverpool)

children were frequently kept away
clothes.

make for sobering reading. On 29
have been aged seven, 'Arrangements
itous children. A mid-day meal is
Union... Breakfast, consisting of hot
with jelly or syrup, is being supplied
iderable. All the infants, save one
breakfast since Tuesday. This is to
unday also.' The stark reality was
hungry. Children died young,
's recording of the death of 'Wee'
e age of just one year and seven
an isolated occurrence.
ople. Anarchist and Class War
famous Glenbuck Bones. His
ve been an influence on the
"My granddad's family were
says Bone "and my dad went
brothers and used to have
Shankly read any socialist
naturally from their fathers
Glenbuck."
explicitly political figure.
ansition from Glenbuck
acked, to put it politely,
had to walk all the way
sign and they gave him
ad drank all the money
also made a prodigious
already fathered four
eturning from service
and going on to have

The Shanklys were a similarly large brood. Out of the ten children, only one, Barbara Alexander's mother Elizabeth, went on to the Higher School at Muirkirk to continue in education. The demands of everyday life ensured few even got the opportunity. At 14, as was so often the case across the country at the time, children were deemed old enough to put their schoolbooks away and head out into the adult world to try and land a job.

Bill was one such boy. He was living in a world of tough realities. Work and survive, or else. He went to labour in the diminishing coalfields, first emptying coal trucks for 2s and 6d, before graduating to the pit bottom.

"He never set out to be a miner," says Barbara. "His goal was to be a footballer, then to play for Scotland, to be a successful football manager. He never went so far as to say that, but he knew he wanted to play football. He would have been just focused on his playing days then. He was such a confident person and he would never stop until he reached his goal. He never smoked or drank, was not interested in women – just completely dedicated and so blinkered."

Shankly worked hard in the mines but never really took to the job. He preferred wide-open spaces in which to express himself, not the airless dark cages of backbreaking drudgery. In the event, he did not have to suffer it too long. The inexorable closure of the mines and the Great Depression ensured Bill was out of the pit – and out of work after two years.

It was a rough, unforgiving place for a teenage boy to have to quickly grow up. Below or above ground, life was a daily struggle. But Glenbuck was no dog-eat-dog small-town dump where individuals battled to look after themselves and no one else. For certain, there was little romanticism about life for the majority of people who were in such situations; the so-called dignity of labour could be a cruel joke played on those who had to endure it. But the unique community spirit of the village provided some kind of safety net from the worst ravages of low pay, unemployment and narrow prospects.

"Glenbuck was an absolutely wonderful place," declares Barbara with unequivocal conviction. "Right from when you were young. If you were five years old and somebody was 15 years old and it was snowing, you went and you sledged with them. There was none of that 'oh you can't come you're only five'; it was just a wonderful place. Everybody looked after everyone else.

"If somebody didn't have coal, another person would give them some; if somebody stole a turnip, the other person got half; if somebody stole tatties, the other person got half the tatties. That's exactly how it worked."

Barbara notices the raised eyebrows at this admission of petty, but essential, theft. "They got them from farms, there were lots of them around Glenbuck. They [the farmers] were not bothered; people weren't really stealing or damaging the crops or anything, there was acres and acres of the stuff."

It is vivid illustration of the hardships the people of Glenbuck had to endure. Life was about survival, and if the paltry wages of the pit or trade could not provide, then more basic subsistence would be required. Children living in one of the wealthiest countries in the world could go dangerously hungry otherwise.

Ian Bone has recalled the family stories told to him about how savage the winters could be. Tucked away in its own micro-world, the community of Glenbuck would be isolated. So people would come together to help each other out and get through it. Matt Vallance echoes that thought. "Villages like Glenbuck, they were on their own, they had to make their own entertainment, and they all fought for one another. Your next door neighbour was likely to be your next door neighbour down the pit – you depended on each other."

That dependence would extend to sharing whatever material spoils were on offer.

"There was poaching going on," says Billy Ward. Sam Purdie cannot resist a mischievous comment to Tom Hazle. "You heard about that, Tam?"

"Ah no, that would be illegal," the older man replies, to gales of laughter. Poaching, however, was vital, supplementing the staple diet with precious protein. So was Bill Shankly much of a poacher? With a chuckle, Tom answers, "As soon as he could walk.

"We all had that skill, it was born into you. We were all hunter-gatherers at one time. You had to kill to eat." Fishing was also a skill youngsters had to learn and perfect. "Without wishing to be crude," says Tom, "there was an old saying: there was only two things to do in Glenbuck – fishing and fucking." "And there's nae fishing in the winter," adds Sam Purdie, to more uproarious laughter. Sam explains how hares would be snared or shot and turned into a delicious soup, and the men gathered around are licking their lips at the thought. The tale has echoes of a piece in the *Muirkirk Advertiser* of 1918 that reported 'a rare occurrence' when Richard Bone of Ladybank, Glenbuck spotted a mother otter and two babies by the side of a stream. Rather than revelling in the natural fauna, Bone killed and skinned the otters, to the paper's obvious approval.

The stories of such poaching, pilfering and back-of-the-lorry bounty are legion, including the legend of a truckload of bananas that miraculously found their way into Glenbuck. Bill Shankly was keenly aware of the vital function of bending the law, and confessed his capers in his autobiography, explaining how he and his co-partners in crime would give the local bobby a fearful runaround. "It was a necessity," says Barbara. "I mean, it was not stealing to sell on or anything like that, it was done out of need. People would all give whatever they snared or shot away to other families who were in need of food. There would be no one in Glenbuck starving. If a neighbour would help, they would gladly help."

Those words again. Need, help, and neighbour. Bill Shankly would pride himself on the value of self-reliance, but he learned very early how individuals could not survive alone. His parents were fundamental in providing that lesson, but it was his sister and Barbara Alexander's mother Elizabeth Shankly, affectionately known as Liz, who emerges not just as one of the most cherished of all Glenbuck's much-loved old characters, but a key influence on the future Liverpool manager.

Despite a seven-year gap Liz and her younger brother Bill were close. He would help her on her paper round, before he went down the pits for his first real job. He would have seen the way she went out of her way to help others. When she married Dave Crawford in 1938, they moved into the small house of a former policeman and set up a coal-fire-heated greenhouse to grow vegetables, and especially tomatoes.

"They were the best ever. Folk would go and get a pound of tomatoes, but my mother would give folk two pounds and charge them half price. There was this family that moved to Glenbuck and every Saturday, the man would come and get a carrot and turnip, and I'd get angry because he never paid anything. They could have grown their own. But my dad just said 'go on, take it'. Some took advantage. But my mum was a people person. Caring. Just the same as my uncle Willie – they would have given you their last."

That sense of generosity had been instilled in the Shankly children by their parents – "A lovely couple – couldn't get nicer," according to their neighbour Tom, and there were other characteristics. "My grandpa John was a disciplinarian, and competitive," remembers Barbara. And proud of Glenbuck's fiercely independent streak, a man who took immense pride in the Cherrypickers, even if he didn't play the game much, and never on a formal basis with his son.

In the absence of playing football together, son and father bonded over the movies. Glenbuck had no cinema of its own, thus requiring long walks to get to the pictures, but the wider area was blessed with a number of places to see films. Tom Hazle recalls that the Shanklys would go to the Taphouse or the Regal, sometimes on successive nights, with both having a fondness for Jimmy Cagney films. They would even act out some of the more exciting gangster scenes. Indeed, it was frequently commented on that Bill had a likeness for the American superstar, who made his name in roles as the combative little tough guy with big ambitions.

These were the affordable treats for Glenbuck's poor. There were not many other paid-for distractions within most people's reach. There were the dances, the socials, the various societies and associations allied to the mining trades, but people had to make most of their own entertainment. Religion tempted few (Sam reckons no place had more atheists per square metre than Glenbuck). Quoiting was a devotional obsession for some, but appears not to have detained Bill for too long. Instead it was that game with the round ball that provided him with his stage and means of escape.

Bill Shankly's world was delineated by a variety of environments and people, but it was football that dominated. He consumed the game from his birth. His older brothers had all gone on to have professional careers of varying degrees of success, so it would have been a surprise if the youngest Shankly boy had not at least grown to like, follow, and play the sport. But for the large age differences, that never-realised family five-a-side team would have been some outfit, competing in a format that was so loved in the village.

Indeed Bill Shankly was an ardent exponent of five-a-sides in his managerial career. It is not a stretch to think that the success of Liverpool was in part inspired by the rapid and hard-working style of passing and movement that was a feature of Glenbuck's football culture. It was a key part of the youthful experiences that informed the way he managed allied to lessons Shankly learned on the Glenbuck pitches and street games.

"Mining was the thing that made the football players in Glenbuck," says Tom. "It was the pit... we were desperate to get out of it. Willie was the same as everybody else. Come out of the pit and have a game of football. Sometimes we had 20-a-side playing. It was a cup final every night, and when it was too dark the game would stop and we just left the ball where it fell, and in the next night would carry on from where the ball was left."

Bill's talent became clear from the outset. He was industrious, full of running and firm in the tackle. He wasn't a wizard of the dribble like Stanley Matthews would become, or a proficient goalscorer like Jimmy McGrory of Celtic. Bill Shankly's specialism was in breaking up play rather than building it. But he was no crude destroyer. He had immaculate timing in the tackle and applied an exceptional degree of evaluation and purpose in his game. He was marked out from the off as a thinker and strategist.

That maturity would have likely earned him a swift elevation to the hotly coveted places in the Cherrypickers team, but by the time Shankly was old enough to pull on the white strip the club was effectively no more. He had a trial at 16, but Shankly wrote in *My Story* that he never actually played a game.

This is contested. Matt Vallance claims that while Shankly was too young to play for the team regularly, he did make appearances. "My uncle Hugh played for the Cherrypickers and he said Shankly definitely played a couple of games. The story is [Bill] never played for Glenbuck Cherrypickers because he played for Cronberry Eglinton, but in 1930/31 there was a Glenbuck pre-season friendly and there's a Shankly listed at centre-forward. All his brothers were senior by then, except for him. So it *had* to be him."

According to James Taylor's *Cairntable Echoes*, a cutting from the *Muirkirk Advertiser* in 1930/31 lists a Shankly as playing in a 3–2 win for the 'resuscitated' Cherrypickers over Cronberry. Given the ages of the brothers, it is almost certain this was Bill.

Whether he played for the Cherrypickers or not, Bill was soaked in the club's culture and values. His father had helped run it, his older brothers had played or trained for the team, and Bill had definitely watched the team play and been part of the unique Glenbuck atmosphere. He recalled the visit of one club that made the mistake of an over-aggressive attitude on and off the pitch, with the young Shankly remembering how he saw his brother Alec whole-heartedly enter the fray as a mass brawl broke out on the touchlines.

Bill did go on to play for Cronberry in 1931/32. By then he could not feature for the Cherrypickers as the club had finally called it a day. There was a touching poignancy that the final Cherrypickers squad featured a Tait, Brown and Bone among their number, resonating with names from the team's glorious past. And how fitting that the team should win the Ayrshire Junior Challenge Cup in that final season, all those years after the Cherrypickers had won the inaugural competition in 1890.

That was for the history books. As far as Bill Shankly was concerned the here and now of trying to make a go of a football career was paramount. He was unemployed, and with the Depression biting, the future looked bleak. He was saved by playing for Cronberry for half a season, making the 12-mile journey by bicycle. Soon his talent was recognised and the scouts came calling.

Peter Carruthers of Carlisle and Bobby Crawford of Preston led the way in trying to lure Shankly into the professional ranks. In the end he chose the lesser club, Carlisle. The family connection with uncle Billy Blyth, who had played for Carlisle and become a director, was evident. But the prospect of a better chance of first team football and the £4 weekly wage that came with it was even more enticing. So Bill Shankly headed off to Cumbria and one of the most celebrated of all professional careers had begun.

That epic saga is well known and has been repeatedly told. From Brunton Park to Preston, back to Carlisle for his first management role and then on to Grimsby, Workington, Huddersfield and then on to glory and European adventures with Liverpool, it is a magical and familiar yarn. There are insights into his playing days at Preston, however, that are less conspicuous. The club's official records, now forming part of the National Football Museum Archive at Deepdale, make for revealing, spellbinding reading into Bill Shankly the footballer.

Hidden away in the minute books that documented the directors' board meetings, inside the carefully scripted pay book ledgers, and the hefty leather-bound collections of almost countless scouting reports, are time-capsule pictures of life for Bill as a player.

The scouting reports or 'watches' are an extraordinary window on the professional game of the period. Listing individual assessments of hundreds of players, they show how Preston sent out an army of football watchers, many unnamed, to trawl the country for talent. The majority of those scouted are mentioned briefly and never again, failing to make it past the first hurdle of the three-stage process that narrowed down the search for new recruits.

'William Shankly', the name elegantly hand-written out in delicate, fading copper script, is one of the few exceptions. In *The Weekly News*'s article of July 1933, The Sentinel wrote that 'Willie, the youngest of the footballing brothers – he is 19 – is a right-half. Recently he joined Carlisle. He has been fixed up for another season.' But something else was going on, unreported.

The first sign of Preston's interest was in late October 1932, when Shankly was 'recommended to Mr [James] Taylor', then the de-facto secretary-manager at North End, and later to become chairman, in a period when the club were effectively run and managed by committee. Shankly was described as a 'left-half, age 19, 9st 10lbs' and was seen by 'Rawlings'. The verdict was brief but put in motion a burgeoning interest. 'Very satisfactory for a young player,' noted the report.

Subsequent reports were not all enthusiastic. 'Sharples', on 9 January 1933 saw Bill in a game against Southport, and said he was 'very useful' with 'plenty of enthusiasm', but also 'no craft. Not promising even for the future.' It seemed damning, but the club were still interested enough to compile a third and more thorough watch. This time three directors or senior officials went on scouting missions. 'Mr Holt' somewhat contradicted himself when he reported on 25 March 1933 that Shankly was 'very good. Poor in defence but well worth following up as a contracted player.'

Less than a week later after a game against Halifax, T. Blackburn was opining that Shankly was 'a good young useful player.' Even though at the end of April, Will Scott, the trainer who would become Preston manager in 1949, cautioned that Bill was 'very fair' but 'slow in execution of work', the various scouts and football watchers had made their collective minds up. Wullie Shankly, by now more commonly going by the name Bill, was targeted for a fee of £500. At first Bill baulked. Preston were in Division Two but still a mighty name, yet Shankly was worried he might not make it into the first team, and the wages on offer were not dazzling. He could earn more money, it was reasoned, from winning one hand in those tempestuous Glenbuck card schools. Thankfully for him and the club, brother Alec made him see sense, and his baby brother signed.

The Preston scouting reports form a portrait of a young player who was perhaps not particularly gifted but worked prodigiously at his game, putting everything into his endeavours to make the very most of what he had. It was an attitude that turned him into a fine footballer. It had echoes of Kevin Keegan who Shankly would so value and cherish after he brought him from Scunthorpe to Anfield in 1971 for £35,000. "Robbery with violence," Shankly said of the deal. He saw something of himself in Keegan, the kid from a mining background not overly blessed with natural talent but prepared to graft and train his way to excellence and achievement.

Bill certainly had to labour to earn his money at Deepdale. He signed on for £5 a week and thereafter, his wages rose only moderately in line with the strictures of the maximum wage. Once he had established himself in the team, he enjoyed parity with the high earners. Fresh from the Great Depression and residing alone initially in the town at 24 Deepdale Road, he lived well for a young working-class man in 'Proud Preston', an archetypal northern textile town. But it was hardly the stuff of fabulous riches. By 1936 he was earning £6 a week basic during the season at a time when a decent average wage was just under £4. In the wartime of 1941, alongside the genius Shankly forever revered, Tom Finney, Bill was on £1 10s; by 1947 the pair were drawing £12 a week basic.

Shankly's best earnings as a player came with the FA Cup runs to the finals of 1937 and 1938. When a Scots-packed Preston won the latter – 'my biggest thrill as a player', as Shankly described it – bonuses for winning the trophy bumped his relevant wages for that week up to £17.

It was some kind of reward for the dedicated service he gave to PNE. He missed only 28 of 319 games in his first eight seasons, and racked up 337 games in total over a 16-year spell. In time they named a stand after him, making him revered at Deepdale more than any other save, of course, for the Preston Plumber, Sir Tom Finney. Bill became a crowd favourite, captain and Lilywhite legend, following in the footsteps of those other six Glenbuck players who played at Deepdale, including his uncle Bob Blyth and the two Tottenham Sandies.

Left-half Bobby Crawford was an uncle to Barbara Alexander on her father's side, and another Glenbuck-Preston notable. 'Laddie' rivalled all of them for service to the PNE cause, lasting 11 years at Deepdale. After a move from Raith Rovers, he made the midfield berth his own but his attacking instincts proved so strong that in 1929 he was switched to centre-forward, responding immediately with two goals in his first game in the position and four in the second, notching 17 in all.

Crawford, who later played for Blackpool, Blackburn and Southport, was an ever-present for all but one game in seven seasons for Preston and left in 1932. He featured in a modern Deepdale mural at the back of one of the stands portraying the club's 'Invincibles' alongside Bill Shankly. Bill had had big Glenbuck boots to fill at Preston, but he did so with his quality as a footballer and his commitment to the colours.

The long and dependable service saw to that, as did the FA Cup win. International recognition also confirmed Shankly's status. In addition to seven wartime representative appearances he won five full caps, in a busy four-month period in the 1938/39 season. There was a 3–1 win against Hungary and most satisfying of all, a 1–0 triumph over England at Wembley, Scotland's first win over the rivals in ten years.

The *Daily Record* of 10 April singled Shankly out for rare praise in its report on the match. It quoted the defender, relating, "'If we had got a second goal in the first half we would have got a barrow load in the second half." Those were the words spoken by Willie Shankly, Reporter Waverley heartily agrees with him. Shankly certainly played a big part in the game, and naturally knew what he was talking about.'

Shankly was closely involved in the move that led to Tommy Walker's brilliant winning goal and then was central to the rear-guard action that preserved the advantage. 'Smith was outstanding,' concluded 'Waverley', 'and need I say more, to his right was the hard grafting Shankly even with the hottest dangerous moments in defence he never forgot his other duties to carry the ball from defence and in difficult times his passing set up dangerous attacks for Scotland.'

This outstanding individual and team performance, broadcast live on 'London television' to the few lucky enough to own a TV set, was followed by a 2–0 victory over Northern Ireland and a 3–2 defeat of Wales, before a 2–1 loss to England at Hampden on 15 April 1939. It made Bill the most successful of Glenbuck's players to represent their country, something that would have made the intensely patriotic John Shankly hugely proud.

His son Bill stayed 16 years at Deepdale, the period inevitably curtailed by wartime service in the RAF. Shankly did not see action. Instead he tried to maintain playing the game as much as possible, turning out for a number of wartime sides including Arsenal. He played 11 games as a guest for the Gunners, a club he had long admired, in the Wartime League South and League Cup South in the 1942/43 season. He would come up to Highbury and sleep in the dressing rooms and then play in games at White

Hart Lane, used for home matches by Arsenal while Highbury was pressed into service as an ARP centre.

Returning as a married man to Lancashire, his playing days wound down. It prompted disagreement with the board, as player and directors saw Bill's future on different terms. Tucked away in the Preston archives are documents and letters of an agreement between the club and Bill, formalising his appointment as a player-coach/trainer on 27 June 1947 for a two-year period, and parity of pay with senior pros. A 'benefit fee' of £750 was also signed 'subject to league sanction'.

When the two years were almost up, another agreement was signed on 4 April 1949, this time cancelling the previous deal. Shankly had taken up a coaching role at Carlisle. The club did not formally stand in his way, but there were severe disagreements over the benefits Shankly insisted he was due. The board blocked his benefit match, to Shankly's bitter and lasting distaste.

An entry in what looks to be a severance form in the 1948/49 season denotes £600 (less tax) paid to Shankly under the heading 'Benefits and accrued shares', and dated 8 October 1948. But the language of the minute books better betrays the attitude on the part of the directors: 'It was agreed Shankly be released to take up an appointment with Carlisle United,' ran the brief note on the leaving of a Deepdale legend.

The curt use of the surname was an unmistakeable illustration of the power relations that persisted in the game. It was a master-and-servant set-up. Even for the abrupt nature inherent to minute notes, there were no tributes to a loyal player, no praise or thanks put on the record. Instead there was a formal note that while Shankly was to be paid his accrued shares his name was to be 'retained on our League list'.

Shankly had got on with the directors for much of his time at the club. He had liked James Taylor's glee in celebrating a previous cup win against Arsenal, warming to the director's sarcasm at rubbing in the scale of 'little Preston's' achievement with his high-status

Arsenal counterparts. The board were a colourful bunch. Hugh Rains for example was a former acrobat, music hall performer and early cinema impresario who also went by the name 'Will Onda'.

But Bill would not be cowed by his supposed social betters. He had ambition, and was determined to realise it, setting off for Carlisle and beginning one of the great managerial journeys.

If the people Shankly left behind thought that was the last they would see of their determined son, they would be mistaken. Shankly never returned to live in Glenbuck, and was not a frequent visitor. The mother he adored died in 1959 and there was less of a draw to return. But he made a point of not forgetting his roots, nor the people who came with them. It seems everyone from Glenbuck then and now has a story or two to tell.

"Him and my father were quite good friends," says Sam Purdie, "and I remember him saying what kind of money he made when he went to Preston North End. My father said, 'What about Liverpool, it's a big club?' 'Oh, it's a big club alright,' says Shanks, 'but I had no idea what I was getting into. So I got the boys out on the pitch, to go around the field dribbling round traffic cones. I won't say the club was in a bad way but the traffic cones won 3–0.'"

There's more. "There was always a bit of friction between Muirkirk and Glenbuck. Ever so slightly! So one time when he was back home paying a visit, they dragged him against his will to see a football match here involving Muirkirk Juniors. The Muirkirk folk wanted him to watch this very likely lad.

"Half-time – Wullie hadn't opened his mouth. Eventually they couldn't contain themselves and said 'what do you think of the wee fella?' 'Ach, the fella with the blonde hair? He plays away fine until he gets the ball.'"

Matt Vallance's cousin Allan Ross played for Shankly's old side Carlisle in goal, and holds the club's appearance record. Carlisle won promotion to the First Division in 1974/75, and Ross later told Matt about his excitement at the prospect of facing Liverpool.

Shankly had stepped down as manager the previous season, but Ross had an approach ready for the great man. "Allan was looking forward to going to Anfield, to finally meet Wullie Shankly, because he had this notion they were 'related'," says Matt, drawing on the convoluted relationships between the various Glenbuck families.

"Our granny Elsie Anderson was originally a Glenbuck Blyth, a sister to Shanks's mother, you see.

"Allan was in the game at Anfield. They [Carlisle] lost and he saw Shankly afterwards. He says to him 'You were nearly my father'.

"'What!?', says Shankly.

"'You were nearly my father.'

"'How come?'

"'You went out with my mother, Elsie Anderson'. [Bill Shankly's cousin and daughter of granny Elsie.]

"'Oh. Aye,' says Willie. 'How's Crilly?' Crilly was the nickname of my uncle Wullie Anderson.

"So they talked a wee while and Shanks asked about Crilly, and he asked about Allan's relatives and all that, and then Shanks had to cry away. His parting shot to Allan was 'Son, see if you *had* been my boy, you'd have saved that second goal.'"

Crilly was something of a Glenbuck legend. He was a driver who had gone down the pits with Bill when they first went to work as boys. Shankly found an out through football, Crilly via an HGV licence and a driving job.

"Crilly told me once about a night he landed in Liverpool when the team were playing someday in the European Cup," says Matt. "So Crilly phones Anfield. 'Can I speak to Willie Shankly, please?'

"'Oh, Mr Shankly's not taking calls today.'

"'He'll take this one. Just tell him it's Crilly.'

"So sure enough Shankly comes on.

"'Aye, wot is it, Crilly?'

"'Hello Wullie, I'm in Liverpool, can I get a ticket for tonight?'

"'Nae bother,' says Shanks, 'there'll be a ticket left at the front door for you.' 'Just one thing,' says Crilly, 'I'm in a big lorry.' Shanks says nae bother. 'We'll sort that out too, don't worry.'

"So that night Crilly's driving down Anfield Road and he couldn't move for folk. This big Liverpool police sergeant comes out and says, 'And where the hell do you think you're going in that!?'

"Crilly says, exasperated, 'I'm going to the game. Wullie Shankly said it was alright!'

"'Oh, you're Shankly's pal!' says the copper. 'Well, in that case just drive it over here and park up where you like.'

"Wullie never forget where he was from."

None did, including those of the last Glenbuck generation. "I'm a lot, lot younger," Barbara Alexander says, "so when uncle Willie was away I wasn't even born." That much is obvious. There's a definite allure of glamour about Mrs Alexander. If Bill Shankly was the last of the old breed, Barbara represented the new generation of Glenbuckians who came out of the benighted remains of the dying village determined not to let its demise hold them down. She married her sweetheart Jackie, moved away, and has lived a good life far removed from the grim days of the Depression. But like her uncle Wull, she never forgot where she came from. And her memories of her famous relation are wonderfully warm and touching.

"He used to come up to Glenbuck before he went to Liverpool, but not so often once he went there and the job took over. When my granny, his mother, died in 1959 that obviously had an effect as well. But it was a real treat when he did pay a visit.

"Mind, he was a terrible, terrible driver, he didn't like driving at all, and eventually he came in a taxi. He used to come in the holidays with his eldest daughter Barbara. We used to go up Douglas Water just down the parish. There's a great pool up there and he used to go in and then he used to take us guddling at Inchie train station near Glenbuck – just happy, happy things."

Mention of 'guddling' provides an intimate and affecting insight into what Shankly was like – not as a famous football manager but a family man simply having fun with his child and niece. Guddling is a Scottish term used to describe catching fish, akin to 'tickling the trout' – i.e. with bare hands, rather than a rod and line, or a net. It would require at least two people – one to tease the fish out of its shadowy hiding place in the lee of a rock, another to catch the fish as it tried to escape. It's the kind of pastime generations of children used to engage in, socks off and trousers rolled up to their knees.

It could need hours of patience, waiting for the moment to strike. When it went wrong and the fish got away, tempers could and did fray, resulting in an exchange of blows. When Shankly was a boy it was an essential means of getting food. And another Glenbuck lesson on teamwork that stayed with him, and one that he would delight in when he returned to his home village. A serious, but rewarding business is guddling.

This was at a time when Shankly was yet to enter his Anfield pomp. Once there his success had a captivating magic for his family and friends, eager to gain insight into the workings of a major club and what their famous relation actually got up to. "Once, a few of us, a couple of cousins, went to Liverpool to my uncle Wullie's to stay," Barbara continues. "I said to him, 'I would love to go to Melwood, uncle Willie.' He said, 'It's no place for lasses Barbara, no place for lasses, but I'll take you, show you Melwood, and then you go home. It's no place for women!'

"He would write letters on an old typewriter which he sent to my mother. She loved the lot of them in her family but I think she singled Wullie out. You could see why. He stayed with us once at Broomhill and he said what a lovely place it was. He was always complimentary to people, he was never nasty."

Sister Liz and her husband Dave were recipients of one of those carefully crafted, affectionate, typewritten letters, in June 1976. It shines a remarkable light on Shankly's state of mind two years after he had stunned the football world by standing down as Liverpool manager.

'A few lines to tell you all the news from this end, and of course hoping that you have now settled in your new home... Well, since I packed it in at Liverpool, I have been really pestered with everybody, it really has tired me out, on top of that I have had an injured knee for about six months... So you see, life has been a little hectic, so much so that I have no notion of going anywhere, until I feel like.'

The letter continues with reference to various ailments and visits to doctors, wife Nessie's spring cleaning, and a tender update on his children and grandchildren of whom Shankly was clearly immensely proud. There is also a desire to visit home and his relatives, but tempered with the line, 'We really cannot promise. My life has not been my own for two years now.'

The accepted perception about Shankly at this time is that he was downcast and lost after leaving Anfield. This is a claim strongly rejected by those who knew him, players and fans alike (see Chapters 12 and 13), and while the letter may indicate a certain world-weariness, it also suggests that the discomfort had as much to do with people not leaving him alone as any sense of personal loss of purpose. In any event a visit from Shankly was something to cherish and enjoy, as he charmed all and sundry. Niece Barbara was similarly captivated, and amused by his hopeless impracticality in certain contexts. "We went on a cruise once from Liverpool and Jack had a wee sports car, a Triumph, and we put it next to uncle Wullie's house. It wasn't a fancy house, just an ordinary semi-detached with a single garage, a two-door car – nothing flash because there was nothing fancy about him.

"Jack left the car in a neighbour's garage. So my uncle Wullie took us down to the dock and there was a young man there who did the entertainment. He said to us in an incredulous tone, 'How do you know Mr Shankly?' I said he's my uncle and the man announced, 'We've got a celebrity here today!'

"Uncle Wullie smiled and said hello but he was more concerned about our car. So, he said he would take it out and give it a wee battery charge. Well, he must have forgot because we had to push it up the hill when we got back. He was just not mechanical. I'm sure he would not be able to use any of these things like laptops. Though he used a typewriter, so he did.

"This was in the sixties when he started winning, but it never changed him. He was always so smart, so dapper. A lovely collar and tie. Oh, and he was very, very house-proud. He set the breakfast the night before and he would be going around with a wee dustpan to brush up the crumbs and everything.

"If Liverpool got beat he'd take it out on the cooker by cleaning it."

The image of the demanding little Scot who dragged Liverpool to greatness by dint of his relentless hard work, mental toughness and fiery-eyed genius might sit uneasily with this scene of domesticity. His routine of exorcising losing demons by scrubbing kitchen appliances has been well chronicled. But it also shows that Shankly was modesty personified. The house he lived in in West Derby was anything but ostentatious. This understated stability was underpinned by the enduring marriage to Nessie.

"My auntie Nessie was also an exceptionally nice lady. She was a very placid person, and she also did a lot for the charities around Liverpool, but she was very much a housewife. They would never say a wrong word to each other. She would go to events with him but neither of them went to many. Fancy footballers of today with their wives and the diamond rings and stuff – I don't think that was the case with Wullie and Nessie.

"They were friends first. Nessie was in the Air Force when she met my uncle Wull, he was stationed at Bishopbriggs, and she saw this man every morning training, she thought he must have been crazy: rain, hail, sleet or snow, he was out there jogging.

"He never drank or smoked; he was just a true, honest-living man. Sometimes I think he missed out a lot because he never did those 'luxury' things; maybe he would have broadened his horizons? But he never mixed with people that never talked about football. If you are not dedicated about things you should not be in it. You hear about all those sports folk like runners or cyclists, there are some so dedicated that they don't have a life outside.

"My abiding memory of uncle Willie? He was an honest man," says his niece with obvious pride. "I think it speaks volumes that he would not go out of his way to harm anyone. He might say a word or two that did not suit people, he would wind a few people up, but everything he would say would be true.

"And again, he was so kind. A kind person. People would never know how much my uncle Wull gave away. He provided well for his immediate family, and when he came back to Glenbuck, he would give most of his family these handouts, like a wee envelope he gave to his sisters. 'Here you go, Liz, a wee something.' Or auntie Bel, 'Here hen, there's a wee something', to my auntie Net the same thing.

"And of course he also gave so much to supporters. There's those stories of fans being on a train in the first class carriage and uncle Wull was there. The inspector came round, started examining the tickets and when he saw the supporters never had a ticket, the inspector was going to throw them off at the next stop. But then my uncle Wull stepped in to pay for all the tickets.

"Tickets for international games oh, you name it, the things he would give away were just unbelievable. And he took nothing in return. And that's how I think he missed out on certain things. I reckon he missed a lot in life because he got the chances. You see these footballers now, they have sponsors. He got the chance to get sponsored suits and lovely shoes, but he didn't take it. Didn't take advantage of it. He could have taken cruises but instead him and Nessie went to Blackpool on their holidays.

"He just played, and went to games, he didn't have a wider experience of anything much other than football. He talked about football all the time. My uncle Bob was different, he could talk about anything. But my uncle Wullie? It was football – just football.

"In his younger days, I do believe when he played with Carlisle and he came up in the close season, he just loved meeting all the folk.

"He loved standing on that corner and telling them ridiculous stories. All those stories..."

There was once a group of lads standing on a street corner in Glenbuck, cracking gags and swapping stories. They saw a familiar figure approaching. He was small but no physical pushover. He was lean, fit, smart – every inch the professional sportsman. He was making a name for himself in the big wide world outside of Glenbuck. And whether the others wanted to hear it or not, well; he had some story to tell.

Chapter 12

Shankly's Fun Factory

IN 1965, Liverpool reached the FA Cup Final for the third time in the club's history. They had never won the trophy that then really mattered, following defeats in 1914 to George Halley's Burnley and Arsenal in 1950. For a club with such a history, and six league titles, it was a glaring omission from the honours list. Bill Shankly had secured one of those league championships the year before, confirming the wisdom of his appointment in 1959. He had not just rebuilt the side, but the whole club, imbuing it with a sense of purpose and an unrelenting hunger for success, and laid the groundwork for the European triumphs that would turn the club into a footballing superpower.

On 1 May 1965, the Liverpool team coach made its way to the stadium to take on Leeds United. On board, as Oliver Holt described in his absorbing twin portrait of Scottish managerial leviathans Shankly and Alex Ferguson, *If You're Second You Are Nothing*, the players were treated not to up-tempo hits of the day appropriate to their generation, but the musical musings of their manager. Over the coach's speakers was played a recording of Shankly's recent appearance on *Desert Island Discs*, so it was the strains of *Danny Boy, The Saints Go Marching In* and the old Robert Burns ballad *A Red Red Rose* that resonated through the coach, rather than anything more contemporary and relevant.

The Beatles, Merseyside's third prong in the cultural triumvirate alongside the football clubs of Liverpool and Everton, didn't get a look in. The selections reflected Shankly's traditionalist tastes but also his enduring passions. The choice of *A Red Red Rose* was an obvious hark back to his Glenbuck days and the lasting affection for Burns's poetry.

Hours after the *Desert Island Discs* on the coach, Liverpool had won the cup, and the Shanks legend had taken on another dimension. Liverpool FC had become Shankly's club. He had engineered its metamorphosis from a humble outfit seemingly resigned to play second fiddle to competitors – even Everton – into the dominant force in British football. As Holt said, "The club united around him: supporters, players, even the board. It was as if everything flowed from his dynamism, his energy and his determination."

Those players were instrumental in implementing the Shankly credo and method. He had signed all but three of them, their progress at Anfield developing in tandem with his top-to-bottom remodelling of the club. Two of the most prominent were the homegrown Ian Callaghan, and Ian St John, the much-coveted striker Shankly signed in 1961 from Motherwell.

The pair had secured the 1965 FA Cup, thanks to Callaghan's cross and St John's brilliant diving header in extra time. A half century on from the Wembley triumph, over 30 years since Shankly's death, and more still since the death of Glenbuck itself, they talked once again of the legend they knew as a real man. They give a fascinating insight into the way he worked and how he turned Liverpool into one of the greatest sides in history.

Amid the stories there is laughter. Lots of it, as the recollections of Shankly the character spill out. "The one thing that shines through is fun," says St John.

It's a word that crops up often in the conversation. Not perhaps one synonymous with the man for whom football was apparently more important than life and death. But then, that was never the case.

"See, that 'life and death' quote?" St John continues, warming to the theme. "Now, I was there when it was originally said; I was in the dressing room and heard it outside in the corridor. It actually came from one of the press lads. He said to the boss, 'This game coming up, this is life or death' and Bill said, 'No, no. It's more important than that.' It was a joke, he said it as a joke, a throwaway gag. He had a wonderful sense of humour; he loved a joke, whether it was in the training ground or the dressing room. He loved laughter.

"The image of him as a stern, tough, hard man who was uncompromising – he was nothing of the kind. He liked nothing better than joking and laughing. There was a time to work, but also to play. You couldn't fart about if you were working, but humour is very much part of football and he loved a laugh as much as anybody. I can hear him chuckling in the corridor now.

"People who didn't know him, and write things about him, they were wrong. Totally wrong. I get annoyed at that quote, the way it's misused. After Heysel, it was quoted then – as if to mock him. People say, 'he said it was more important than life and death, well look at what happened'. It was a *joke*.

"The press conferences were done in the corridor and I heard it, I heard the tone. It was so obviously said tongue in cheek. It's been totally misconstrued over the years and it gets brought up when there are tragedies. You think 'you people, you're putting the boss's name to this and it's giving a totally false impression of Bill Shankly and what he thought about people – and life'.

"It's a quote that should be wiped off the record books."

St John's insistence is forthright and clear. But what the record books do reflect accurately is a remarkable run of success for Shankly built on the efforts of two great teams. The first won two league titles and that FA Cup during the heady, thrilling footballing days of the 1960s, when a series of great club sides featuring wonderful players swapped superiority, and managers like Matt Busby, Bill Nicholson, Don Revie and Shankly locked horns. His second great Liverpool team prospered at the start of the club's period of long domination and near monopoly of trophies, with another league title added to an FA Cup and Liverpool's first European title, the UEFA Cup, which served as a warm-up act for the club's conquest of the continent under Bob Paisley.

St John would play for Liverpool for a decade but not survive the rebuilding, in contrast to Callaghan, who as Liverpool's longest-serving player with 857 appearances mostly in all red – the colour Shankly insisted the team wore – transcended the two Shankly eras. But while the faces changed, the fundamental way of working did not.

"He got teams together," Callaghan says, with emphasis on the last word. Fresh from an annual reunion of the England 1966 World Cup squad, he's been reliving the glory days, and he's more than willing to sing Shankly's praises. "He came in '59, went up in 61/62, bought Ronnie Yeats, Ian St John. He built the side and how we played. He had Bob Paisley with him; who was a great tactician. The two of them together complemented very well. They were different characters. Bob was a quiet man."

The contrast was stark, with Paisley the steady, diligent and unassuming background figure, doing wondrous things behind the scenes, in contrast to Shankly the garrulous extrovert. "That's the thing about him," Callaghan continues. "He came to Liverpool, he promised things and the people took to him. Because he was so out in front with what he said. He made promises but crucially he kept them.

"Liverpool were going nowhere when he came, they were a Second Division club. Within a couple of seasons we'd won the Second Division. Within a couple of seasons more we'd won the league and then the FA Cup for the first time, which I think he said was his greatest achievement."

"Lots of things have been said about what makes for good football management," St John says, "but I think the abiding thing about the boss was just his love of the game. His love of the game never left him and that all started way back, as it does for every one of us. You start off as a kid, kicking a ball around with your mates when you're just a toddler. Up at Glenbuck, in those villages in Scotland, there was nothing else to do. That was all you did, you just played football.

"The pitches would have been terrible – I know, I've played on them – but they would play on scraps of ground, any sort of space at all. If there were only two of you it would be one versus one, then somebody would turn up and it would be two versus one, and so on until you had a proper game. That was the way it was and everybody looked forward to it, getting up in the morning and playing.

"Bill was the same as everybody else. He would have been one of those kids first out in the morning, making sure he had a ball, because he had older brothers who were all footballers so there was always, always, plenty of action going on with his brothers and other pals in the village. His whole life was made up with football – from the beginning it was all football, football.

"If anyone thinks back about Bill Shankly, the one thing they think about was his love of the game. He couldn't understand if you didn't have it. He could not comprehend anybody not having this love for the game. The first thing he wanted to know about every player was not the skill and what have you; he wanted to know how much you loved the game and wanted to play. And he wanted to win, that was the important thing. He had to see that in players, he had no time for people who didn't have that in their make-up, who didn't have that inherent love for the game."

Shankly made sure that those off-the-peg players he signed, like St John, or those nurtured through from the youth ranks, shared that total commitment to their sport, and a hunger for success. It was built on the fundamental faith in teamwork, relentlessly drilled into the players, allied to an abiding belief that football is best practised using a football. A very Glenbuckian approach to the game.

"Although he had star players," Callaghan says, "he emphasised all the time how much it was a team game. You needed different players, mentalities and attitudes to make the team, and he used to emphasise this and he wouldn't go over the top about one player. It was always about the team."

For St John, Shankly was a revelation. "He was my second pro manager. The one I had at Motherwell, Bobby Ancell, got a very good team together but was the total opposite of Bill Shankly. [Ancell] was a desk man. We never saw him, we never saw him at training.

"The complete opposite was the boss, who couldn't wait to get out of his office, get a tracksuit on and be mixing it with all the players. He had to have his football fix every day, he had to play every day, the five-a-sides at training and then in the summer they were playing in the car park, him, Bob Paisley, Joe Fagan, Reuben Bennett – even the milkman was roped in to make up one of the teams in the car park. That was the difference between the boss and other football people or managers who were desk managers. He was a football-pitch manager.

"And he could have been a manager in any era. Today it's supposed to be all about 'we've moved on', this, that and the other, but I disagree. I think any club that had Bill Shankly as a manager would have a successful team. He looked at players and evaluated them, and you had to have that determination, a will to win and that natural enthusiasm – that was his great expression, 'you must have natural enthusiasm' – and he simply could not understand anybody without it."

Callaghan too had been a close witness to the transformation Shankly made. The Toxteth-born youngster first joined in 1958 as an amateur and played in the junior and other teams outside of the senior squad.

It was Shankly, arriving a year later and taking a more active interest in the Anfield youth, who saw Callaghan play and signed him as a professional in 1960.

"He changed things. I was an amateur two nights a week but when I signed pro, we all saw how he changed training. Everything was done with a ball."

"He wasn't so much a tactics man," adds St John. "Bear in mind we were the first to play a flat back four. In the old days it was two full-backs and a centre-half. The flat back four came about because we were in Europe and started learning from European teams and the different tactics they were employing.

"So the boss wasn't averse to changing things, trying out new ideas and certainly, we were the first team to play a back four, a 4-4-2 and pushing up. He was ahead of the game as far as that was concerned. But he wouldn't put tactics down as the be all and end all, if you didn't have that natural enthusiasm, a will to win; tactics meant nothing without that."

What tactics Shankly did want to impart he communicated using a board with the familiar little numbered men – red for Liverpool, white for the opposition.

St John adds, "He would run through it with us and explain to people what he wanted from them, the positions etc. He made it clear; he wasn't a baffler. I went to Lilleshall years later to get my coaching badges and they were talking a different lingo. He hated that. All this organised coaching as if it was the answer to everything. To us he was just talking common sense; he would describe it as that.

"In training it was all ball work. You warmed up, and pre-season you did a bit more running, but for most of the rest of the time it was all ball work. Which again was something new in the game. Professional footballers before my era and even during it, they were still running round the track; still running up and down the terraces."

Mention of the five-a-sides provides a link to Glenbuck and the form of the game its players took to with such gusto. St John says that Shankly and his coaches made sure the small-sided contests were competitive. Occasionally he'd even join in. "I don't know why," St John says chuckling, "but he was a good player still, even in his 50s. And still very fit."

The Shankly system worked with purring efficiency. St John describes how Reuben Bennett, former goalkeeper and who was at Motherwell with the striker, was himself in the running to get the manager's job at Anfield but took a trainer/fitness coach role instead. He put the players through their physical preparation and then Paisley and the other coaches would oversee the ball work. "'Coach' wasn't the word as such, because it felt like everything was planned before we got out on the training ground," says St John.

"Shanks was very careful. This business about players getting injured in training, he couldn't understand teams where that happened. 'What are they doing?' he'd say. We worked hard for sure, but there would also be days where the pace would be light, where we weren't pressed as much physically, days where we would go up to the saunas, get massages and all the rest of it. It wasn't a case of every day being putting through torture machines.

"He was mindful of the games we had coming up. Once we got successful we were playing twice a week because we had European games and cup ties. So it made sense that you have to rest as well as work. Again that was all very new in the game. Other managers didn't think about that, they just tried to kill you having you running up and down the terraces all the time."

This was an illustration of Shankly's understanding of players and what made them tick, drawing on his extensive experience – but also the lessons learned from his runner father John. His youngest son was not so ahead of his time on nutrition, swearing by a diet of red meat, but far from being stuck in a pre-war time warp, he looked firmly to the future.

"He was an innovator," St John insists, "ahead of the game because he was thinking about it all the time. The fitness of the players and keeping them fit, that was essential. If you look through the period we were always classed as the fittest team in the league.

He would laugh because people said we were the fittest because he was running the legs off us in training, when it was the opposite."

In the 1970s, British Pathé filmed some wonderful footage of Liverpool players being put through their paces by one of Shankly's lieutenants and eventual successors, Joe Fagan. There is no sound, just images, providing a mute insight into the hard work put in at Melwood that was integral to the team's consistent success. A tracksuited Shankly can be seen only briefly, but of perhaps greater interest is in the background where wooden structures drift into view. They look like some combination of fences and cricket sightscreens, supported by angled struts and with painted lines or numbers on one side.

These are the famous Melwood boards, used for various drills in which players would be tasked with hitting balls at a specific target or completing a varied routine of, for example, using their left foot to hit the ball against one board before striking the return at another.

"That again was his idea," says St John. "They were the size of full-size goals. If there was no keeper you'd batter balls against it, control it and then whack it again. I suppose it was like being a golfer out on the practice range and giving it a whack. You're honing your skills."

The boards, the notorious sweatbox exercises – "very, very hard, though it was always with a ball", remembered Callaghan – and of course the Anfield boot room: they were all signifiers of Shankly's impact at the club and the way he moulded an environment dedicated to getting results. The boot room is the stuff of legend, a place of footballing hallowed ground whose mythical status has only increased with Shankly and Paisley's passing. The reality was prosaic – "just a room for boots" laughs Callaghan – but it had a reputation as some holy of holies where footballing miracles were divined.

"You'd go in and there would be manuals, notes on what we'd done that day, what we were going to do tomorrow," says Callaghan. "That's where the training or whoever we were playing on a Saturday was all discussed. The players didn't go in. You'd go in only if you were invited; even when I was coming to the end of my career at Liverpool and I wasn't playing as much, you'd have to be invited in. Which I was towards the end; I'd go in after the game, and the opposing managers would come in – it was a buzz for them to say 'I've been in the boot room', because it had such an iconic aura about it."

St John confirms the status Anfield and its manager enjoyed as the reputation of both grew. "Other managers liked him because he played the game at the highest level and he was a character. Other players from other clubs loved him because he liked to talk to the star players of other clubs. He was a football fan.

"When Bobby [Moore] and the West Ham boys came up, or Chelsea, it would be all 'Hi Bobby, you alright?' from Shanks. They all loved him. They thought Shanks was the greatest and that we were lucky. They all thought they would love to have been playing for Bill Shankly.

"It's a funny thing. It's like [Jose] Mourinho gets that now – people say they would like to play for Mourinho. I mean, even Steven Gerrard said he would have liked to play for Mourinho. It was the same for our club because players wanted to play for Bill Shankly. That's a good selling point, isn't it?"

With another laugh, St John answers his own question. Shankly was one of life's natural salesmen. He convinced players to join him, persuaded directors to stump up the money to sign them, and inspired an entire club to follow his direction. And first impressions counted.

"Dynamic" is St John's succinct description of his first impression of Shankly. "A very dynamic man. You meet a lot of people in your life, some who are very quiet with little to say for themselves. Well, he was the complete opposite. He was a whirlwind. He would just take over."

It's an uncannily similar description to the one Glenbuck's Tom Hazle used to describe Willie Shankly in the village, holding sway over the lads gathered on street corners as he held forth on football and all else besides. St John adds, "He knew what he wanted, he could convince people like me to come to Liverpool, convinced the fans we were going to be the best team and as it turned out... well, he did it. He said 'I told you before, I told you. If you didn't believe me then you believe me now, eh?'"

Callaghan concurs. "He was charismatic. You walked into a room or he walked down a corridor, and you'd see him dressed immaculately – he was just one of these guys you listened to.

"I didn't see an awful lot of him as an amateur, he used to come down occasionally and watch us train. But he asked me to sign professional. I said, 'Well, I'm an apprentice, you'll have to come down and see my mum and dad.' As soon as he walked in the house, he promised my mum and dad he'd look after me, which he did do. I had 14 wonderful seasons with him.

"He had a great effect. We were very young, I was only 17 when I signed... and he had an effect on your life, really. You respected him. He had this way about him, an extrovert without going over the top, but when he spoke you listened.

"This was one of the things about the Liverpool team when he was there. He could motivate people like nobody else. He could get people to go out and play for him, give that '100%' all the time. That's the way he was. It was his greatest strength. Whatever walk of life he was in he would have been able to motivate people. He had this gift.

"He just had this way about him. You respected him so much and wanted to win for him as well as for yourself and everyone else. If you gave everything – even if you hadn't actually played well, but put the effort and commitment in – he was made up with that."

Shankly and Callaghan had a strong bond. They had effectively joined the club at the same time and grown into their Liverpool careers together. The manager once said of the player, "He is everything good that a man can be. No praise is too high for him. Words cannot do justice to the amount he has contributed to the game. Ian Callaghan will go down as one of the game's truly great players." How could anyone resist that and not give that '100%' and more every time, all of the time?

Callaghan tells a story that speaks volumes about the relationship between player and boss. "There's an incident which will stay with me for the rest of my life. It was when we won the FA Cup in 1974 against Newcastle. That year I was the first Liverpool player to win the Football Writers' Player of the Year.

"We were down in London and the awards were on a Thursday evening. We weren't going to go to the dinner; we were going to go just after for the presentation because it was before the Cup Final. I remember getting there and just sort of looking in and they had a top table of players – well, what a line-up, a table full of players who'd won the award before.

"My bottle went. Shanks must have seen this and he just put his arm round me. He said 'Son, you get out of this game what you put in. Now go in there and enjoy it – you deserve it.'

"And it calmed me down because I had to give a speech. He had this way about him of saying something or just touching you on the shoulder which reassured you."

That closeness Shankly had with his players brought difficulties too. When the time came to change things, to bring in new blood, and implement the unavoidable removal of the old guard, Shankly found the process tough. His natural instinct as a people person who loved company, and especially that of footballers, was at odds with the brutal but necessary cull of players deemed to be past their useful best.

It was the case with St John. The two were similar in many respects. Small in stature but committed and competitive as players, and with a shared Scottish heritage, they had an inevitable bond, intensified from the beginning. When the board hesitated at spending the record £37,500 transfer fee needed to bring St John south, Shankly is said to have exclaimed 'we can't afford not to buy him'. St John rewarded the outlay and Shankly's faith. He was pivotal to the success of the manager's first successful Liverpool side, scoring and creating goals aplenty. But the end was messy.

"Oh, my departure, you mean?" St John laughs on being asked about the handling of the parting of the ways when it came in 1971. It's a different take to previous comments, when St John has expressed no little anger over how he was dropped by his manager. Perhaps the years have mellowed the resentment, for his reflection now is more philosophical and fatalistic.

"The truth is he got close to all his players. We were his first team. He'd managed elsewhere of course, at Carlisle, Grimsby, Huddersfield and that, but we were his first team that brought him what he wanted in football; the winning of championships, cup finals, being in Europe – the glory. All the things he wanted of his teams as a manager. We were the first team to deliver that. So he had a closeness with everybody.

"The break-up when it came – he couldn't really handle it. It was the first time he had to do it. It wasn't as if he was just letting a lad go who had been a year at the club or whatever, or wasn't good enough. Me and the rest of the lads had been the team that had got Liverpool where they were. The time comes for us all and we all knew that, it happens to everybody in football, but you're the last person to know, really, that *your* time has come. You always feel you've got another season in you and I did. Obviously he didn't, but he couldn't handle it. He couldn't sit me down and talk about it. He did it in a strange way of announcing the team and I wasn't even in the dressing room. He could have told me the day before, he could have told me the morning of the game.

"I didn't understand it and he didn't want to face it. He just didn't want to face it. It wasn't just me, it was with Roger Hunt, Ronnie Yeats, Gordon Milne, all the lads that played through that ten years with him, he never did it right with anybody."

It's a familiar refrain, of the rejected player. Listen to any ex-pro and it's rare to find one who'll say their demise was handled right. But St John maintains things could have been done differently.

"Its never going to be palatable for the player, but I think a manager should sit down face to face with a player and say 'look son, I'm going to have to leave you out, we've all got to move forward', that sort of stuff – a bit of fanny, really, if you like, how you've been great for him, that kind of thing.

"Bob Paisley pulled me aside the day it happened. He said, 'Look, it happens. You know what happened with me? I played in the FA Cup semi final [in 1950 against Everton], I scored and I never got played in the final.' It made me realise, Christ, that's a worse story than mine. That was the way to do it.

"It's hard to take. It's like a bereavement. It is. Like a bereavement. Being left out. You're not playing, something you've been part of for ten years. All of a sudden you're not part of it. It needs somebody to put a hand on the shoulder. But the boss could not do that, he turned away from it. As if it would manage itself. You're supposed to just accept it and walk away."

St John peppers his references to Shankly with the term 'the boss'.

"I would never call him Bill, or even Mr Shankly," he says, laughing again. "It was always 'boss'. All the boys called him boss, to this day we do. I suppose it was like the Mafia, he was the boss of bosses!"

More laughter. And more affectionate memories. "He loved the gangster movies. On a Friday night before a game we'd watch a film. We were all brought up on the gangster movies and he absolutely loved them. He was a big James Cagney fan and he'd sort of impersonate him. Without him realising it, I think, he had his mannerisms. He looked like him – didn't have the accent, mind."

The smiles and laughter, and the enduring terms of endearment show the pain of being dropped has dissipated. "I had a fall-out with him but it didn't last long. It wasn't long before we kissed and made up. After that he would always seek you out and have a chat. When I was on the television I went down and did interviews with him and he was great."

In those interviews when St John became a major TV star, the past was left where it was. The break-up was never discussed. "No, because that would be like me saying 'you made a mistake'. It was water under the bridge, what was done was done. I think he knew he hadn't handled things well, but you can't go back on it, we just picked up the friendship on a different level.

"In fact, he helped me when I was manager at Motherwell and then, unfortunately, he tried to help me with Portsmouth as well. The chairman John Deacon had asked the boss about who he should get the [Portsmouth manager's job, in 1974] and Shanks put me in the frame. So he phones me up, Shanks, and says, 'I've got this man from Portsmouth, I've told him you're the man. It's a great club.'

"Of course he remembered it from the war when Pompey were a big team because they had everybody in the army, air force and navy turning out for them – they had the pick of Britain. So Shanks was thinking they were still great and dropped me in it! I told him that later on and he said, 'Oh, I know son.' So at the end of the day he done me twice! But as it turned out I went into TV and another career. So in that respect it turned out fine."

On the whole it turned out very fine for all those Shankly brought to Liverpool, including the Scots among them. There were four in that 1965 cup side, among a roster of outstanding Caledonian talents in Division One like Denis Law, Dave Mackay, Billy Bremner, and Frank McLintock, continuing the fine tradition of Scotland sending its players down to England to teach the southerners a thing or two. Shankly had been one himself and there was a deep understanding on his part of the culture they came from.

Callaghan did not notice a particular tendency for Shankly to confide in his compatriots, but St John was made fully aware of what 'the boss' thought about some aspects of their shared heritage.

"The first thing I remember him saying in the dressing room – and there was a few Scots in there, including Ronnie and myself

– Shanks said, 'If anybody mentions Celtic or Rangers in this dressing room, they're out.' Being Scottish we were all brought up on that bloody Celtic–Rangers bigotry. It's a terrible thing and it could split football clubs way back then. He said 'if I hear anybody mention it, they're out the door'. So he put the clamp right on it. Nobody would dare mention Celtic or Rangers, meaning of course Catholics or Protestants.

"We would never ever know Bill Shankly as anything other than a football man, he was never into all that bloody bigotry. He hated it."

This was another legacy of Glenbuck, the determination to instil collective purpose and ignore any sectarian divides. It begs the question – did Shankly talk much about his home village to the players?

"Sometimes. When he moved south as a professional, he would go back in the summer, for longer breaks than they have today and he'd have plenty of time. So he'd go back home and get the football going there again. He'd see his parents and that and just play football. That's what he did for his summer holiday!

"He would talk a bit about being a miner and all the fellas up there, the great characters that he knew. He got a love for the gambling up there. I remember as a kid myself, people loved a gamble with the 'tossing schools'. You'd have them all squatting or sitting in a circle. A guy would have a little piece of wood with two coins on it; he'd toss them and you'd have bets on two heads, or two tails, whatever, and they would sit there doing that for hours. Miners were used to crouching from working in tunnels and tiny passages.

"So Shanks would be up there in the summer, when he came home and he'd be there for the tossing schools. I'd seen the same thing operating in Motherwell. The boss liked a bet – he did. He wasn't a compulsive gambler or anything like that, but he'd like a little bet. And he liked the card schools, they had those and the tossing schools at Glenbuck. He played cards on the coach with the lads. I'm laughing at the memory, he'd squeeze the cards so close to his chest to keep his hand hidden, even if you were standing right behind him you couldn't see what he had. I think that was how he was brought up in those Glenbuck card schools, you didn't show anyone what was in your hand.

"They only played for shillings. But he stopped the gambling on the coach eventually because he was losing too much, not *that* much, the most you'd lose would be a pound. He reckoned the players were fixing it. I wasn't a gambler; I just used to stand there watching and he said 'this is a fix!' But the ban only lasted two weeks and then they started playing again."

More laughs. More recollections of the fun to be had under the boss of Liverpool FC in the 1960s. Not so much of the dwelling on the past, and the tough life Shankly had left behind.

"Did he talk about childhood, and working down the mines? No, only that he was glad he got away from it. For his generation it was a mining village and it was the only work they had, really, and they wanted to get out of the pits. He had a great admiration of miners. He would occasionally talk about people who worked up there, but not that much, really.

"You see, people get injuries in football and knocks, things like that. They are so trivial by comparison. Shanks knew what being hurt really meant – pit accidents, roof falls, people dying in the mines for Christ's sakes. So you could not, believe me, ever moan about anything. You could never moan about an injury. No. Because the comparison with the miners – well, there was no comparison. 'Don't you moan about bloody anything', was what he'd think. He'd tell us we were blessed, to be running about in the fresh air kicking a ball. Other guys are going down a pit."

Shankly, the great communicator and football evangelist, made sure his players knew they were privileged. They admired, respected, loved him for it. Even opponents did. "He's a universal figure," says Callaghan. "Even Everton fans, they all loved him. Brian Labone was a big mate of mine who lived in the next road, and he loved Shankly. He used to love to meet him. He said it was a joy to meet him, because he was so charismatic. That's how Everton fans, everybody just liked him, respected him.

"The fans relate to him and Liverpool today, which is a worldwide club, and this man was there at the start of it. Without him where would it be today? The man was very special; there'll never be anyone like him again. They broke the mould when they made him."

Back in the 1960s when Liverpool were gathering cups for fun and after the formal occasions to mark the triumph were dispensed with, the players often celebrated as they did at the time with a pint in the pub among the people who paid to watch them. It was an age far removed from the social chasm that now exists between footballer and supporter. Shanks, of course, the teetotaller, wouldn't have been in the pub, but he would allow his players their celebrations and understood full well the joy shared with the fans. Because, as St John says, "He was a man of the people. That's been said a lot, but what's key is that, OK, he had been a player and manager, and very successful, but at heart he was still a fan. He was a fan of it all, he loved meeting players whoever they played for. You half expected him to get out an autograph book and get them to sign it, because he was such a fan. The greater the player, the greater the awe.

"You had to meet him and know him to understand what football meant to him – the players and fans. Not the administrators and directors.

"It was the people."

Chapter 13

Man of the People

WHEN the 1965 FA Cup Final was won, the joy on the final whistle among the Liverpool fans was manifest. One man more than any other understood the elation. Amid the celebrations at Wembley, Bill Shankly ventured on to the muddy turf and went straight to the massed ranks of delirious supporters from Merseyside, as they hailed the victory and its chief architect. Arm aloft, fist clenched, Shankly communed with his congregation. He always – always – maintained that it was the fans he and the players were working for, and now he shared in their delirium. Robert Burns, Glenbuck, the dedication to collective endeavour – that rainy May day in 1965, Shankly's ideological circle was firmly squared. He said of that moment, "I went to the supporters because they had got the Cup for the first time. Grown men were crying and it was the greatest feeling any human could have to see what we had done. There have been many proud moments in my career, wonderful, fantastic moments. But that was the greatest day."

Shankly also once said, "If you're a member of the Kop, you feel as if you are a member of a big society... I identified myself with the people because the game belongs to the people." Shankly was speaking specifically about Liverpool, but his sentiments rang true for fans of all clubs in all kinds of communities, and beyond borders. What applied to Liverpool was equally valid for Barcelona or Buenos Aires. It was the solidarity of the tiny pit village writ large – the ethos of Glenbuck on a global scale.

Shankly took to the fans and they reciprocated with unswerving devotion. As the *When Saturday Comes* book adeptly put it, 'No other manager before or since has attracted such an evangelical cult of personality, both among supporters of [Liverpool] and in the wider culture of the game: wisecracking, passionate and political, and defiantly a man of the people.'

So, on a bright, sunny spring day some of the people have taken their reverent place at the foot of a gentle hill. A lone piper strikes up a familiar tune and emotions swirl in harmony with the high, echoing notes.

Amazing Grace has its characteristic effect, the hymn adopted as an African-American spiritual prompting a strange kind of inspirational sadness. Then the piper plays another, altogether contrasting medley, adapted from of all things a reactionary film from 1968.

The Green Berets was John Wayne's portrait of America's military role in Vietnam. In the 1980s, a man called Phil Aspinall stripped away the gung-ho jingoism, took the film's theme tune and adapted it for a group of men who proudly wore and supported different colours – the deep, crimson red of Liverpool FC.

A Liverbird Upon My Chest was Aspinall's arrangement, with lyrics celebrating the grand achievements of one of football's most famous clubs and in particular, the influence of one man. The piper plays the refrain. 'We are men of Shankly's best', chorus the small crowd. Over a century on from the birth of the man in the place where he was raised, right beside his memorial, modern devotees of his unique legacy are still singing his praises.

"It was a great day; a great day," says one of those in attendance. Peter Hooton, singer, songwriter, author and activist, was speaking of how he and a group of Liverpool fans had paid a visit to Glenbuck in 2015. Hooton is better known in some circles as lead singer with

The Farm, the enduring musical pride of Merseyside. The band were formed during the indie heyday of the 1980s and flourished amid the heady era of Britpop, but have lasted longer than many of their contemporaries. The Farm are still playing to decent crowds, and Hooton is still eulogising the man who made his football club what it is.

"Bill Shankly built Liverpool Football Club. The club in the 1950s was Second Division, and I don't think [the owners] knew what they were hiring. They were hiring a whirlwind – almost a revolutionary."

Shankly might have been gone for a generation but he lives on in the hearts and minds of people like Peter and his fellow travellers. They described their visit to Glenbuck as a kind of pilgrimage, and Hooton talked of it with an inescapable reference to religiosity.

"He was Liverpool's spiritual leader and had this connection with the Kop that was like a communion. And he used to talk in those terms, saying 'people don't go to church anymore, they come to Anfield'. So there was a real connection between the crowd and Shankly. As far as people were concerned, like my dad and granddad who talked to me about Shankly, he was the leader. He was more than a manager; he was the embodiment of Liverpool's revival.

"People go to Lourdes or to Mecca, and some Liverpool fans go to Glenbuck. It's the myths that surround him. Shankly has become an iconic figure."

It's a view shared by another proud Liverpudlian whose life has been shaped by Shankly. Tony Evans used to play in The Farm's horn section before becoming a journalist, going on to become the long-time football editor of *The Times*, and an author who has written extensively about the club.

He talks volubly and with personal insight about the man who, like so many of his generation do, he identifies as key in creating Liverpool FC as a something more than just a team that plays football. In their and Evans's eyes, he turned the club into a cultural and political symbol.

"He was absolutely crucial," Evans says of Shankly's importance to the identity of the club. "He came along at just the right time to not only transform a second-rate team and a second-rate club, but to provide a sense of momentum for the whole city. It was a precursor of when the city was about to explode on the world scene in a way that it hadn't done before.

"Shankly grasped almost instinctively what made the fanbase tick – the mentality, what excited it. He tuned into it, harnessed it, focused it behind the club and turned the second team in the city into not only a team that won things but a flag bearer for a sense of identity – a sense of scouse. For an outsider to do that, a Scot, it's amazing, really, notwithstanding the Scottish influences on the city, he understood the scouse mentality, probably in a way no one else seems to, and certainly no one else coming into the city.

"He had a great sense which he always conveyed to you, that you weren't a fan – you were a part of [the club]. When you see it in black and white – 'the Kop sucked the ball into the net' – it can look trite. But when he said it, he made you feel that this fanaticism on the terraces mimicked his and vice versa. He really made you feel you were part of it, which built ties to the club the marketing men of today could never imagine, ties that are impossible to break.

"As much as the club's moved away from what I believe it should and what it stood for, for me... well, this is where I wonder if it was a good thing, I can't drag myself away; the spectre of Bill Shankly drags me back."

Tens of thousands of them keep coming back. Liverpool have been relying on past glories of late, but the club that Shankly built generated such success and support, that its global fanbase is second almost to none. Following on from the shattering blows of Heysel and Hillsborough, the Premier League hasn't been particularly suited to Liverpool and, for whatever reasons, the club has struggled to fully exploit the new league's unequivocally commercial ways. For all the cup successes, the league title Anfield once held to be its own has been elusive. But Liverpool FC is still an undeniably huge club. And for the long-standing supporters, it's about more than glittering prizes.

If anything, Evans believes, Shankly's central role in the story of the club and the city was magnified when he was no longer such a prominent part of it. Jobs started leaking away, and the city came under pressure, politically, economically and socially. "The scouse accent had once again become associated with theft and violence and yet, he created this thing, this flag bearer for us. We'd go to other cities and we'd sing, 'They all laugh at us, they all mock us, they all say our days are numbered but I was born to be scouse, victorious are we.' And you'd feel ten feet tall.

"The team became a sort of political symbol for us, in a way I don't think many other teams are. We're a left-wing fanbase and it was all brought about by Shankly. There endures an idea among supporters of my age that Liverpool is an anti-Establishment flag bearer for a city that no longer is, unfortunately.

"We try to pass it on to the next generation, but it fades and fades as the years go by and the game changes. You could say he was the symbol of another age, but in another way there wasn't anything innocent about it. He knew how it all worked, and he knew that you had to fight for everything you got. And that's a form of socialism – if you don't ask you don't get; if you stay quiet, then no one will hear you."

Evans explains how he feels Shankly created a wider politicisation of the fans. "When Shankly arrived this was a city that didn't really know what to make of itself. Bear in mind that where I came from had an Irish Nationalist MP [T.P. O'Connor] until 1929. The potato-famine generations had gone, the Irish had become scouse, but they weren't quite sure where politically, culturally they stood. There was a confusion in the city.

"So Shankly was really important in creating the modern notion of what it meant to be 'scouse'. It was a derogatory word for people who ate 'scouse', a stew, but was turned into a term of pride. Shankly took the quite directionless thing and centred it around the club...

"He focused and fostered that sense of not being 'Establishment' so that Liverpool fans became the symbol of 'scouseness'. Everton fans will argue that, but while their fanbase was politicised, it wasn't quite as politicised as ours.

"If it was just about football that would be fine, but it was more than that. Football was politics to him and politics was life, football was life. I was aware of it from when I was very young that I was a socialist and aware of the team I supported. The iconography as well – the Liver Bird, the symbol of the city on the shirt, the blood-red, and at the top Shankly, one of the greatest left-wing orators I'll ever come across."

It helps to illustrate why Bill Shankly is so revered in Liverpool beyond his footballing achievements, though those successes are, naturally, fundamental to his appeal. Together they perhaps explain why Peter Hooton and a coachload of other fans made the trip up to Ayrshire on the 50th anniversary of the 1965 FA Cup win, a victory some Reds fans maintain really instigated Liverpool's rise to dominate English and European football.

"You've got to remember that the cup victory was very symbolic, says Hooton. "Shankly used to say it was an absolute disgrace Liverpool had never won it. Evertonians used to give Liverpool fans a lot of stick because they had won twice before, whereas we'd been to two finals and lost.

"There was this mythology that Liverpool wouldn't win the cup until the Liver Birds flew off the Liver building and all that type of nonsense going on. So Shankly, by winning the cup, he went down as a legendary figure anyway, even if he did nothing else.

"That's why we came up. We wanted to recognise the 50th anniversary by going up to Glenbuck which is Shanks's spiritual home. Everyone came away saying that's one of the greatest away days we've had."

Around 30 Liverpool fans made the trip. Among their number were plenty of Anfield fan legends including Aspinall. The piper was Hooton's friend from Glasgow, Celtic supporter Andy Devers. The pair have a shared background in the field of community work with disadvantaged young people and, naturally, a love for football. The combination of the two men's experiences, in a place where football did so much to claw young people from the dispiriting grip of poverty, gave the occasion added poignancy.

It was a grand day out, even for a venture into the place that was once regarded as bandit country for proud Glenbuckians. "We went to Muirkirk," said Hooton. "Everyone was so welcoming; they put on pea soup and scouse, and loads of sandwiches. I think they were just made up that he is remembered that way. My philosophy is you've got to learn off people like Shankly – the way he lived his life, his take on life in general, not just football."

Indeed, for Hooton and others of similar mind, Glenbuck's most famous son has provided inspiration way beyond football. For men like Evans, it is political. He recalls how in his childhood Shankly was an 'over-arching figure' who filled his view of football much more than the players. Evans believes that while Shankly journeyed from a very small and mining community with a 'mono-culture', into a big and diverse city, there was a strong shared identity.

"What they had in common was socialism and a very left-wing attitude. People mistake socialism and what it stands for. Shankly is the perfect example of what it should be about. It's the socialism of aspiration, where you know what, you'll get the opportunity to go as far as you can and you want to go to the top. It's not a case of taking from people, you want to earn everything, but it is a collective effort, and that for those who don't have the ability, there's a safety net for them. It's almost an 'American Dream' point of view – you work hard, and you go as far as you like.

"Shankly with his strong socialist belief, was about getting as far as you can do, but by working together. The message he sent out to everyone was it wasn't about sitting still; it was about going forward – being the best. It came at a time when the Beatles were projecting the city worldwide."

Evans pours scorn on the accusatory cliché that Liverpool is the self-pity city. "It's quite the opposite. It's where the people say they're the best in the world and they're not going to take anything lying down, they're going to fight back. Shankly had that mentality. There's not an ounce of self-pity, he picked up on that and said 'alright, let's do it together.'

"It's the power of the man. You see football managers who have charisma, people like Mourinho. And he does have charisma, albeit with political views at the other end of the scale. You think 'he's great – but he's a football manager'. Shankly was more than that. His intensity never took a day off. What he did was he transplanted something as stupid as football, a daft game, so deep in your sense of self and your sense of politics that in fact I often wonder if it was a bad thing. It's coloured and influenced my entire life. Bill Shankly has, in many ways, sent me in every direction I've gone. You've got people who are religiously fundamentalist saying 'what would Jesus do?' You'd ask yourself 'what would Shankly do?'"

Evans laughs at the notion, but he's not alone. Hooton too finds humour in his own devotion. "I grew up as a kid with Shankly. My family were always trying to get me pulled away to Mass, but he appealed to me more. I always think, even now, if there are any dilemmas and conundrums, you should always ask yourself 'what would Shankly do?' Because if you take his philosophy, you won't go far wrong."

It is an ethos that also underpins the work of a burgeoning supporter movement in which Hooton, his colleagues, and like-minded supporters across the nation, are engaged. The fan activism that is behind campaigns such as the 'Twenty's Plenty' ticket pricing scheme, designed to peg the price of away tickets to £20 in England, is imbued with the spirit of the early days of supporter fanzines in the 1980s, a period again when Hooton was prominent.

He was one of the originators of the famous fanzine *The End* – a hand-made publication that transcended Merseyside, northern and even national football rivalries to give a voice to people hitherto ignored by the football and journalistic mainstream. *The End* championed terrace culture, warts and all, revelling in its fun, thrills, and glories while being painfully honest about its darker aspects. It was innovative, irreverent, and hugely influential, cited as an inspiration to everything from *Loaded* magazine to much of how newspapers cover football today.

Hooton had and continues to have a prime role in the celebration and championing of that football fan culture, and in particular for a group named in honour of the man whose views on the sport and life in general chime with so many supporters – the Spirit of Shankly.

Set up in 2008 as the first supporters' 'union', it has a series of short- and long-term aims, from ticket pricing to the ultimate ambition of fan ownership. The nature of the group is avowedly political, carrying one of Shankly's famous maxims as a motto: "The socialism I believe in is everyone working for each other, everyone having a share of the rewards. It's the way I see football, the way I see life."

Formed amid the chaos of the Tom Hicks and George Gillett regime at Anfield, the Spirit of Shankly (SOS) aims to put those principles into practice. Not every fan supports its activities – no supporter group has ever had universal support – but in response to the naked commercial speculation that has been running riot through the game, SOS have tapped into a discontent widespread across the sport.

"When Hicks and Gillett took over, it became obvious the Americans had put debt on the club like the Glazers did with Man Utd," says Hooton. "They said they weren't going to do that. We started getting leaks and claims saying no, they had done exactly what the Glazers did – borrowing assets against the club. There was a period in January 2008 where there was a lot of turmoil – people on forums and fanzines, people who ran coaches to games – trying to work out what to do.

"I found out that there was this Liverpool network that said they were going to hold a meeting – a select group of people. So I got in touch and said 'it's a good idea, this, but why don't you open it up for the wider fanbase – that's what Shankly would have wanted.'

"So I said 'look, let's do it as a mass meeting, don't have little vested interests, lets just open it up to anyone who wants to go. Some people were umming and aahing, saying 'don't want to do that, it'll be chaos', etc. But in the end we did it. I got a chair in called Paul Rice who has sadly passed away. He chaired Broadgreen Labour Party during the days of the Labour Council in Liverpool, so I knew if he could chair the Broadgreen Labour Party, he could do anything.

"He chaired it, it was a great meeting, 300 people, all different factions and it wasn't just people who write for fanzines, or people who write on forums, there were all sorts there – it was a cross section; business people, urchins. All sorts.

"We thought we're going to try to save the club, because we owed it to Shankly. He built it, and if we go into liquidation, all those years of hard work and what had gone on since 1959 when he came to the club would have been lost.

"We did it in his honour really, that's why it could never have been called the Spirit of Dalglish or Spirit of Paisley, it had to be Shanks. Because he built the club up. He called it the biggest toilet on Merseyside when he arrived. Within a few weeks he was out with all the groundstaff painting it. They didn't even have running water at the training round at Melwood – it was just a shed."

The degree to which that spirit has survived the commercialisation of the modern game is variable. "If you want to draw a family tree now that Steven Gerrard has left," Evans says, "he was brought through by Steve Heighway who was brought into the club by Shankly – so you could say the break is happening now. The last boot-room manager in a sense was Roy Evans and then they brought in [Gerard] Houllier, but he had been teaching locally in the 1960s and 1970s. He went to watch Liverpool and was fascinated by this phenomenon happening around him. The last vestiges have gone now, the sense of the importance of the club to the city and in part that's due, I think, to the globalisation of the game. The ownership are more interested in a foreign fanbase than a scouse one.

"Shankly was very keen on making Liverpool a very fierce source of civic pride. Steven is the last of that breed that had that civic pride in being scouse. Shankly never underestimated the importance of that, even though he himself wasn't."

Evans believes Rafa Benitez "got it, though not at first. He became exposed to the support base during the war with Gillett and Hicks and found in the supporters' group the Spirit of Shankly, the spirit of Shankly! And became kind of obsessed with it. He's manager of Real Madrid [but] if Liverpool offered him the job tomorrow, he'd leave. He hasn't got the same charisma [as Shankly] but in his own way he's got the same one-eyed insanity. He saw the belief, passion from young lads like James McKenna to people of my generation like Peter Hooton, Benitez saw what the club meant. So, as much as a Spanish outsider can, he gets it."

Evans's former band-mate also recognises the significance of Glenbuck in the story. "If you look at the village, it had what, 1,000 occupants? It was an isolated village, just imagine what it was like when Shankly was born in 1913. They all had to work together because of the hardships, they all had to club together, and in a village like that it was everyone co-operating. He said it about the greatest form of socialism being a football team.

"I think that's been lost in the mists of time because that's what it is. If you've got one person who isn't pulling his weight, or even two people, it's not as good a team.

"Everyone has to pull together, and share the weight. That's the teamwork. Socialism is a word that has got various connotations now because of various factors, but if you look at what teamwork is it's what Shankly was talking about.

"Certainly it shaped his philosophy and he took that into his managerial career – that was everyone working for the same ends, wearing the shirt."

The pride in Shankly is obvious and convincingly asserted. A common perception about Shankly's Liverpool sides and those of his successor Bob Paisley is that they were functional rather than expansive – the 'Red Machine' of football lore. Hooton rejects that, pointing to players such as Keegan, Heighway and later Kenny Dalglish, but concurs with the wider view that it was collective effort that was at the heart of the side.

"They were schooled in the team ethic. And they were very aspirational. People talk now about the Labour Party having to respond to aspiration – that to me is the biggest insult to working-class people. Are they saying working-class people aren't aspirational? Of course they are... when I hear people say that I shake my head. They haven't got a clue.

"Shankly was totally aspirational – he wanted to build Liverpool into a team and quoted Napoleon about conquering the bloody world – what's more aspirational than that?"

Today Glenbuck, tomorrow the world. It's a pretty remarkable story. The kind of fable that can capture the imaginations of star-struck kids and inspire them to do the best they can.

Tony Evans should know. He was there. He was one of those kids who would gather outside Anfield, hoping to catch a moment with their idol. Not Keegan, or Toshack, or Heighway or Hughes, but the little Scotsman in the tracksuit or the understated but smart suit.

"He was awe-inspiring but accessible. You only had to go up to the ground during the school holiday and he'd talk to you. I met him loads of times. He had more than charisma, there was something of the messiah about him, there was a conviction and a belief and he wasn't going to let you not believe.

"You'd have your book for autographs. He'd come out and he's say 'Ah son, son, no, I've got to get back to Nessie.' So you'd say 'OK, but Bill, just before you go, how good's George Best?' And he'd go 'Ah George, great son, he could play, had everything George Best.' So then you'd say, 'Was he as good as Finney?' And he'd stop dead, give the 1,000 yard stare, and he'd go 'Tommy... Tommy was the greatest!' and he'd be off.

"It was infectious. The kids would be silenced. There was something of the prophet about him, the preacher. I'd imagine him as a benign demagogue dictator or a fundamentalist preacher. He had that ability to shut up a crowd with a word. We sometimes have those moments, in the pub or whatever, when you know you've got your audience there's silence and you know you have people's attention. You have it for a second and then it goes. 'I had charisma there for a second!' you think. Shanks had it. He exuded it. When you saw and talked to him, you could not help but believe."

Shankly practised what he preached. Not simply in his well-documented generosity but his willingness to utilise his position and influence. Evans recalls the family of a friend who lived on the corner of Kemlyn Road and Anfield Road and who were experiencing repeated problems associated with living right by a football ground. "His mother was always going round to see [club secretary] Peter Robinson. Whenever she encountered a dead end she'd collar Shankly and he'd sort it out. There were stories, and they're true, of people who couldn't get housing from the council; they'd ask Shankly to help them, and he'd go down and cause havoc, next thing they knew they'd have a house."

At the heart of it all, though, was the total love of the game. Barbara Alexander and the extended family saw it, so too did Ian Callaghan and Ian St John. And so did the group of wide-eyed little scouse kids hanging around Anfield and hanging on his every word.

"There's a story that when a policeman kicked a scarf off a pitch," Evans remembers, "Shankly said, 'Don't do that, you're kicking someone's dreams.' He believed that. There was an innocence about him in that sense. If it had gone the wrong way it could have been a really dangerous thing. But there was also a warmth and an inclusiveness about him. He appeared to love people, he wanted to talk to them, encourage them.

"If you turned up at the ground on a day when you should have been at school, he'd tell you off. 'Aw, I was sick today, Bill.' 'Well, then you should be at school this afternoon!' And it was a good telling off.

"We lived quite near the ground, it was only ten minutes' walk. You'd go to Anfield and wait for the bus to come back from Melwood. They'd all go off with the kit, shower, have something to eat and then come back out about 45 minutes, an hour later. Most of the time he'd talk. There'd be 30 or 40 kids, little boys trying to have a word with him, getting him to sign hundreds of autographs.

"Shankly would say 'I've got to go,' but more often than not he'd get distracted and stay and talk. It would almost be like a mini seminar, talking football, life, politics – everything.

"Most of the time he'd talk about football. We quickly picked up that if you asked about the 'Preston Plumber', [Shankly] would go off all day. During the three-day week, when they couldn't play games under floodlights, he'd say, 'Terrible times, terrible times – but the working man's got to fight.' He would talk predominantly about football, for obvious reasons, but there was no sense of a one-track mind.

"He had that robust intellectualism of the working class – there was nothing smart-arsey about him. He never patronised you. He'd talk about almost anything. There was a lot of the comedian about him. Very interested in history; he'd just chat. He talked to us as equals.

"The first time you spoke to him you'd be nervous but he had that way of speaking that was both portentous but also put you at ease. Here we are, 40 years on, I can still see him on a sunny day, a circle of boys around him, talking to us and absolute silence when he talked. No one drifted away from the group, no one said 'what's this old fella on about?' When he talked, you listened."

It seems a world and an age away – something for the sporting history books rather than very much living memory. But what would Shanks make of the modern game?

"I think," Evans says, "he'd be really disappointed by the lack of application from some players. He'd be very perturbed by the lack of atmosphere. As for the commercialisation of the game, I think he'd see the positive side of it and the players getting paid. It's a myth that in terms of the finances of the game, that the players are the problem. People have always taken money out of the game, and the players have had the least of it. So I think he'd be pleased about that.

"What would shock him, I think, is the anger and the lack of pleasure people take out if it. The modern supporter relates to the game largely through television, and I think Shankly would be shocked by the rage for their own team and the opposition.

"You see, what people don't understand, the thing that keeps getting thrown up is that quote 'the matter of life and death'. When he originally said that it was a press conference and Shankly quipped 'no, it's more important than that'. Everyone laughed, and he started doing it as a party piece. When I met him, even though I was a kid, I knew few people who knew more than Shankly that football *wasn't* a matter of life or death. Yeah he wanted to win – by God he wanted to fight to win, but he bounced back up the next morning, rallied the troops and went on. He realised this was not the be all and end all."

It's why Evans refutes the commonly held perception that in retirement Shankly was lost and depressed. "This portrayal of him as a sad and lonely old man. Shankly was irrepressible.

"One night I'd been to an Everton game at Goodison about 1975. I was hanging around the players' entrance; I would have been 14, looking to get players' autographs. Shankly came out. The place was full of Everton fans. He started signing a few autographs

216

and walking along and people start following him, asking him questions.

"Off Goodison Road, up around Stanley Park we get to Anfield Cemetery and there's about 30 people following him. He was like the Pied Piper. Before we know it we're up by Bellefield near his house. He says, 'Boys, boys, I'm going to have to say goodbye to you now. I'd invite you all in for a drink, but Nessie wouldn't like it.' And he'd bid us all farewell. You'd walked three-and-a-half miles out of your way but you didn't mind because Shankly was holding court. There'd be two or three Liverpudlians there, but the vast majority of them Evertonians and they followed him all the way.

"Bill didn't have to sit all lonely in cafes. People were attracted to him. I can see he would have had disappointments, but when you saw him around town, he'd have that Cagney swagger. No one was keeping Bill Shankly down, and that was the message from him: 'No one should keep you down.'

"That's why he's more important than football. Football isn't a matter of life and death but behaving in the right manner, acting in the right manner not taking things lying down, and fighting for yourself and what you believe in, is. That's what he gave to people of my generation, and that's why he's so important to us. He got that from where he came from, without a doubt, from that small mining community.

"Even in a city which was so much bigger, he made you feel you were part of a close-knit community centred around a football club – even for those Everton fans walking back with him that night. In many ways I often think he missed his vocation. He should have been a politician, a socialist leader. I'm sure they would have tried to grind him down into the ground, but he would have come back. In many ways it's a disappointment he was a football manager.

"Although, the years of pleasure he gave me through that, I'll take it."

Chapter 14

Scars

IN 1913, the year of Bill Shankly's birth, the field workers of the Royal Commission of Housing (Scotland) came calling to Glenbuck. They rooted around the houses on Grasshill Row. The dwellings were owned by William Baird and Co, who as part of the Baird's and Dalmellington group, later held domain over a number of Ayrshire pits in pre-Nationalisation days.

The officials were not impressed. For seven shillings a month, the residents of the 33 two-roomed 'apartments' (three were empty) were housed in conditions worthy of a Dickens novel set a century before.

There was, the commissioners reported, 'a dry-closet for every four tenants, formerly without doors but now protected by sparred gates, with locks. The peculiarity of these closets is that each of them could accommodate two persons; in fact are seated to do so... the ashpits were very dirty... The footpaths are unpaved and dirty, with dirty sluggish open syvors [sic] in front... the sewage runs in an open drain until it reaches the main road 20 or 30 yards away, and, we are told, smells badly in the summer.'

About the same time, Alec Douglas Home, future 14th Earl of Home, Prime Minister-in-waiting, and distant descendant of the medieval Douglas clan that hunted the Buck of the Glen in the 14th century, was finishing his prep-school education before moving on to Eton. Six hundred years on from those days of lord and peasant, and Glenbuck was still very much a 'them and us' kind of place. The 'us' were finding it hard going.

The story of the end of British coal mining is dominated in modern minds by the 1984 strike and the bitter showdown between the free market and organised labour, but the industry's decimation began much earlier in little backwaters like Glenbuck. Save for bursts of activity, usually fuelled by wartime demand, coal production in Ayrshire started to decline.

The common term for the reason is 'exhaustion' which tells only part of the story. There was and still is a substantial amount of high-quality coal in the region – so good that it was said you could light a lump of the stuff directly with a match, rather than need kindling – but it became uneconomical or impracticable to mine under the models of both private and public ownership.

The last Glenbuck pit, Grasshill, finally closed for good in 1934, but the die had been cast earlier. The village still provided a home for miners but now they had to travel to Muirkirk, or further afield to find work. The Kames pit was where many headed, like Sam Purdie in 1953, the last in a long line of miners. He followed in the footsteps of his own father, who was one of those Glenbuck pitmen now having to head west. Purdie's grandfather might have joined them, had his spine not been broken in the Grasshill in the early 1930s.

There was great hope for the miners on 1 January 1947 on 'Vesting Day' – the day the industry was finally nationalised. At the coalface however, little changed. "The same men were working in the same pits for the same wages and the same managers. *Plus ca change, plus c'est la meme chose,*" as Purdie pithily remembers it.

Tragedy awaited. On 19 November 1957, Kames was the scene of a terrible disaster, when poor ventilation and lax inspection contributed to an explosion deep underground that claimed 17 lives, among them two Glenbuck veterans, Tom Burnside and Bill Smith, and 18-year-old Tam Casey.

Kames was rebuilt and modernised. But other mines in other places could not preserve Glenbuck. People started to leave around the time the Cherrypickers were doing their finest, and the population figure began its long slow descent to zero. By 1922 the mining companies were selling off property. Two of the best known, Vass's Place and Auchenstilloch Cottages, better known to all as Monkey Row, were being auctioned off for £150 and £177 respectively, but with no takers. It was left to a local farm owner to buy them in a private and presumably knockdown-price deal.

Life in the village was always testing but it had got harder. As if to magnify the problems the villagers had to endure, Glenbuck played host to a dreadful saga that exists in complete contrast to the happy success of its footballers. On the afternoon of Thursday 2 April 1908, a young woman who had been in Glenbuck to visit her mother and father on Grasshill Row walked to high ground on the village outskirts. She was joined by a man familiar to her – all too well-known, in fact – and the pair headed towards the railway station before a torrential downpour made them take shelter in a farm shed. There they were heard arguing by a local shepherd who advised them to go home. They headed off in the direction of Muirkirk and the woman was never seen alive again. The man had savagely attacked her, kicking her to death.

The awful story had begun three years earlier in 1905 and the marriage of one of the Bones, Thomas Jnr, nicknamed 'Jew', to a local woman called Agnes Campbell. He was 25, an occasional miner and a frequent troublemaker who had already done time for violence and criminal damage. She was 17 and a second cousin of Bone. Right from the start, the relationship was troubled and, despairing of Bone changing his dangerously aggressive ways, Agnes left him for her own safety. Increasingly possessive and enraged, his mood often worsened by drink, Bone stalked Agnes, relentlessly pursuing her in a vain attempt to win her back. It led to various threats, attacks and charges, from malicious mischief to assault. He was imprisoned four times, but nothing appeared to dissuade him.

On the fateful day in 1908, Agnes's mother Helen had written to tell her not to visit, knowing Bone was back in the village and still brooding over the rejection. Tragically, Agnes did not receive the letter in time.

After their fateful meeting, Bone strode back to the village and was seen washing his hands in the burn. He then went home to his aunt Mary's house where he admitted his crime to her and his cousin, bizarrely offering a handshake. The cousin refused in disgust. Bone then confessed further to other relatives and neighbours, and reportedly marched off up to the abandoned Lady pit to throw himself down the shaft left open by the owners when the pit closed. By now a confused and excitable crowd had gathered. Bone pulled back from committing suicide and continued to describe what he had done. A group of miners set off to find out what had happened and 500 yards away discovered Agnes's corpse. Her body was said to be so horribly battered that some of the men broke down and collapsed.

Police eventually arrived and with the women of the village aiming what the *Cumnock Chronicle* described as 'a perfect roar of detestation and indignation hurled at the object of their hatred', Bone was taken away. When he went on trial for murder in Glasgow just a month later he pleaded guilty. The stunned judge, Lord Ardwall, asked him to heed the advice of his counsel and reconsider. 'No,' said Bone, 'I have a higher poo'er [power] to face nor [than] you, an' for that reason I plead guilty.'

The trial went ahead regardless, with a number of witnesses testifying to Bone's temper, rage and threats to 'kick the bloody head off her.' Their names included Davidson, Weir, Bone, Milliken and Bain, members of long-standing, inter-related Glenbuck families horrified at what had happened in their close-knit village. One had seen Bone on the ridge, silhouetted against the sky, stamping at something on the ground; the witness thought

Bone might have been killing a rabbit. He couldn't have imagined it was a human being. Glenbuck people helped each other; they certainly did not murder each other.

The case was as clear-cut as it could be. The jury deliberated for just ten minutes before finding Bone guilty and Ardwall sentenced him to death. Bone was taken to Ayr to await execution, but, in a sign of the times when there was some reluctance to carry out the sentence for capital crimes, this was commuted to life imprisonment by the Secretary of State for Scotland on the eve of the hanging. Bone, on being told of the decision, burst into tears, crying that he wanted 'to be with my wife'. He would have the final say. Four years later, he was found dead in his cell, having apparently hung himself with a knotted bed sheet.

The brutal murder was a senseless aberration, a dreadful stain on Glenbuck's reputation for otherwise relatively peaceful co-existence. Agnes was mourned, Bone reviled. The episode hung over the village like a threatening cloud. But life, as always, went on. People got back to their own day-to-day concerns, their work in the diminishing coalfields and sought refuge in the game they had taken to with such alacrity.

The village continued to roll out footballers from Burnside Park. Right-half David Henderson played 18 times for Motherwell between 1920–22 before signing for Royal Albert and Mid-Annandale in Lockerbie. John 'Deedie' Murdoch had a brief spell at Clyde in 1931/32, scoring once in six league and cup games.

Left-back John 'Jock' Mackenzie was another who ranged far and wide in pursuit of his professional ambitions. At the late age of 24, he signed for Carlisle, then Norwich a season later, following manager Bert Stansfield. Jock spent five Southern League seasons in East Anglia, missing just four out of 190 matches. He was utterly dependable and became captain and the first Norwich player to play 200 games for the Canaries, skippering the side to a famous 3–2 FA Cup win over Spurs in the second round of the 1915 FA Cup.

It was one of his final games down south. He headed back to Scotland and played 25 games for Hearts in the 1915/16 season, before becoming one of that generation of the club's players who famously swapped football kit for battle fatigues to fight in the First World War. Out of 31 players, seven were killed or died in the conflict. Mackenzie, a gunner with the First Lowland (City of Edinburgh) Royal Garrison Artillery, survived to have a trial with Millwall Athletic and finally made his Football League debut at the age of 36 with Walsall in 1921/22, for whom he played four times.

There were still more players. Some registered with a club only to not feature for the first team like Walter 'Wattie' Ferguson at Sheffield Wednesday, and James Muncie at Middlesbrough. James Weir turned out just twice for Cowdenbeath in 1924–26, while his namesake John played 52 times for Edinburgh's long-lost St Bernard's in the same period. Others plied their trade with lesser-known or more obscure clubs. John Menzies played for Cumnock's short-lived club Lanemark, and John 'Hardy' Taylor at Bathgate.

John Barr played for the semi-pros of Belfast Distillery FC, who later brought Tom Finney out of retirement for an unlikely and very brief European debut in 1963 in a match against Benfica. It was almost as eye-catching a move as Cherrypicker Alec Park's to the pre-Second World War American Soccer League, where he played for Fall River FC in Massachusetts in the 1930s.

By that time, the Cherrypickers were no more. The economic fundamentals had knock-on demographic realities and there were simply not enough people in the village to sustain a club. The father of newspaperman James Taylor was the last goalkeeper signed by the Cherrypickers. "He reckoned Bob Shankly was a better player than Willie," James says, but thereafter, if Glenbuck footballers wanted to take up the game seriously, they had to find a team elsewhere.

Census figures starkly illustrated the village's decline. In 1921, in the 'land fit for heroes', the population had fallen to 713. The coal strike that year exposed the vulnerability of a small community dependent on mining. Once government control of the industry had ended with the cessation of global conflict, a new battle raged in British industry. The colliery owners wanted to cut wages, which the miners not surprisingly opposed.

The cost of living around the time was actually falling, with basic foodstuffs like flour and butter almost halving in price. But this could not disguise the endemic poverty and the villagers were not luxuriating in nutritional abundance. During the three-month lockout, soup kitchens had to be set up to provide 'communal feeding'. Small wonder Bill Shankly, Tam Hazle and the rest had to be such effective 'hunter gatherers'.

Glenbuck's miners were staunch in their support of strike action and till the end rejected the 1921 pay offer by a clear majority of 17 to 63 despite the considerable hardships they and their families were enduring. They would be similarly militant throughout the disputes that dragged on as the coal industry experienced slumps and strife, notably the General Strike of 1926.

By 1931 Glenbuck's population had fallen further still to 551. The Great Depression was at its most vicious. The *Muirkirk Advertiser* reported that for those still in some form of employment, short-time working was the norm in the local pits. A hot summer put even greater pressures on the demand for coal. In October 600 people signed on at the Labour Exchange – a huge figure in a parish whose population was just 4,358. Times were bitingly hard.

Mining in Scotland was in freefall. A survey by the Clydesdale Bank showed that just before the First World War, there were 139,424 men and boys employed in the pits. Twenty years later, that workforce had shrunk to 80,350, though that figure was more accurately described as workmen on the 'colliery books' i.e. registered as available for work, rather than actually working. The real unemployment rate among Scottish miners at the time was just over 25%.

Glenbuck miners would not be cowed. In November 1936, while the rest of Ayrshire's miners voted in favour of a new pay deal by a majority of two to one, colliers in Muirkirk and Glenbuck voted substantially against. The former was split 350 against to 242 in favour. In Glenbuck the margin was 27 against and only 16 in favour.

But the figures are also telling in another regard, in that they showed how few miners were living in Glenbuck by that time. To all intents and purposes, mining, the industry that had given proper birth to the village, was dead, and dragging Glenbuck down in its wake.

And yet the village still, even then, produced footballers. The last hurrah came with a player too young to have even seen the Cherrypickers play in regular earnest, but one who lived up to its fine traditions. It was another Brown, Thomas Law Brown, son of John who had played for the Cherrypickers. Born in April 1921, Tommy began his career as a wing-half with Cambuslang and had a trial for Rangers in 1936. That came to naught but he signed for Hearts in 1938 and looked set for a long career until war again interrupted a promising career before it had a chance to blossom. Yet he still managed 44 games and five goals for the Jam Tarts, and two appearances for Scotland in wartime internationals with England, to add to his three Schoolboy caps.

After the conflict he tried his hand with Millwall for whom he played 67 times in the league. The crowd at The Den admired his skills, but as David Prole in The Millwall History Files website so tellingly put it, 'A delightful ball-player, Brown was a bigger version of that latter-day phenomenon, Tommy Harmer. Unfortunately he often trapped himself in trickery, and a goal from him was a rarity.'

Even so, he was deemed good enough to make the step up to Division One and a two-season spell in south London with Charlton. He cost the Addicks £8,500 and played 34 games, before a final berth at Orient in 1950. He fell just two games short of a century for the Os when he retired from league football in 1953.

Brown brought the number of Glenbuck-born, raised or played-for footballers up to a round half-century. There is evidence, not included in Faulds and Tweedie's history, that there were three additional pros with definite Glenbuck links (see Appendix 1) that makes the productivity of the village even more remarkable. But with Brown's retirement the active story of Glenbuck Athletic/Cherrypickers effectively came to an end.

The village itself was not dead just yet. It continued in some form of habitable existence up to the 1970s and before then there was still plenty of life in its streets. Sam Purdie was among the last generation and he saw the wholesale destruction of his home, but also enjoyed its unique character and characters. He grew up in those same rows as the Cherrypickers who preceded him, went to the same school, sought treats from the same shops and was schooled in the same hunter-gatherer ways.

Sam has partially written his own memoir. It deserves to be finished and published, for his is a fascinating life well lived, and the insights into his childhood in Glenbuck before he moved temporarily to Glasgow at the age of eight are vivid and told with great articulacy. His skill as a writer must in part at least stem from his education.

He was one of the last Glenbuck schoolchildren, recalling that the master "'Sanny' Sloan was an educator, a mentor and an example to us to this day." But the roll had fallen to just 36 pupils by 1943, and in 1951 this public amenity that had been so hard-fought for shut for good, with Sam and the remaining students bussed to Muirkirk school from then on.

There were some efforts to improve the villagers' lot. The announcement in 1928 of the building of the new council houses that the Shanklys and Hazles would move into, was a notable advance in that regard. Even so, the Glenbuck world of Sam was barely different to that of previous generations stretching back decades.

There was still no electricity and villagers had to ration their listening on battery-powered radios to hear the news, especially during wartime. Sam recalls hearing the words of Winston Churchill assuming "a massive significance... Those of us who had fathers and uncles overseas hung on every word for even a hint of how the war was going. We were young but, we knew how desperate our situation was. We knew that we were in a fight for national survival.

"I visited Coventry where one of my uncles was engaged in war work. I celebrated my fourth birthday in Coventry on the same night that the Luftwaffe tried to flatten the whole city." Purdie had also been among the boys in Glenbuck who had seen a strange red glow on the northern horizon the night Clydebank was razed to the ground.

The wartime blackout for Glenbuckians was nothing new, since there was still no street lighting in the village, though there were some compensations. "We could appreciate what 16 hours of wintertime darkness is like without street lights. We sometimes had the moon but thinking back, I've never had so much privacy in public places. We were out of sight of the big folk but we were equally certainly not out of mind; in our little community, everyone knew what everyone else was doing – and with whom. A loud sneeze reverberated from one end of the village to the other and if any young girl should happen to catch a 'cold' we all knew who had given her the 'smittle'."

Life for younger kids like Sam revolved around playing football in the big-sided street games, occasional visits to Ayr or bigger towns, but more often to sample the wares of the local shops. The main one was the Co-operative Store. It provided the much-needed 'divi', the twice-a-year share out based on accumulated purchases. But the Co-op, run with wondrous efficiency by the multi-skilled A.V. Hazle and his family, offered so much more.

"It sold almost everything needed to survive. Any items which were not in stock such as bicycles or furniture could be ordered through a catalogue. There was paraffin and methylated spirit for cooking stoves and lamps, large pats of butter and whole cheeses, which stood on the marble back-counters side by side with whole sides of smoked bacon. Hanging from the ceiling were brushes, shovels, pots, paraffin cans, working boots and miners' lamps.

"The alternative and only competition to the Co-op was Bain's at the other end of the village. Convenience kept it going plus the fact that there was a telephone, which everyone could use. 'Open all Hours' really was the motto of the Bains. They lived next door to the shop and would open up at any time to answer an emergency. The store was run by the Bains' spinster daughter Annie and I can never remember seeing Annie walk anywhere, she was always at the half-trot.

"She was consistently helpful. One time after the war when I was just a boy, I had to phone my father to give him some terrible news; my dear grandpa had just died. Annie gave me a mint imperial and a cuddle as she saw me to the door. Gentler times, gentler people."

There was also Aunty Jinnet's tin-shed fish and chip shop, which also sold sweets and tobacco. "She was the whole village's Aunty. A heart as big as a hill." The chips cost from two old pennies a bag. Summer weather allowing there was also the hand-cranked ice cream maker. "Ice cream has never tasted so good since," says Sam.

Annie and the Bains were Glenbuck legends in their own right. They had gone into 'trade' when George Bain had been hurt down the pit. "He was my grandfather," says Peggy Bain. Born in 1929, she is another of the last of the Glenbuckians, 86 now but still with a pin-sharp recall of what the realities of life were like.

"You see in those days you never got paid for when you were off sick. I think they used to get a penny a wean, but that was only for so long. So they sold apples out of my granny's room to make money to feed the family. My father's name was Richard (Dicky) Bain and his father was George. My granny was Irish, Annie McLeary Bain, and most of the grand weans were called Annie after her. People would come to the door and ma granny would sell the apples from her room."

This embryonic fruit business mushroomed. Having been hurt down the pit, George Bain refused to put his sons through the same experience and so set Dicky to work with a horse and cart. This became one of the most familiar and much-loved sights in the village and surrounding area as man and beast trod the roads to bring wares to a grateful populace, especially to those snowed in during the winter.

When she was old enough, Peggie would help out with the horse and cart, working long and demanding hours. The poor girl would be on the receiving end of her father's physical ire for any error. It was as if he cared more for the horse than he did his own daughter. "He said, 'Let me tell you, when you're feeding nine of us I would think of you more!'

"Och, him and that horse. Floria was her name, she ruled our house. When my father was doing his rounds hawking round the villages Floria would only go her way: the same way every single day. She would not listen to anyone else expect my dad. When Floria would have a stone in her hoof my father would tell me to take it out. I would say 'come on Floria move and lift your leg up!' Floria would put her weight on me and not let me back up. Och, she was trouble... she would stand on folk's feet all the time and she knew all the doors to go to and she would not move from the door until she got a piece [of bread] with jam."

The Bains' shop also sold clothes and alcohol, "A bad thing for my grandfather as he was keen on the booze. I guess that's why my father hardly ever took a drink, only on special occasions," says Peggie. She also recalls the grinding poverty of the village. "I never thought how poor people were, with us having the shop we would always have our dinner tatties, but there were houses that never had tatties.

"I just took it for granted that everyone was the same in my day. I guess in my father's time it would have been even worse. Families were big in those days. I remember the Kerr family and Mrs Kerr had trouble with her legs so all the lassies would help with dinner.

The Kerr men always came home to a big plate of tatties, one meal a day. If you were lucky you would get a piece with jam later on."

One of the Kerrs, Liza, continued to attract lodgers to her boarding house near Burnside Park. Miss Kerr, Purdie recalls, was a devout Christian who ran a resolutely 'proper' house. One lodger couldn't tolerate the discipline and in reprisal, taught Miss Kerr's parrot to squawk 'Liza's an old whore!'

The Bains had made up for the loss of Milliken's as far back as 1916. That shop had barely survived two years since the death of Leezie Milliken, a hugely-popular Glenbuck character. 'It was the rendezvous of the youth and beauty of the place,' lamented the *Muirkirk Advertiser* – 'the local Westminster and the headquarters of all the Football Associations.' Glenbuck people saw their shops as the lifeblood of their community, not just for its provision of life's essentials, but for its social heart, much more so than the church which closed its doors in 1954.

The shops were still in some sort of business but other symbols of village life and history were disappearing. Glenbuck House, home to the Howatsons, was demolished in 1948. The railways went the way of many lines across Britain; the 'new railway' linking tracks to Leshmagow and Muirkirk hadn't even been used due to practical obsolescence as soon as it had been completed. So the line's rails and sleepers were torn up, its viaducts demolished.

When Glenbuck was hit by bad weather – not an infrequent occurrence – the place took on the image of a frontier town all but cut off from civilisation. There was a dreadful winter storm in 1940 that forced the residents to form a human chain to bring vital supplies from the railway line up to the village stores. A terrible rainstorm in August 1963 caused widespread flooding and tore up pavements and kerbstones, abetted by the flooding of old mine workings.

Politics stood firmer for those clinging on. Purdie, who himself was an early activist in the Scottish National Party and stood twice for Parliament, remembers one Tory candidate being made rudely aware of the village's militancy in the election of 1945. "He was a newly retired major. Years later I met him, by then representing a safe Home Counties seat. He recalled his alarm on seeing Soviet flags displayed on most of the outdoor washhouses on the 'Long Raw'. He confided that between the flags and the barracking he suffered from big women with no teeth and wearing black all-in-one overalls he feared he'd arrived in Russia by mistake."

It's a typically comic Glenbuck story, but years later, people like Purdie and Peggy Bain are in no mood to laugh about what happened to their village. The anger at its casual degradation is manifest. "The apparatchiks decreed that the demography would be much tidier on paper if they killed off small local communities, without a single thought in their pea-brained heads of the societal consequences," Sam says.

People continued to move away. Houses and buildings fell into disuse. When Glenbuckians moved to Muirkirk en masse in 1954, to a street of new houses called 'Hareshaw Crescent', they found the adjustments hard, not to say confusing. "When they moved into two-story houses, it was a big change for them," says Sam. The first time there was a storm and the wind really blew, they panicked and ran out into the street, thinking the houses would blow down."

Some kept the memories going, and still remembered their local footballing heroes. One such was John Hastie, who in 1962 celebrated with his wife their golden wedding. The couple had been living at Glenbuck Public Hall where John had been caretaker for 30 years, the pair remembered by the *Muirkirk Advertiser* as 'a kindly couple'. They were popular and well known, but had got on with their lives quietly and modestly, without John proclaiming his earlier achievements. For Hastie was yet another of those old Cherrypickers, who had made the professional grade.

He and his family had arrived in the village when he was four and his football schooling in Glenbuck earned him a place in the Cherrypickers side. This in turn led to him signing for one of the biggest clubs possible – the mighty Glasgow Celtic. Hastie's time at Parkhead was another of those rather short-lived careers for the village's players, but it was further evidence of the remarkable quality of the Cherrypickers academy.

Hastie played 19 times in two seasons before he moved, on loan first of all with Raith Rovers and then into Junior football with Nithsdale Wanderers. But any selection for the Celtic team of this period was some feat. This was the Bhoys of the Willie Maley Edwardian era, when the club had been propelled to greatness with the aim of making Celtic giants not just of Scottish football but a side of international renown.

When Hastie joined in 1910, the club had won six league titles in a row and was in a period of brief transition. A problem position had been inside-left, and Hastie was signed to address that specific need. In truth he struggled to make a lasting impact. He did however, play his part in the victorious Scottish Cup campaign of 1911. He played in the goalless final against Hamilton Academical, a match commonly regarded as one of the most boring in the history of the competition, and paid the price by being dropped for the rather more entertaining replay which Celtic won 2–0. Yet Hastie was able to pick up a winner's medal. He joined the continental tour of 1911 and played his last game for the club at Montmartre in Paris against Etoile Rouge.

The French capital was a long way from Glenbuck but it was another illustration of the collective journey Glenbuck footballers had made. In retirement, Hastie settled back into life in the village with his wife, an enduringly popular district nurse.

They were among those Glenbuck couples who joined in the reunions attended by many of the old village clans. Taits, Browns, Bones, Knoxes and all, came from far and wide – Canada, America and Australia – to reminisce and laugh. But they were returning to an old country for old men and women. Glenbuck was on its way out.

By the mid-1970s, when Bill Shankly's ghostwriter John Roberts paid a visit to the village, it was virtually abandoned. He painted a desultory but descriptive picture. Sheep roamed the shells of buildings, some now used as farm outbuildings There were 20 people left, among them Liz Shankly. A dozen houses, eight of them the council-built homes, remained occupied. Other than that the village was a ruin.

It was to get worse. The Bill Shankly memorial, funded by Liverpool and Scottish Coal, was unveiled in 1997, but it was to a backdrop of mechanised leviathans tearing the heart out of what was left of Glenbuck. The open-cast mining operators had moved in. First Scottish Coal, then other companies looking to exploit the coal reserves by stripping away whole swathes of the land, dug out vast grey holes and scraped the hills of vegetation.

The mining companies soon got what they had come for. In 2013 Scottish Coal went bust and Glenbuck was left to its own, deeply scarred devices. The old pits – Lady, Galawhistle, Spireslack and Grasshill – had all been consumed. The remnants of the streets and buildings disappeared or were left as empty lots with a few bedraggled stones. Glenbuck became a lifeless, uninhabited moonscape.

Burnside Park, that once rang with shouts and cheers of footballers and fans, fell deadly, eerily silent.

Chapter 15

Rebirth

TOM Hazle is chuckling to himself. Asked why, he says, "Ah, Willie Shankly, he was very good to me. He used to call me 'Thumper'." Because Tom was a cute kid and like the lovable character in the Disney movie, *Bambi*? "No, it's because I was very noisy and thumped around a lot. He could hear me through the walls of the house making a racket."

Tom chuckles again. It's hard to see his expression, obscured as it is by dense and pungent smoke. He's puffing away on a pipe filled with the meanest tobacco this side of Havana. 'Thick Black', it's called, and rightly so. It is an oily, coal-like blend special to Ayrshire and its miners, who smoked it by the bucket load, though hopefully not at the coalface. It's a wonder it didn't kill them but Tom looks very well on it for his near-90 years.

It is high summer 2015 and we are sitting in Tom's front room, the heating turned up to maximum and the fire ablaze just the way gentlefolk of his vintage like it. If it feels like being in a greenhouse, Hazle is making his substantial contribution to global warming with his pipe. Puffs of black smoke rise to the ceiling and stick there as glutinous tar. "It has enough CO_2 emissions to give the Greens heart attacks and is a guaranteed deterrent against all flying creatures," declares Sam Purdie. So rare is 'Thick Black's' dark, mysterious alchemy that it can only be bought now from a specialist supplier in Ayr. But also because there are not enough miners around to keep up demand.

Tom is reminiscing again about Glenbuck and its footballers. There are stories to tell, often going off into tangents and unconnected sagas, but the conversation is lively, funny, and engaging. It always is with Glenbuck people. Their village might have gone but they aren't going to let its astonishing, inspirational, moving story head the same way. And that story might, just might, have a few more new chapters to run.

The importance of Bill Shankly to the ongoing tale is vital. It is his origins in Glenbuck that draws visitors up the A70 to peer at what the fuss was all about. The inscription on the black granite memorial reads, 'Seldom in the history of sport can a village the size of Glenbuck have produced so many who reached the pinnacle of achievement in their chosen sport. This monument is dedicated to their memory and to the memory of one man in particular, Bill Shankly.'

Shankly's descendants are active in keeping that memory alive. His granddaughter Karen Gill is patron of the Spirit of Shankly and chair of the Liverpool Supporters' Committee. A teacher by profession, a disciple of her granddad by belief, she has also authored a fine book, *The Real Bill Shankly*.

"I have been to Glenbuck twice in my life," Karen says. "Once with my granddad on an extremely rare family holiday when I was about eight years old and once last year with my sister Pauline and some friends. Both times were very special, but there was a hint of sadness the last time I was there as there was nothing there but the wonderful memorial to help me conjure up images of the place I'd heard so many stories about from my granddad."

Another of Shankly's grandchildren, Christopher Carline, told the journalist Martyn McLaughlin, "The importance of Glenbuck to my granddad is a point that should be continually made. Everybody thinks of the period between 1959 to 1974, when he delivered so much success to Liverpool, but there's no doubt whatsoever that the upbringing he had gave him his morals, his mindset, and lifestyle. That was the making of him, and without it, would he have been the same person? Probably not."

Carline and relatives have also set up the Shankly Family Foundation, a charity which supports grassroots football and young people. It 'aims to promote community participation in healthy recreational activities through the provision of facilities', and 'to help young people develop their skills, capabilities and responsibilities in society through education and leisure.' The foundation is also looking to bolster the links between Liverpool Football Club and the village, and abide by Shankly's mantra about teamwork, football and life.

It is why the foundation is interested in supporting the Glenbuck Academy. Set up by one of the authors of this book, Robert Gillan, in honour of the village, the academy is intended to be the first of its kind in the country. It will encourage local children to become interested in and playing football, utilising the story of Glenbuck.

The academy will not just be about training and coaching. It is seen as a means to revitalise grassroots football in a rural area where jobs and opportunities are thin. There are hopes to draw in children from Lanarkshire towns like Douglas, Rigside, Coalburn, and Lesmahagow, and the Ayrshire communities of Muirkirk, Lugar, Logan, and Cumnock – all places that were part of the Glenbuck story. Ultimately, the aim is to have a dedicated football park, with changing rooms, floodlights and top-quality pitches.

It will also work to help the community come together to help youngsters channel their energies to get into sport, work on their fitness, encourage healthy eating and to keep kids out of trouble.

It is a familiar ambition, and not dissimilar to that of the Victorian worthies who saw the social virtue of football. But Glenbuck Academy will try something different, by using the stories of the Glenbuck players, the village and its heritage to help to educate youngsters, and learn about the wider history of the sport in Scotland.

It has the support of Karen Gill: "When I heard about Robert's initiative, I felt hopeful that once again the name Glenbuck could be associated with the dreams and ambitions of aspiring young footballers, because it truly was an incredible place and deserves to have a happier end."

Karen's view is shared by her relative Chris Carline. "As the founder and chair of the Shankly Family Foundation, I have placed a huge emphasis on celebrating and educating people as to the values that my grandad lived by. These values were developed and honed in Glenbuck so when we found out about Glenbuck Football Academy we knew the potential was there for a partnership.

"We recently took our foundation team to Glenbuck, to play a tournament against local teams from the Ayrshire area; and to educate them as to what Glenbuck was like and the local surrounding area. It was a great experience and is something we will look to do each year as we continue to build the partnership between the foundation and Glenbuck Football Academy."

Eventually, under the auspices of the Glenbuck Academy, select Ayrshire-Lanarkshire sides are envisaged, to compete against youth sides from the professional leagues, but the immediate target is more basic. Hiring pitches and facilities, bringing in properly qualified coaches, and putting in the time to organise such an academy's work requires, of course, money. In an era when the professional game is drowning in cash, it would cost a fraction of the Premier League TV deal to sustain a project like the Glenbuck Academy. But, as it is for so many working at the grassroots level across Britain, making ends meet is an ongoing and often debilitating struggle.

Amid concerns over Scotland's Club Academy system and the perennial complaints about the lack of talent being produced by the various initiatives and schemes in England, is the fundamental divide between the elite game and the sport at its grassroots level. *The Herald* reported Jim Fleeting, SFA director of youth development, as saying, 'I have the utmost admiration for those volunteers involved in our grassroots and that's the reality of it: volunteers. Some people write us off as if it's some big operation but the support we receive from unpaid coaches is very beneficial for the future of these kids.

'Davie [Moyes] was here to discuss development; we talked about the time, effort and resources being put into the game and agreed that the game wouldn't survive without volunteers devoted to grassroots development.'

Where the players are coming from is another question. The constant flow of supreme Scottish talent to English clubs has virtually dried up. Once, a top-flight team depended on Scots; now they are even rarer among the elite Champions League sides than decent English players.

Glenbuck Academy might not provide the answer to that particular problem but there is support for its aims. There might even be an opportunity for Glenbuck itself to be revitalised via the academy. And this is where a Dumfries and Galloway-based academic enters the scene.

Professor Russell Griggs OBE could be just the champion to rekindle the spirit of the Cherrypickers. An academic and businessman, he has a background in a variety of areas including banking, textiles and design. Latterly he has been heading the Scottish Mines Restoration Trust (SMRT). In part funded by one coal company, Hargreaves Services, this is a body set up in April 2013 by the Scottish Government to, literally, clean up the mess left behind by open-cast mining.

The savage despoliation caused by colossal trucks and diggers, has rent the landscape across the former coalfields straddling the borders between East Ayrshire, Lanarkshire, and Dumfries. Companies that were supposed to put the land back together after they had finished open-cast mining went into liquidation, without leaving behind the money necessary to fund the clean-up. The story of how this came to pass is often dispiriting and a window on to the scandals that can arise with the consequences of post-industrialisation. It is also a very long saga. Suffice to say that something has to be done, and Professor Griggs is intent on making it happen.

At a stroke, when he was made head of SMRT, he also became one of the country's biggest landowners, with 10,000 acres at his disposal. With additional funding from liquidators, the Trust is now engaged in a variety of projects and is considering various proposals to restore the land and regenerate it. Wind farms, woodland and nature reserves, farming and assorted commercial operations are all in the mix. The public and private sector, landowners, government, local communities and young people are involved – one wind turbine scheme will be overseen by a committee of pupils from the Sanquhar Academy.

Glenbuck is now in the SMRT's sights, and, considering the physical state of the area, surely one of the toughest challenges.

"Our biggest single site is Spireslack and Ponesk," says Professor Griggs, outlining the plans for the open-cast complex of which Glenbuck is a part. Sitting in his home in Sanquhar, he offers a realistic and honest take on what can be done with the legacy of open-cast.

The process has presented a multitude of problems for Scotland, from pollution leaking out of vast and deep pools, to the visual blights of those enormous scars on the hillsides. "But by nature I'm a glass half-full person," says Griggs, and he is positive about Glenbuck's future.

The British Geological Survey, says Griggs, have said that on the whole road from Douglas through to Cumnock, only about 20% of the landform is natural. It has been mined for about 1,000 years and most of the hills are effectively man-made. Human activity over a long period has shaped the landscape and now people are looking to adapt and use it once again. The Trust is a partner in the restoration of Glenbuck Loch. "It has been nicely restored," Griggs says. "Over time that will convert into an energy park, and the Duke of Buccleuch is looking to put in a pump-storage hydro scheme." At Ponesk, the Trust is 'hopefully' in the latter stages of putting out a tender, with the intention it will then be sold on to a local farmer who will put chicken sheds on it, creating jobs for around 12 people. Jobs are much needed but, to be blunt, there's something potentially far more exciting in store for Spireslack and Glenbuck.

"I got a call one day from the guys at the British Geological Survey (BGS) in Edinburgh," says Griggs. "They said I should be aware that there are two sites you've got that have things of special geological interest on them. Those are Mainshill and Spireslack. Mainshill has one wee bit of absolutely unique geology where the rock strata are vertical, not horizontal – very, very unusual. Oil and gas geologists from around the world will come there because usually you only see that kind of geology 3,000 feet under the sea.

"Now, Spireslack has what is politely called the 'Grand Canyon', which is the big piece up the middle of it. This again has strata of interest to geologists all round the world. They've had, oh goodness me, universities from all over the world looking at those sites. Apparently at the last count we've had 50 research proposals in. So our view over time is to turn Mainshill and Spireslack into a geo-park.

"A geo-park can be many things, in particular the 'geo' bit. But what you then do is develop everything else around it."

A team from a consultancy firm, Glamis, led by Colin Smith, have been engaged to explore ideas and proposals, and one of them has huge relevance in a football context. "In terms of Spireslack," Griggs says, "since we started we've been trying to merge the local industrial and social history together. There is no open-cast mine museum in Scotland. There's an underground one but not an open-cast, and Spireslack has within it all the geology to show people what it is.

"So what we're trying to do is develop some sort of museum to tell the industrial and social history of that valley because it's been in mining for 1,000 years. There is visible geological evidence that you can bring people to see. We also want to do something to tie in with that at Glenbuck and the history of football. One of the proposals is to restore the pitch."

It is a comment to pull the listener up sharp. Come again?

"There are daft ideas which turn out to be not so daft. I think there is a market, if that pitch is restored, for people to come and play football matches at Glenbuck again. You could build two rows of cottages where players could stay over the weekend, a restored pitch, somewhere to eat – who knows maybe you could have Everton 'teams', some from Liverpool, all sorts of different teams coming to play on the pitch and stay in the village. There would be an economic benefit because you'd need people to look after it and all sorts of other things."

It raises the possibility that Burnside Park, unused, neglected and then abandoned, might one day be a proper football pitch again. Glenbuck could even become a viable community once more. "My role in all of this as we restore the mines," insists Griggs, "is to leave some lasting benefit to the community."

If it is to happen the major issue will inevitably be money. Just to maintain the sites and uphold health and safety costs the Trust £1m a year. The SMRT raises income as various projects get underway, and Griggs says he does not want the Trust to stay as a landowner, but to convert its assets into cash that can be used for other projects. As a charitable institution, SMRT can go to various bodies like Heritage Lottery to source funding, but a cast-iron case has to be made. Thus Glamis is not just conducting a feasibility study but carrying out market testing to evaluate if the project is viable.

"You have to have everything in place," says Griggs. "We're not pushing against an open door but if we can show there is a market there... I really am committed to this. We've got the support of government, we've got East Ayrshire council on our side, all the interested parties are on our side. We're now speaking to Liverpool

FC because they must have an interest, but it's all about whether Glamis can show there is a sustainable future here. The view from Colin Smith and his team is that this is a day out from Glasgow.

"The geo-park provides lots of things. It can let young people know what their history was, to learn how coal was created and taken out of the ground. And there is a huge scientific interest all around the world.

"We have the undivided enthusiasm of the BGS. They've had experts from universities the world over. One of them from Wisconsin, an eminent professor in his field, said 'Spireslack is to the geological community what the Large Hadron Collider is to the particle physics community.'

"The BGS will have a number of research proposals, but I don't want for it to be just a geology site. I want to develop the Glenbuck end as a social amenity – and my goal is to get that football pitch back."

Too good to be true? The road to coal-mining ruin is paved with good intentions, and the history of the industry suggests some significant setback or disappointment is just around the corner. Mining folk, and especially those from Glenbuck, have heard about grand plans and bright new tomorrows many times before. But Griggs, the glass half-full professor, offers some hope for rebirth and revival. The suggested timescale is three to five years. It is possible that once again Glenbuck will be a place where football is played.

"There has to be some restoration to these big holes that industry has just left behind," he reasons. "As a businessman, I don't think that's a good thing for industry to be doing, to be walking away from its obligations. The other point is that mining in Scotland has been part of its history for centuries. All you get nowadays is talk of how awful coal mining is. We don't have somewhere where we can celebrate what this has brought in terms of jobs and economic benefit to Scotland... we need to tell that story. Spireslack and Glenbuck is a great place to tell that story."

That story has come full circle. Centuries on from what first attracted people to Glenbuck, they are once again exploring opportunities to make the land work and provide.

For now, humanity is absent and the place is empty and silent. Walk along its abandoned lanes, and such is the impact open-cast mining has had on the place, it is a struggle to make sense of the village's old geography. You need an experienced guide to point out its long-lost features. Someone like Sam Purdie. There's where the pub was, he says, where the bar had dimples in its surface to deter pilfering of pint pots. Over there is where the Co-op used to be, and Annie Bain's, and kindly Aunty Jinnet's. Down there is the site of the school and the church, with its monument to the Covenanters. Look further on and you can see the still-standing 'Mating Tree', where many a Glenbuck betrothal had its passionate roots.

Surrounding it all are the places where they used to dig for coal. Grasshill, the Lady, Galawhistle, the Davy. In between is where the houses used to stand, like Monkey Row. On a specific spot is where the Shanklys, the ten boys and girls, were raised. You can tread where its bare floor was but, shamefully, scandalously, there's no blue plaque here to mark its importance.

And over there, beside the gurgling Stottencleugh stream, running a rusty red with one of the spoils of the industry that once dominated this place, is a flat green, sodden field, overgrown with grass and weeds. It is Burnside Park, home of the mighty Cherrypickers and Glenbuck Athletic. The football nursery that produced over 50 – count 'em, over 50 – professional players.

Now, narrow your eyes, listen close and let your imagination run away. For there are ghosts looking on, and waiting for the next part of their tale to be told. It's already been some story.

Appendix 1

The following is a list of professional footballers who played for Glenbuck Athletic/Glenbuck Cherrypickers and/or who came from/were born in the village.

It is commonly accepted that the total number of players is 50, but in the course of research for this book, three more have come to light. According to official records John Bailie, Charles Lawie and Robert Woodburn also came from Glenbuck.

Note: not all of the following played first-team football for the clubs listed.

Information taken from A Record of Pre-War Scottish League Players *published by PM Publications, http://www.pmfc.co.uk/prewar. html*

The Players

JOHN ANDERSON: Kilmarnock
JOHN BAILLIE: Kilmarnock
WILLIAM BAIN: Solway Star
WILLIAM BANKS: Kilmarnock, Portsmouth, Manchester City
JOHN BARR: Belfast Distillery
WILLIAM BARR: Ayr United
JOHN BISHOP: Ayr United
ROBERT BLYTH: Cowlairs, Middlesbrough Ironopolis, Glasgow Rangers, Preston North End, Portsmouth

WILLIAM BLYTH: Portsmouth, Preston North End, Carlisle

JOCK BONE: Aston Villa

JOHNNIE BONE: Everton

SANDY BROWN: St Bernard's, Preston North End, Portsmouth, Tottenham Hotspur, Middlesbrough, Luton Town. *International Caps: 1*

TOMMY BROWN: Leicester Fosse, Chesterfield, Portsmouth, Dundee

TOMMY BROWN: Hearts, Millwall, Charlton, Orient

ROBERT CRAWFORD: Raith Rovers, Preston North End, Blackburn Rovers, Blackpool, Southport

JOHN DAVIDSON: Solway Star, Coventry, Kilmarnock

JOHN CROSBIE: Ayr United, Birmingham City, Blackpool. *International Caps: 2*

JOHN FERGUSON: Sheffield Wednesday. Hamilton Academical, Cowdenbeath, Dunfermline Athletic

WALTER FERGUSON: Sheffield Wednesday

GEORGE HALLEY: Kilmarnock, Bradford Park Avenue, Burnley, Southend

JOHN HASTIE: Glasgow Celtic, Raith Rovers

ARCHIE GARRETT: Hamilton Academical, Millwall

DAVID HENDERSON: Motherwell, Royal Albert

HUGH KNOX: Greenock Morton, Sunderland

THOMAS KNOX: Hamilton Accademical

WILLIAM KNOX: Everton, Liverpool

CHARLES ROBERT LAWIE: Forfar, Aberdeen, Crewe Alexandra, York

ALEX McCONNELL: Everton, Woolwich Arsenal, QPR, Grimsby Town

JOHN McCONNELL: Kilmarnock, Brentford, Grimsby Town

PETER McINTYRE: Rangers, Preston, Sheffield United, Portsmouth, Hamilton Academical, Abercorn FC

JOCK McKENZIE: Carlisle, Norwich City, Hearts, Walsall

JOHN MENZIES: Lanemark

WILLIAM MUIR: Everton, Third Lanark, Kilmarnock, Dumbarton, Dundee, Heart of Midlothian, Bradford City. *International Caps: 1*

JAMES MUNCIE: Middlesbrough

JOHN MURDOCH: Clyde

JAMES NISBET: Ayr United. *International Caps: 3*

ALEC PARK: Fall River, USA

ALEC SHANKLY: Ayr United

JAMES SHANKLY: Portsmouth, Halifax, Coventry, Carlisle, Sheffield United, Barrow, Southend

JOHN SHANKLY: Portsmouth, Luton Town, Blackpool, Alloa, Greenock Morton

ROBERT SHANKLY: Alloa, Tunbridge Wells, Falkirk

WILLIE SHANKLY: Carlisle, Preston North End. *International Caps: 5*

HUGH SMITH: Solway Star

SANDY TAIT: Ayr, Royal Albert, Rangers, Motherwell, Preston North End, Tottenham Hotspur, Leyton

ROBERT TAIT: Nithsdale Wanderers, Motherwell, Cowdenbeath

JOHN TAYLOR: Bathgate

ALEC WALLACE: Airdrie

BERT WALLACE: Hamilton Academical, Bathgate, Plymouth Argyle, Torquay United

JOE WALLACE: Newcastle United

JOHN WALLACE: Partick Thistle

JAMES WEIR: Cowdenbeath

JOHN WEIR: St Bernard's

ROBERT WOODBURN: Third Lanark, Clyde

Four players won the English FA Cup:

Sandy Tait 1901

Sandy Brown 1901

George Halley 1914

Bill Shankly 1938

Appendix 2

Ghost stories are legion among the coal miners of Britain. This is one such tale. It relates to an actual fatality at the Kames pit.

The Auld Pit

A story passed down by old miners

By Sam Purdie

The men trudged down the path to the Auld Pit for the night shift as their fathers and their fathers before them had done, every night for almost a hundred years. The blowing snow muffled the steady tramp of the steel shod boots, froze on the coats and stiffened the moleskin trousers. These strong men walked in silence. Thinking on the jobs ahead, there was no need for talk.

They walked by the pure white flame of their carbide lamps which cast meagre circles of light a pace ahead of each miner in the silent file, like cloistered monks bearing candles to their vespers.

They drew closer to the pithead and as they rounded the massive pit bing, the feeble gas lights at the end of the sidings came into sight. The bing gave the men a little shelter as they reached the jumbled collection of low buildings huddled around the two shafts. The pithead wheels were still spinning in the dark and the deep bark of the huge old steam winding engines dominated the other noises of the coal screening machinery as the last of the dayshift coal was wound a thousand feet to the surface, screened for size and loaded into wagons.

The men crowded into the bothy where the only furniture was two long tables with forms either side and hooks around the four walls for the overcoats. The focal point was the big open fire built into one corner. The burning coal was piled high and the front bars glowed red. The bothy was a welcome opportunity to thaw out, breathe some warm dry air and "cry a ben" or call out your turn to go down. The iron rule was that you came back up in the same place in line as you went down, strictly first come, first served.

The "ben" was relevant as the cages only held four men crouched together on each of the two decks, a rate of fifty men an hour. Coming to work an hour early meant being home for breakfast before some of the men had reached the surface.

The next step was to pick up explosives and their Davey safety lamps. Each face worker picked up two zinc boxes of gelignite. The lamp cabin was the last stop before the cage. The flame safety lamps were the first line of defence against the twin silent killers, black damp which snuffed out life by suffocation or fire damp which threatened a violently explosive death in the confined space of the pit. Just as each man left the lamp cabin, they performed an age-old miners' ritual. They picked their token from a huge board on which hung hundreds of brass discs, one for each man and boy in the Pit, a number allocated on his first day and surrendered on his last day up the road provided the Pit did not get him first. This was the infallible system, which located every man. A token on the board meant that a man was on the surface, an empty hook meant that a man was underground.

The tokens were bright with the polish of use except for a few which were dull and unused. These were the tokens, which had belonged to men killed in the Pit, by tradition these numbers were kept on the board never to be used again.

The descent into the depth of the auld pit was a grim business. The number one shaft was the downcast or fresh air shaft. The freezing air was forced down the shaft by the rotation of the huge paddles of the steam fan. The incessant beat of the paddle blades, as they each passed the duct in the sealed pithead, was the life pulse of the Pit. The fan could never be interrupted, air had to be blown continuously into every corner of the workings before it was expired, polluted and stale from the number two shaft.

The cold air rushing down the old shaft at this time of the year sometimes created giant, 60 feet icicles in the shaft, formed in the constant torrent of water rushing downwards to find a temporary resting place in the deep sump below the pit bottom before being caught and pumped back to the surface in man's constant, fruitless effort to defeat the inexorable forces of nature.

The cages were built to carry coal, not men. Each was the size of a one-ton hutch, three feet high and less than three feet wide. Four grown men could only be fitted into this space by hunkering down and interlocking their knees with the man opposite. Thus freezing, cramped and soaked, the miners were dropped a thousand feet to begin each shift; carrying food, water, explosives. A totally inhuman transport to the ultimate dehumanised way of life.

This was the start of a normal shift for the Kelly brothers. Having reached the pit bottom in separate cages, as was the custom such that any unforeseen incident in the shaft would only cost one family member at a time, they waited for the Oversman.

He was the section foreman who gave them their job for the night. They would be going where they went last night but they had to wait to be sent. The Oversman had to know where everybody was. The Kellys were assigned to the old North Brae section. This section had stood idle for years but was now being reopened.

The Coal Pit is a constantly changing system of tunnels. The original coal Barons went for the "easy" coal first so that the working faces got further and further from the Pit Bottom. Occasionally as in the case of the North Brae the coal that had been left could be as attractive to recover as the newer, more distant coal faces.

They tramped the familiar roadway in the company of men bent double in roadways just high enough for hutches to pass, headed for the main workings two miles inside. Their work led them to branch off before the rest of the men and climb the long brae to where they were repairing a branch roadway at right angles to the main brae. The brothers were "Brushers", the tough men who kept the roadways open, continually removing the rock encroaching from the roof under the monstrous weight of a thousand feet of rock and renewing the supports in a constant battle to hold back the mighty forces of gravity and geology.

Such thoughts were far from the minds of the Kelly boys as they worked steadily at their task. The brothers could be said to be typical, they were third generation miners and now by virtue of their father having been crippled by a roof fall, they were the main breadwinners.

Like every family in the village, they knew that the auld pit would claim its blood money. They were reopening an old road, which would be used as access to the planned new workings. The workplace was deserted. They had a visit from the fireman, who was the area supervisor and safetyman. After a brief word, the brushers were left on their own. The work involved some repair but the intruding roof rock had to be drilled and blasted to restore the roadway to the six feet needed for an ingoing airway. "Piece-time" on the night shift was 2am.

The routine was that the holes were charged and blasted to coincide with the snack break so that the worst of the explosive smoke would disperse while the men were on their break, the elder brother lit the fuses and followed his mate to a safe distance. The men were glad to sit down near the end of the road where the air was better. They cleaned and recharged their carbide lamps and ate their bread washed down with cold tea from enamelled flasks.

The explosion came on cue and there was the thunderous rumble of broken rock crashing to the floor followed by a cloud of smoke and dust. The ensuing silence was disturbed by the creaking and groaning of the recent wooden supports as the roof settled into its new balance. Then there was the silence that's only found in the non-productive areas of the pit.

As the brothers sat quietly with their own thoughts in the small circle of light given off by the flames of their lamps, they heard the footsteps of the fireman climbing the main brae to make his mid-shift check. The footsteps stopped and the fireman did not appear, probably he was answering a call of nature.

For some reason, the hair on the back of Jimmy Kelly's neck began to tingle. The footsteps sounded again, this time faster than before. They exchanged glances. Curiosity overcame them and without a word they rose and went to the road end to see what game the fireman was playing. When they reached the main brae there was no sign of a light. This meant that the fireman was hiding. With his light out, a miner is invisible.

Suddenly the floor started to shake and there was a thunderous roar of falling rock. The blast of air displaced by thousands of tons of debris blew out the brothers' lamps. They were now choking and totally blinded. After a scrabble the carbide flames were sparked into light but the dust cloud was so thick that the lamps were all but useless.

There was only one way to run and that was down towards the pit bottom in the hope that the roadway was still standing. As they ran, they met the fireman hurrying upwards to see what damage the huge rock fall had caused and what had happened to the Kellys, the only men in the section. He told them that he had not been near their place since the beginning of the shift.

The three men retraced their steps cautiously and were aghast to see the wreckage of what minutes before had been the roadway; it was closed almost to the edge of the main brae. The place where the miners had been eating had disappeared behind a solid wall of rubble. Whether they had heard footsteps or not, they had moved just ahead of the massive roof fall. The brothers had lost all their belongings including their tools.

Nothing could be done now but head for the pit bottom.

They went into the pump room where the huge pumps drove 3,000 gallons a minute to the surface. The massive electric motors gave off a background heat, which was a small comfort, given that their jackets were entombed with the rest of their belongings at the top of the North brae. Now that they had time to think about what had happened, the chill in their bones was not entirely due to the fresh air at the pit bottom. They did not discuss all the circumstances of the roof fall, even with each other.

They went to the surface in their ben. Near death experiences are no excuse to break the rules. They checked their tokens and left the lamp cabin and collected their coats from the bothy, now full of dayshift men waiting to continue the endless cycle of coal extraction. The fire was even more welcome than usual.

The veteran who was in charge of the lamps took note of their token numbers and did a quick double check of the board.

He reeled back in horror. The old, unused token of the senior Kelly brother, drowned in an inrush of water five years before, was off the board.

According to mining custom, the long lost Bill Kelly was once again underground.

© Sam Purdie 2014

Appendix 3

List of Glenbuck mining fatalities

The following is a list of those who lost their lives working in Glenbuck pits. This is a guide, only: proper records were not maintained throughout the period of mining in the village over the centuries.

It does not include those from Glenbuck who died at other pit villages or mines. The list of serious injuries is too long to include.

DATE	PIT	NAME	AGE	CAUSE
18 June 1884	Grasshill	David Haugh	20	Engine injuries
17 June 1887	Davy	J. Dunbar	N/A	Roof fall
"	"	D. Dunbar (son)	N/A	"
24 April 1893	Davy	A. Woods	22	Fell from cage
17 Oct 1894	Galawhistle	T. Davison	20	Roof fall
15 April 1899	Galawhistle	W. Reid	N/A	Roof fall
9 Jan 1901	Ponesk	G. Samson	28	Roof fall
25 Jan 1901	Davy	W. Wilson	21	Roof fall
July 1914	Grasshill	J. Dempster	N/A	Roof fall
July 1922	Grasshill	A. Allison	18	Runaway
May 1923	Grasshill	J. Cameron	N/A	Runaway
Dec 1928	Grasshill	A. MacDonald	N/A	Roof fall

Bibliography

Books

If You're Second, You Are Nothing: Ferguson and Shankly; Oliver Holt; Macmillan, 2006

Shanks: The Authorised Biography of Shankly – Dave Bowler; Orion 1996

Shankly: It's Much More Important Than That – Stephen F Kelly; Virgin Books, 1997

Shankly: My Story – John Roberts; Trinity Mirror Sport Media 2011

The Real Bill Shankly – Karen Gill; Trinity Mirror Sport Media 2007

Old Muirkirk and Glenbuck – David Pettigrew; Stenlake Publishing 1996

Mining, Ayrshire's Lost Industry – Guthrie Hutton; Stenlake Publishing 1996

A Dictionary of 20th Century World Biography – Consultant Editor Asa Briggs; OUP/BCA/Market Books 1992

Lost Ayrshire – Dane Love; Birlinn, 2010

The Mineworkers – Robert Duncan, Birlinn, 2005

20 Years Down The Mine – Ian Terris; Stenlake Publishing, 2001

Bash the Rich – Ian Bone; Naked Guides Ltd; 2006

Cairntable Echoes and Cairntable Memories – James Taylor, 2002

Encyclopedia of British Football – eds Phil Soar and Martin Tyler; Collins 1974

The Football Grounds of Britain – Simon Inglis; Collins Willow, 1996

Inverting the Pyramid – Jonathan Wilson; Orion, 2009

Rothmans Football Yearbook, various edtns – ed Jack Rollin; Headline

Athletic News (various editions)

Keir Hardie: A Biography – William Stewart, The National Labour Press, 1921

Garan 1631 to Muirkirk 1950, Thomas Findlay; 1980

When Saturday Comes: The Half Decent Football Book; Penguin 2005

Cherrypickers – Glenbuck nursery of footballers – Reverend MH Faulds and William M Tweedie Jnr; Cumnock and Doon Valley District Council, 1981

Pompey People (Portsmouth Who's Who) – Mick Cooper; Yore Publications, 2001

Pompey – Mike Neasom, Mick Cooper & Doug Robinson; Milestone Publications 1984

Portsmouth FC – An A-Z; Dean Hayes; SB Publications, 1997

Proud Preston – Ian Rigby and Mike Payne; Carnegie Publishing, 1999.

Who's Who Of Preston North End – Dean Hayes; Breedon 2006

The Spurs Opus – various; Kraken, 2008

The Spurs Miscellany – Adam Powley and Martin Cloake; VSP 2008

Tottenham: The Managing Game – Norman Giller; normangillerbooks.com, 2011

Tottenham Hotspur: The Complete Record – Bob Goodwin, Breedon Books 2007

Tottenham Hotspur: The Official Illustrated History – Phil Soar; Hamlyn 1997

Tottenham Hotspur: The Official Biography – Julie Welch; VSP 2012

A Century of Great Soccer Drama – John Cottrell; Sportsman's book Club 1972

The Juniors 100 Years. A Centenary History of Scottish Junior Football Paperback – David McGlone and Bill McLure; Mainstream, 1987